Images of Woman in Literature

Also by David Holbrook

Imaginings
Against the Cruel Frost
Object Relations
Old World, New World
Chance of a Lifetime
Selected Poems

ON EDUCATION

English for Maturity
English for the Rejected
The Secret Places
The Exploring Word
Children's Writing
English in Australia Now
Education, Nihilism, and Survival
English for Meaning
Education and Philosophical Anthropology

Images of Woman in Literature

David Holbrook

NEW YORK UNIVERSITY PRESS
NEW YORK AND LONDON

Library of Congress Cataloging-in-Publication Data
Holbrook, David.
Images of woman in literature / David Holbrook.
p.   cm.
Bibliography: p.
Includes index.
ISBN 0-8147-3460-X (alk. paper)
1. English drama—History and criticism.   2. Women in literature.
3. Shakespeare, William, 1564–1516—Characters—Women.   4. Barrie,
J.M. (James Matthew), 1860–1937—Characters—Women.
5. Psychoanalysis and literature.   6. Death in literature.   7. Fear
in literature.   I. Title.
PR635.W6H65   1989   89-34366
822.009'352042—dc   CIP

New York University Press books are printed on acid-free paper,
and their binding materials are chosen for strength and durability.

Book design by Ken Venezio

For Peter Lomas,
who helped me understand

Contents

CONTENTS

CONTENTS

Images of Woman in Literature

Introduction

Through various circumstances, I have been obliged to bring certain interests together. I have left my desk as a creative writer to teach adults, undergraduates, and children—some of these less able children. I have been brought to admit the profound influence of psychotherapy in my life and so have explored the investigations of human nature made by subjective psychology. How do these insights illuminate the experiences one has, from time to time, of woman as an inspiration on the one hand and as a threat on the other? How do the insights of psychoanalysis illuminate certain cultural phenomena: the child's preoccupation with witches or Shakespeare's perplexities about woman? What is the relevance of psychoanalysis to literary criticism?

Out of these perplexities, I have written already a number of studies: of Dylan Thomas, Sylvia Plath, Gustav Mahler, George MacDonald, and C. S. Lewis. One significant theme emerges from all these, aspects of which I have not yet satisfactorily explained to myself: the association between woman and death. Or, to put it another way, the focus is on woman's relationship to 'being-in-being' and 'going-out-of-being', concepts that are inseparable from the problem of a man's relationship with his female element and the phantom woman of his unconscious.

These are the themes that I intend to explore further here, especially within the dramatic experience—first, by looking at two plays by James Barrie, the author of *Peter Pan*, and then by looking at a selection of Shakespeare's plays.

I once titled this book *Literature and the Problem of Woman*. Hearing of my title, an intelligent colleague remarked at once that the book should be called "the problem of man," since this study actually addresses the problem man has with woman.

In this book I shall be trying to bring to bear on literature some insights from psychoanalysis about gender. In this sphere, *gender* is a phenomenological concept—that is, it is an aspect of consciousness, of the *Lebenswelt*. I realize, of course, that I have been doing this work in the context of a society in which there is a good deal of intellectual and political interest in woman's situation and the history of attitudes to woman. (For example, a paper entitled "The Literary Representation of Woman" was included in part 2 of the English Tripos at the University of Cambridge in the 1980s.) [1] All of this interest is valuable and will generate insights and new forms of understanding. But my explorations do not belong to this movement; they are not "feminist," though I hope, naturally, that they may contribute to understanding and so perhaps aid the debate on equality and self-realization. My investigations are concerned, rather, with the nature of human nature and with symbolism. I am concerned with the realities of consciousness, a sphere of truth not always attended to by radical movements. In my sphere, woman is a symbol. She represents in our consciousness inescapable experiences, since we all are created from a woman's body and being; and what she *is* leaves its pattern, ineradicably, as a legacy in the very nature and form of our consciousness.

It will no doubt be asserted that I ignore a great deal of feminist writing, and this is true. In making my own particular exploration of aspects of consciousness, I flinch from the problem of absorbing the great library of feminist discourse, because I apprehend from the outset that it is not in my dimension and would be almost impossible to engage with because it belongs to a different paradigm.

Introduction

Of course, it is important for woman to define herself. The feminine modes of 'being' are of great importance in studies that belong to the humanities. But my doubts about feminism came to a crisis when I began to help students prepare for the Tripos paper "The Literary Representation of Woman" (referred to previously). Those conducting this course evidently believed that certain aspects of the question were already solved; all the students had to do was to cover the literature. This literature included a number of comments on Freud's case study of Dora; but the syllabus did not indicate that it was of primary importance to come to grips with Freud, while figures such as Carl Jung, Melanie Klein, and D. W. Winnicott were conspicuously absent. There seemed to be no intention to help the students to appreciate what a psychoanalytical approach to problems of gender was but rather to select aspects of discourse in the area that endorsed feminist approaches. For example, Roman Catholic approaches to Mariolatry and other Christian perspectives were absent. And while the syllabus contained references to many sound and important literary works dealing with woman, it was essentially a campaign document.[2] As with most campaigns, it was assumed that the proper approach to the subject was already decided and that truth was already established. All the student had to do was to absorb the political literature.

In practice, those conducting the course sought at one stage to hold seminars that were to be attended only by women. They had to be reminded that by university ordinances—that is, by law— every teaching occasion at the University of Cambridge must be open to all, irrespective of religion, sex, or race. This attempt at exclusiveness did the feminist cause no good at all; later, the Tripos paper was properly changed to one that addresses literature and gender.

Political polarity, with all its bigotry, is no service to the Socratic dialogue by which, we assume, truth may be found. One hopes that by seeking truth one will arrive at a more tolerant and understanding relationship between the sexes, races, and classes of men and women. In the study of human makeup, one is trying implicitly to promote sympathy and so, one hopes, a better world. But where such a deep subject as attitudes to woman are concerned, the troubles that cause injustice are deep and cannot be removed by political slants, nor by verbal juggling (such as referring to a "person-eating tiger" or "person of war").

As in so many spheres of human affairs, if we pay attention to the insights of psychoanalysis and other such phenomenological disciplines, we find that the social and moral issues are far more complex than is often assumed, not least by passionate reformers. Above all, we find the issues dogged by fear—and the problem of woman is no exception. The fears arise often out of childhood logic—for example, if woman as mother creates us, may she not also have the power to destroy us? It may seem perverse, to common sense, but then we all find the baby perverse, as when he begins suddenly to disobey us and to hate us as well as love us; huge debates arise around the question of where that hate comes from. And so it is with woman, who is naturally equipped with special and mysterious powers by which to respond to the many moods and needs of the infant. There is no point in denying that woman has these special powers and that the sanity of the world depends upon them. Many problems that psychotherapists strive to deal with arise from the way in which, inevitably, these processes go "wrong"—and it is they who learn how much we take for granted in the mysterious developments by which the human consciousness is formed.

If we are to understand the symbolism of culture around the figure of woman, we must attend to these processes of consciousness and find new modes of understanding that will bring together the explorations of the therapists—working under a deep and grave engagement with severe problems—and the interests of the literary critic who tries to investigate the truth of human experience.

PART ONE

Insights from Psychoanalysis

CHAPTER I

The Mirror and the Witch

The study in depth of the image of woman in art has profound relevance for problems of the modern consciousness and everyday life. The present search by women for their own freedom and independence is at one with the need to unravel modes by which men project their images and fantasies onto them. In men, this projection relates to their need to come to terms with the woman in themselves—their own feminine element. At a deeper level, we cannot solve the problem without understanding love and hate. (Alas, too many feminist organizations have been founded on hate itself.) [1]

As we shall see, in the unconscious woman represents aspects of our immanent physical and psychic history. We all emerge from a woman's body and are created by her creative power; we are drawn out by her psyche. Therefore, in the symbolism of our perceptions of the world, she is both a great mystery and an ideal positive power. Women is also the creature we are terribly afraid of because she once had the power of life and death over us. She was once the creative mirror in whose face and response we saw our being emerge. But because she had this power and because we could have seen only a blankness in her face, we are afraid of her for she could be a witch. Because we are afraid of her, we are often hostile to woman. Yet, we tend to idealize her because we admire and are in awe of her.

These extremeties in our attitudes to woman underlie our perplexities and our cruelties. Moreover, they affect deeply our relationship with ourselves and the world. Undoubtedly, these problems differ in the consciousness of men and women. (However, from my study of Sylvia Plath, I have learned that such deep unconscious fears and preoccupations about woman are as present in a woman's consciousness as in a man's.) Let me now turn to the writings of some psychotherapists and suggest how their insights illuminate problems of the philosophy of being.

Karl Stern makes some valuable points in the first chapter of his book *The Flight from Woman* (1965), which I will discuss later. For millennia, Stern says, women have suffered atrocious forms of social and legal injustice. The trouble is, however, that many assume that the problem would be solved if we simply deny woman's special nature: "The cry for *equality* has changed into an assertion of *sameness*" (14). The word *discrimination* has taken on the flavor of discrimination against.

The irony is that, in the field of human rights, the "model" of woman has taken on a Cartesian character. This is profoundly ironic, since, as Stern shows, Descartes had a profound fear of woman as a result of his mother's death when he was a baby; and his sense of man's relationship with Mother Earth is one of total alienation. From his scientific mode, an attitude to woman has developed that removes all feminine qualities in favor of a mechanism:

> The idea that anatomical differences are nothing but a matter of accidental implements of the body, interchangeable, as it were, is a touch of Cartesianism—something that imperceptibly creeps into many of our modern views of people and the world. (14)

Thus, we find women themselves denying the primary truth about woman—that she creates us and that she has a special function, not only to create each one of us in the womb but also to create our consciousness. For this reason, the phenomenological dimension needs to be added to the study of woman, to enrich it.

Stern quotes Simone de Beauvoir, whose view of woman, which rejects sexual polarity, leads, Stern declares, to "an extraordinary impoverishment":

> What began in feminism as a movement of liberation is bound to end in a slavery worse than the first. (15)

In the denial of the special nature and role of woman, of the *participation mystique* between mother and infant in which our being grows, and in the denial of woman as the *mysterium tremendum* lies a new depersonalization—in a false emphasis on interchangeable sexual sameness—that might permit political and social policies that could become new forms of slavery. One does not have to go far to find feminists whose attitudes and behavior make this clear, in their aggressive denial of what D. H. Lawrence called "disquality," or *la différence*—so that, like Marxism and Sartre's kind of existentialism, militant feminism ends up with an atmosphere indistinguishable from that of scientific positivism, in an implicit denial of the very truths of inwardness and the strange mysteries of 'being,' which are the proper object of our quest for inner and outer truth. For example, D. W. Winnicott's great discovery of *primary maternal preoccupation*, that special state in woman that enables us to find our identity in creative reflection, would obviously be anathema to feminism. As Stern says, "the alleged mysteriousness of the feminine is treated with benevolent jocularity in feminist literature" (17). Yet, it is this special characteristic of woman that is the key to our understanding, on the one hand, of why woman has been ill-treated in the past and of what she has contributed to human civilization, on the other. True understanding is here the clue to her freedom.

Perhaps the open discussion of the nature of woman nearest to my point of view is that pursued by Ann Belford Ulanov in her book *Receiving Woman: Studies in the Psychology and Theology of the Feminine* (1981). Ulanov is an American Jungian therapist and teacher at the Union Theological Seminary in New York City. I differ from her in that she believes in God and I am an agnostic; but her view of feminity, based on her own experience, her experience of patients, and on the psychology of Jung, Winnicott, Melanie Klein, Harry Guntrip, and others in dynamic psychiatry seems to me most illuminating and right.

Ulanov believes that both the chauvinist and feminist attitudes to woman are partial. The hard-line chauvinist would take away from woman her physical power, her intellect, her ambition, and her capacity for free assertion. He wants to do this out of fear of these elements of her 'being.' The misogynist cannot bear a woman to have both those capacities that are womanly (the creative capacity to bear and nurture children) *and* the capacity to assert her independence and culturally creative power.

The hard-line feminist, on the other hand, abstracts woman from her own particular life at the dependent, vulnerable core of human 'being'. The feminist may reject any recognition of the differences between sexes and may believe that any recognition of such differences must become translated into forms of political discrimination. This is but a manifestation of the fear of those aspects of 'being' that belong specifically to the female and that cannot be defined in male terms. There is a sense in which the new stereotypes of feminity upheld by "hard" feminists are themselves too male to account adequately for woman.

The way to understand woman, says Ulanov, must come from woman herself, as Freud ultimately decided. Although Jung made the illuminating discovery that a man tends to experience the deep aspects of the unconscious as presented to him in the feminine images of the anima archetype, which he feels as something like his own soul, the obverse, Ulanov believes, is not true of woman, who does not experience her own soul as the animus.[2]

Ulanov believes that woman should be capable of receiving, or acknowledging, all of herself and believes that women have done so cutting across stereotypes throughout the ages. She pays a particular tribute to the heroines of the novels of Elizabeth Gaskell, as I too would wish to do. These novels show, as Ulanov says, "the vigors of introspection that put every feeling and perception into that inner order which produces a woman of great inward authority, one who can change the world around her through her impact on persons who come into contact with her" (Ulanov 1981, 21). This is especially true of Margaret Hale, the heroine of *North and South*. These heroines, Ulanov says, "trust the life in them to take its proper shape. . . . [they] *trust life to come into being* [italics mine]" (21). In this, I believe, she points to the most important aspect of woman, both in life and in art: *she is the focus of the fulfillment of that which we have within us to become;* or, as Goethe put it, "woman lifts us up."

Here it will help to discuss certain psychological and emotional processes that are especially relevant to the problem of woman. Some of the highly valued psychological and intellectual processes in our society are considered by some psychologists to be eminently male: they are those processes that are analytical, logical, mechanical, and intellectual. But others are especially female: intuition; the capacity to respond and to 'be for'; creative powers; the use of poetic modes, such as symbolism of a metaphysical kind; empathy; and telepathy. In our growth toward becoming ourselves as adults, we undoubtedly depend upon female-element powers, both in ourselves and in others; in men and in women.

One of these powers is the capacity to identify with another person. Of course, the way boys grow up is different from the way girls grow up; but in both, identification with the male and female aspects of father and mother is important. The development of *gender* clearly is closely bound up with identification. (In her studies of homosexuality, Elizabeth Moberley [1983] finds that identifying with the parent of one's own sex is the most important factor, homosexuals often being orphans for one reason or another.)

As we shall see, these early imaginative processes are the basis of our sense of identity and of our capacity to relate to others and to the world. It is important to bear in mind that these processes are related to female-element 'being' and to the mother's influence in this. Our capacity to become ourselves and to relate effectively to the world are drawn out in us largely through the powers of the mother. This why woman is both so mysterious and terrible. And because she has the power of life and death over us and is only human, she is feared.

In association with these imaginative processes, there is an important psychological phenomenon, which Ulanov considers, that is crucial to the consideration of woman, her nature, and her position in society. This is *projection*.

Projection is a normal process, and it is unconscious. We only discover it when we find ourselves doing it. It is a way of defending the ego against unconscious impulses, affects, and perceptions that we fear will be painful if admitted into full awareness. We deny recognition of these internal elements and perceive them as originating outside ourselves.

Closely related to these processes is the fact of *ambivalence*. We are all a mixture of love and hate, and love and hate are always closely related. Hate is not the opposite of love; indifference is. Hate is a positive but inverted dynamic, intended, when love is denied, to compel the other to give what, it is felt, is due. If necessary, the impulse to compel may pay the final tribute of annihilating the object. Whenever our harmony is threatened and the frightening impulses to hate become disturbing, we are liable to expel these and to ascribe them to other persons or to causes external to ourselves:

> To some degree we treat the other person as a blank screen onto which we can cast various aspects of our personalities that we somehow cannot yet consciously acknowledge. (57)

This spares us the pain of recognizing our own ambivalent emotions as one source of conflict within us. But "exporting" the problem may have worse consequences. In marriage,

> by seeing our partner as the cause of tension, we can persuade ourselves that if only he or she would change, harmony would be restored. We thereby protect our own self-image as good, free of negative reactions and troublesome attitudes. We do so by projecting the bad onto someone else. (58)

It is this dynamic that lies beneath racism and pornography, especially of the sadistic kind. And as Ulanov points out, it is also the underlying problem behind wife-beating:

> In the case of wife-beating we see projection working in its most primitive form. There the husband projects onto the wife fearful images in himself that he violently repudiates. He then punishes her

for having them while indulging those impulses in himself in the beating process. (58)

What such a man may be projecting is a dread and fear of his own female element.

It is common, Ulanov suggests, for men to project onto women feminine aspects of themselves, "along with their unconscious expectation that the female will manage these parts of life for them" (58).

> Many marriage problems begin when a woman refuses to carry out such projections. A major thrust of the woman's movement points women towards recognizing themselves as persons, no longer to be defined in the images men project onto them. (58)

It is necessary to examine some complex papers in psychoanalysis in order to make it plain that the whole problem of woman is bound up with one's attitude to oneself. Those familiar with psychoanalytical concepts of introjection and projection will have no difficulties here. We often find in literature male writers struggling with the ghost of the bad side of the mother; but, of course, this is not happening out in the world, though it may be projected onto the world. They are struggling with a dynamic within themselves, and to grasp this requires an understanding of how human beings experience splitting and other processes in the psyche. One of the most important insights from psychoanalysis is that in each of us there is an inner reality in which is dramatized, by way of endopsychic dynamics, subjective problems that both echo external realities and are projected out over reality.

On the question of the split-off elements in an individual's gender identity, one of the most important papers is by D. W. Winnicott (1971a), in which the author discusses the male and female elements.[3] Winnicott's paper, entitled "The Split-off Male and Female Elements to Be Found Clinically in Men and Women—Theoretical Influences," is an important phenomenological one. It was Freud who pointed out that each partner in a sexual union brings two images to bear on it—that is, the father and mother of the woman and the father and mother of the man. We know this from our own sexual experience, for example. This indicates that within us, since

Insights from Psychoanalysis

we built up our personality largely by identifying, we have male and female characteristics. In family life, certainly, it is often startling to see how much a child identifies with the parent, at all ages, and how much the child's concepts of maleness and femaleness are taken from the parents, mostly in unconscious ways.

Since all depends upon the 'core of being' developed through identification with the mother, 'being' comes first. Thus, female-element capacities come first or are most important. On them depend the capacity to find the world and to relate to it in an objective way, in what Winnicott calls "male-element" terms, which are those of rationality, analysis, and "doing." Self-realization and a sense of identity depend upon the experience of identification with the mother and upon the shared emotional experience with her. From this security the infant develops his or her capacity to "do." Thus, as Winnicott says, 'being' comes first; "doing" comes later.

By contrast, writes Harry Guntrip, there is another kind of upbringing in which problems result because 'being' does not come first:

> The not very maternal, busy, bustling, organizing, dominating mother, who is determined that her baby shall "get on with his feed" . . . will present him with a "pseudo-male element breast" which seeks to "do things" to him. (Guntrip 1968, 250–51)

Here we have the roots of much of the inability to accept femininity, as well as the roots of a false kind of male "doing" as a substitute for 'being'. (It would seem likely that the prevalent cult of the breast symbol reduced to part object and the hard-bitten, "doing" trend in our culture are related to the increasing inability of many modern women to 'be for' their infants—that is, to give their babies "female-element breast." The result is a fundamental failure to achieve security of 'being'.) [4]

The worst consequence of this failure is illustrated by Winnicott in a fascinating case history. Winnicott had a patient who seemed to find it impossible to complete his analysis. Something made it impossible for him "to put paid to the whole thing." Yet the patient couldn't cut his losses, as the sacrifice would be too great.

Suddenly Winnicott became aware that though his patient was a man, he was talking about penis envy. Penis envy is a concept in Freudian theory that describes a certain kind of envy of male potency to be found in women. Even if we disagree with Freud's view of these matters, what Winnicott heard was a mode of symbolizing that was not male but female. It should not have been found in a man. Winnicott was a therapist who was willing to go mad if need be; thus, he said, "I am perfectly aware that you are a man but I am listening to a girl, and I am talking to a girl."

After a while the patient said, "If I were to tell someone about this girl I would be called mad."

Winnicott replied, "In fact it was not you who told this to anyone. It is I who see the girl and hear a girl talking; when actually there is a man on my couch. The mad person is myself" (Winnicott 1971a, 73 ff.).

By saying this, Winnicott spoke to both parts of the man, his male self and his split-off pure female-element "girl." Winnicott also put himself in the (mad) position of the patient's mother who wanted a girl and made her son fit into her idea of a girl. Winnicott admits he cannot prove all of this. He believes, however, that in the mother's early management of her son, she "held him and dealt with him in all sorts of physical ways as if she failed to see him as a male" (74). Her first child had been a boy, and now she wanted a girl. Thus, she treated her second child as if he were a girl; in a sense, she "created" a girl in the area of the psyche.

The "girl" in the man did not, of course, want his analysis, his self-discovery, to end. "She" wanted him to find out he was a girl; therefore, it was a stalemate. In this patient the dissociation between male and female was almost complete.

This frightening case suggests many insights into problems of maleness and femaleness.[5] There does seem to be the possibility that some individuals simply cannot accept their male or female element. The theoretical interpretation also explains certain forms of sexual behavior. For example, a man with a split-off female element may need to seek sexual relationships with an endless sequence of women, to whom he desires to give sexual satisfaction while finding none himself. The women represent only his split-off female element, and so the affairs are simply narcissistic—the 'other' is never found. Winnicott suggests that because of such problems we need to reexamine completely our ideas about homosexuality. The existence of this split-off female element in his patient, he suggests, may even have prevented homosexual practice, as this would have established a maleness the patient never wanted to acknowledge. The classical psychoanalytical diagnosis of the Don Juan type of individual, whose compulsive promiscuity is motivated by a hatred of women, is that such a person is essentially homosexual. It could be that such an individual is trying to solve the problem of a split-off female element. However, the problem could be, instead, that such a person is trying to integrate a split-off female element. It could be that underlying Shakespeare's problem with woman is a split in his personality. If the sonnets are autobiographical, as seems certain, we may assume that Shakespeare was as deeply involved emotionally and sexually with a man as well as with a woman. Although we do not know the exact details of the relationship to which the sonnets refer, the poems themselves speak of profound forms of tormented uncertainty and disillusionment—involving the poet in profound disturbances of the reality sense and with problems of meaning in relation to time and death, involved with ambiguities about gender.

Besides considering male and female elements as aspects of the personality, we may also see them as relating to modes of knowing the world and dealing with it. As Guntrip puts it, there are two ways of relating: knowing and communicating. The male-element way of relating is expressed by active "doing," knowing by thinking, and communicating ideas through verbal symbols. In other words, it centers on the intellectual processes. (As we shall see, Karl Stern, in his *The Flight from Woman* [1965], believes that this is too exclusively the thought mode of our era.) The female-element way is that of relating by identifying and sharing in a sense of 'being', knowing by feeling, and communicating through emotional empathy:

> All this is reorganized in the familiar line, "Thoughts that do often lie too deep for tears," or for any expression in words, an experience common in earliest motherhood, profound friendship, and true marital love. (Guntrip 1968, 262–63)

The Mirror and the Witch

It is becoming apparent to many that there is another kind of thought, another way of knowing the world—the female way. This is not to say that this way is a prerogative of woman, though it is clear if we contemplate the French Impressionist painters that there is a special delicacy and perception in the paintings of Berthe Morisot because she is a woman. Yet, it is as obvious that Renoir, Pissaro, and Sisley are equally able to see and portray the world in a "female" way—that is, their paintings illuminate 'being.' Much of the art of the last one hundred years, including the art of the Impressionists, has been existentialist in that it emphasizes the uniqueness of individual 'being' and perception. Poetry and the novel can be also essentially rooted in female modes, as, (for example) in the works of Blake, Dickens, Lawrence, and Tolstoy. That this is so is foreign to our male-dominated thought modes; and this accounts for the hostility to the poetic to be found in certain traditions of predominant thought in our society, from Galileo to Bentham and beyond. Continental philosophers, phenomenologists, and existentialists have striven for a century to restore the reality of the 'I', the uniqueness of 'being', and the creative consciousness of the human person to Western thought in their philosophical anthropology. In this they have striven to restore female-element 'being' to recognition in a situation in which modes of thought have been distortedly masculinized—so masculinized as to be at times hostile even to the very recognition of feminine modes of apprehension (a hostility often clearly manifest in empirical psychology).

I would like here to discuss in detail the psychoanalytical theories of Harry Guntrip. Guntrip was himself a therapist, but his written work is most remarkable for its comprehensive account of the work of others in psychoanalysis. His work clearly relates the experience of mothering and of woman to problems of dependence and ego weakness. Notably, he relates the work of W. R. D. Fairbairn, with whom he was in analysis, to that of Winnicott. Using these authors, Guntrip tries to penetrate to the heart of the schizoid problem—that is, the universal problems of identity and 'being'. His first work of this kind was *Personality Structure and Human Interaction* (1961), and the second was *Schizoid Phenomena, Object Relations, and the Self* (1968).

17

Insights from Psychoanalysis

The sections of the latter book that concern us are in the chapters entitled "Failure in Ego-Development" and "Foundations of Ego Identity." Later in this chapter Guntrip gives us a historical, schematic account of the way psychoanalysis has, as he sees it, worked in from the "outer" elements of the problem ("The Individual in Society") to the very core of the self ("The Absolute Start of the Ego"). (See the diagrammatic analysis of the process of psychoanalysis in Guntrip 1968, 246–48). At the heart of these problems is the child's relationship with the mother.

Guntrip's account brings together a number of concepts. One is the very idea of a 'core of being'. This is associated with the female element, which develops out of the experience of the mother. Where there are psychological disorders it is in the female element, in both men and women, that the trouble lies. Guntrip associates the 'core of being' and the female element with the *true self*. The idea that there is a true self within us, either securely "there" or waiting for the opportunity to come into being or deeply hidden and frustrated, is developed further in Peter Lomas's *True and False Experience* (1967) and in Marion Milner's *Hands of the Living God* (1969), in which Milner seems to associate a true self with what she calls a "formative principle."

Guntrip begins chapter 6 in *Schizoid Phenomena* from the experience of ego weakness in himself and in his colleagues. This is not something clear-cut that enables therapists to distinguish between mental illness and health, but it is a recognized problem. Moreover, ego weakness is something of which we are all afraid. The patient's intense fear of ego weakness makes him resistant to therapy. To others who experience it, it is a source of tension. To overcome ego weakness and to hide it, individuals force the self to cope with outer reality; they develop courageous and unremitting modes of activity to keep their daily life going. The problem is, however, that these modes do not feel authentic; they feel as if they belong to a false self. And in individuals with deep ego weakness, there lurks, beneath the active surface of the compensatory dynamics, a center of the identity that is experienced as a weak infant and as a fear of dying.[6]

Guntrip reports from his clinical experience that the fear of dying may turn into a wish to die. Looking at cultural problems, we may associate this with the longing for 'nonbeing' and also the inclination to suicide, which Masud Khan (1979) detects as a significant theme in modern European culture. According to Guntrip:

> The ultimate unconscious infantile weak ego is very clearly experienced as a *fear of dying*, when its threat to the stability of the personality is being felt. (Guntrip 1968, 215)

This is felt, says Guntrip, in less uncompromising terms as a longing to regress, to escape from life, to go to sleep for an indefinite period, or, more mildly still, as loss of interest and active impulse—that is, a wish to get out of things and avoid responsibility.

This Guntrip calls the problem of the "regressed ego." But he suggests it is still more complicated than that. There are, he suggests, three contributory causes (1) *repression* of the frightened infant because this ungrown element of the self represents a threat to the adult self; (2) *withdrawal* of the frightened infant from a world he cannot cope with; and (3) *unevoked potential* in the primary natural psyche, which has never been "brought to birth" because the "maturational processes" have not enjoyed a "facilitating environment."

Guntrip then discusses the phenomena of schizoid suicide, quoting patients who say "I don't want to die, but I need to be able to escape from the strain of keeping on living for a while." Schizoid suicide, Guntrip explains, is not really a wish for death as such, except when the patient has lost all hope. "Even then there is a deep unconscious secret wish that death should prove a pathway to rebirth" (217). I have used Guntrip's insights to discuss poems by Sylvia Plath, Ted Hughes, and Dylan Thomas and Gustav Mahler's Ninth Symphony. These insights are also relevant to those writers, such as C. S. Lewis and George MacDonald, who are preoccupied with the world of death (because the lost mother is there) and the hope of finding the opportunity to be born again.

What Guntrip finds in patients with schizoid problems is the feeling of being absolutely and utterly alone. It is not just a question of not being able to make friends, or whatever. It is an absolute, final sense of aloneness, which is accompanied by a sense of horror. Guntrip relates the dreams of patients in this condition: images of a black abyss at their feet, or of being a baby in a coma, or of being a paralyzed, isolated, and lost self. In some of these cases, Guntrip suggests the possibility that the therapist has contacted the hidden, isolated core of the patient's self.

The basic problem that confronts the therapist, says Guntrip, is the feeling such patients have that can be described thus:

> I can't get in touch with you. If you can't get in touch with me, I'm lost. But I've no confidence that you can get in touch with me, because you don't know anything about that part of me. No one has ever known and that's why I am hopeless. (220)

"In every human being," says Guntrip,

> *there is probably, to some extent, a lonely person at heart, but in the very ill, it is an utterly isolated being, too denuded of experience to be able to feel like a person, unable to communicate with others and never reached by others.* (220)

It is interesting that at this point Guntrip quotes Martin Buber. The human being needs confirmation, and Buber's memorable phrase is "from man to man the heavenly bread of self-being is passed." The individual who is well mothered feels a profound sense of belonging and of 'being-at-one-with' his world. Such a feeling is not thought out but is the persisting atmosphere of security in which the individual exists within himself. Such a person is able to be alone and is able to trust the world. The person grows up with a natural, unquestioned, symbiotic quality in the experience of himself and his world.

It is because the majority of people function in this way that society can go on at all. It is impossible for a human being to exist as a human being in isolation. Guntrip quotes Winnicott:

> Only if there is a good-enough mother does the infant start on a process of development that is personal and real. If the mothering is not good enough, then the infant becomes a collection of reactions to impingement, and *the true self of the infant fails to form* [italics mine] or become hidden behind a false self which complies with and generally wards off the world's knocks. (224)

According to Guntrip, the capacity to be alone, which Winnicott believes to be a mark of the well-mothered and secure person, is also a capacity to enjoy privacy and a sense of reality within oneself. The person who is basically ego-related never feels mentally alone within himself, even when he is with people with whom he has nothing in common or even when there is no one with him at all. Such a person will have a conviction of the reality and reliability for him of *good objects* (as in Kleinian psychoanalysis) in the outer world.

Two subjects are discussed in the last pages of Guntrip's chapter. The first is privacy. A certain strength of identity is necessary before an individual can enjoy privacy—being alone, enjoying benign memories, or enjoying being in touch with oneself. The individual who has a serious degree of ego weakness may feel a fear of loss of contact when alone and therefore feels threatened. Such an individual may need to develop *bad* fantasies (in the Kleinian sense), which act as a defence against unreality. The person also may develop feelings of depersonalization, emptiness, and loss of ego. Guntrip draws a specific distinction between "compulsive anxious defensive thinking" and "enjoyable remembering of good experience."

The other subject that Guntrip discusses is Winnicott's concept of a core of the identity that is "incommunicado"—"an isolate permanently non-communicating, permanently unknown, in fact unfound" (236ff.). Guntrip's position is so firmly an object-relations one that he finds it difficult to accept this. Guntrip believes that any such isolated core is a primitive fear phenomenon.

Whether or not we accept Winnicott's view that the center of the self is incommunicable or not, it is clear that both he and Guntrip felt there is something in healthy people that can be called the 'core of being' and that this trait is a product of the special kind of responsiveness in the mother, which Winnicott called the "primary maternal preoccupation." If this sphere of 'being' is established, "doing"—the male capacity—follows naturally from it. But in people with profound psychological disturbances, "it is always the female element that we find dissociated, in both men and women, and that the fundamental dissociation is of the female element" (253).

The artist employs a kind of knowing like that of the mother. But this also requires a kind of retreat from the world, an entering into secrecy, and attention to that core of the self that Winnicott found to be incommunicable. There are dangers in this exploration for anyone and especially for the individual of weak or insecure identity. (I shall discuss further the way in which the creative artist must collaborate with the female element of 'being' within himself or herself in subsequent chapters.)

Here, I believe, we have the clue to certain puzzling manifestations in the arts. Art that attends to the 'core of being' is felt to be dangerous, as indeed it is. Blake, for example, is a poet whose work is clearly dangerous, in the sense that it challenges so many assumptions and conventional acceptances. There are those who enter into the disciplines of art only to find they cannot persist in exposing themselves to the existential themes aroused—the demands and perplexities of 'being'. They are defeated by the encroaching comforts of falsification. Arnold Bennett is a case in point, as he lost his capacity as an artist to bear the torments of creativity, which he was able to bear when he wrote his remarkable novel *The Old Wives' Tale*.

But there are also those who, because of their vulnerability, must turn to *bad* remembering and forms of male-element "doing"—in the form of fantasy and thinking—as a defense against the feelings of vulnerability and dread they would experience if they allowed themselves to be alone with 'being'.

In light of these insights, a great deal in our contemporary culture needs to be explained in terms of the development of modes of false strength, which are based on a certain kind of male dynamic. Where there is a deep insecurity of existence, this male dynamic is employed as a substitute for female-element 'being'.

Play, culture, interrelationship, and our capacity to see and deal with the world are thus all bound up with complex processes. Our creative powers emerge through the mother's capacity for creative reflection, and our capacity to engage with the reality of ourselves and the world is developed in play with the mother, as Winnicott argues in *Playing and Reality*. The possession of symbolism, which is the basis of all thought, is an achievement that belongs to the *participation mystique* between our own female-element powers and our mother's responsiveness. Therefore, at the heart of all creativity we would expect to discover a problem of woman, and literature is no exception.

CHAPTER 2

'Being for' and
Other Primary Processes

It is necessary to open up for discussion crucial experiences that have been up to now either taken for granted or have remained cloaked from us. It seems clear from psychoanalysis, especially from the study of infants, that a normal, sane existence is established as the result of a special kind of creative relationship in infancy. This relationship requires the special state in woman, to which D. W. Winnicott gave the name *primary maternal preoccupation*, which enables the mother to give *creative reflection* to the emerging being.

Without the experience of the mother's capacity to 'be for' us, there would be no hope for us to become autonomous creatures. It is this alone that gives us ego strength and enables us to go on to the later experiences, which are also important, of imaginative play between mother and infant. It is this imaginative play that equips us with independence and cultural resources, including the manifestations to which Winnicott gave the name *transitional object phenomena*. We find reality, a personal culture, and a sense of a meaningful existence only through woman's intuitive gifts. She knows how to use these gifts through tacit and mysterious powers. Doctors and nurses, says Winnicott, only think they know; the mother *knows*. This may be uncomfortable to a masculine society; yet, it goes on, often under a heavy, tacit denial of its importance.

In his valuable historical survey of psychoanalytical theory in *Schizoid Phenomena, Object Relations, and the Self* (1968), Harry Guntrip suggests that Winnicott brought psychoanalytical thinking to the 'core of being' (Guntrip 1968, (246–48). Freud explored the individual in society and the oedipal problems; Melanie Klein explored the infant's inner world and consequent forms of splitting in ego development and; W. R. D. Fairbairn explored the deeper schizoid problems of the very origin of identity. But in Winnicott's work over a lifetime; in his work at Paddington Green Hospital in London as an analyst of adults and children; and above all in his observation (as he estimated it) of twenty thousand mothers and infants, Winnicott penetrated to the "beginnings of the ego":

> The differentiation of subject and object out of the state of primary identification . . . the Absolute Start of the Ego . . . in . . . which the infant cannot yet experience an object relation but can experience . . . as *symbiosis, identity* with (in favourable cases) a stable object, the good enough mother. (248)

The psychotherapist, of course, sees adults and children who have not completed certain processes that in normal life are simply taken for granted. The psychotherapist is thus able to ask what the processes are by which the experience of 'being' or security originally is established between mother and infant in the first months of life; he thus reaches down in his study of human nature into the realms of primitive emotional development.

Winnicott's theory is that the mother is capable of creative reflection. Besides physical parturition, there is also psychic parturition. At first the baby does not sense himself and is not aware of himself as a whole being at all. The baby simple experiences disconnected experiences. Where there is no 'I', there is also no 'thou'. Only as the baby comes together as a whole continuous being does he become aware of the *object*—that is, the mother and, later, the world with which he is in relationship. As he finds the object, he also puts a self together.[1] At first, the baby and his world are, so to speak, all *subject*. And at first the mother "allows" the baby to believe, and to behave as if, she is simply part of him—his *subjec-*

tive object. This is infant *monism* and *narcissism*. Gradually, the mother "disillusions" the baby, thus allowing him to develop a self in relation to the world by finding her as the *objective object*.

The terms are difficult because what is being opened up are states of existence that are (to borrow a term from Maurice Merleau-Ponty, the French phenomenologist) *antepredicative*. That is, these states belong to a shadowy realm that lies in the area before it is possible to predicate anything from 'I' in relation to others and to objects. It is impossible to speak clearly of such states, since speaking clearly of anything itself belongs to a state in which the 'I' is speaking of the 'other'.

Nor is it possible to speak clearly of the original state of the mother in psychic parturition because this belongs to the kind of knowing which, in Michael Polanyi's terms, is tacit and ineffable. The psychic condition has, however, physiological concomitants:

> It is important to examine changes that occur in women, who are about to have a baby or who have just had one. These changes are at first almost physiological, and they start with the physical holding of the baby in the womb. Something would be missing, however, if a phrase such as "maternal instinct" were used in description. The fact is that in health women change in their orientation to themselves and the world, but however deeply rooted in physiology such changes may be, they can be distorted by mental ill-health in woman. (Winnicott 1970, 52)

Winnicott is reporting here on one kind of experience a psychotherapist has to face, despite all its disturbing truth: while the physiological processes may proceed in a pregnant woman, it is possible, because of mental ill health, that she may not develop properly her capacity for psychic parturition. Normally,

> soon after conception, or when conception is known to be possible, the woman begins to alter in her orientation, and to be concerned with the changes that are taking place within her. In various ways she is encouraged by her own body to be interested in herself. The mother shifts some of her sense of self onto the baby that is growing within her. (53)

Winnicott points out that in dealing with patients who have not sufficiently experienced the mother's attention in this way, the analyst becomes sensitive to their needs in ways similar to the sensitivity of the pregnant or nursing mother. We may note here that Winnicott's insights are those of a man willing to accept the female mothering role in his way, and his theories develop from his own experience of primary maternal preoccupation.

Winnicott refers us to his paper "Primary Maternal Preoccupation," in which he discusses the common recognized fact that "there is found to be an identification—conscious but also deeply unconscious—which the mother makes with her infant." He says that in the earliest phase, "we are dealing with a very special state of the mother, a psychological condition which deserves a name" (Winnicott 1958, 301).

> It gradually develops and becomes a state of heightened sensitivity during, and especially towards the end of pregnancy. It lasts for a few weeks after the birth of the child.
> It is not easily remembered by mothers once they have recovered from it.
> I would go further and say that the memory mothers have of this state tends to become repressed. (302)

The mother takes a risk: she can only get into this state if she is healthy; and she can only recover from it if she is healthy. If the baby dies, the mother's state "suddenly shows up as an illness" (302). Woman's exceptional courage, I feel sure, has to do with her ability to dare to enter naturally into this mysterious state and to take these risks.[2]

There are women who cannot allow themselves to enter into this state: "When a woman has a strong male identification she finds this part of her mothering function most difficult to achieve" (302). Such a woman often has "alternative interests" and may for this reason be so unable to 'be for' her child that the child grows up with psychic difficulties. Winnicott explains, "They do therapy instead of being parents" (303).[3]

When things go wrong, the infant experiences reactions to impingement, which interrupt the infant's 'going-on-being'. These reactions are experienced as a threat of annihilation. This, suggests Winnicott, is a very real primitive anxiety, "long antedating any anxiety that includes the word death in its description" (303).[4]

Insights from Psychoanalysis

Here, we may reflect on an insight from psychoanalysis: We all tend to fear woman because we were once totally dependent on a woman. In some the memory of such a dependence is a memory of a reaction to impingement—that is, an awkward kind of substitute for 'being for'—which contained a threat of annihilation. As will become evident, I believe that such unconscious memory lies behind the fear of woman expressed in the works of some authors.

Where the mother fails, there is a failure of a particular female mode; and this is an imaginative failure. It is clear from this chapter and from Winnicott's later work on play that the process in which the human identity is formed is one in which imagination plays a large part.

> Only if a mother is sensitized in the way I am describing can she feel herself into the infant's place, and so meet the infant's needs. These are at first body-needs, and they gradually become ego-needs as a psychology emerges out of the imaginative elaboration of physical experience.[5] (304)

What is important is that through identification of herself with the infant, the mother knows what the infant feels and so is able to provide almost exactly what the infant needs in the way of holding and in the "provision of an environment generally." With the "care that it receives from its mother," each infant is able to have a personal existence and so begins to build up "what might be called a continuity of being" (Winnicott 1970, 54).

An individual who has experienced adequate mothering in this way can have a "belief in the benign environment" (Winnicott, 1970, 32) (the individual's world *can* be Mother Earth). Such a person can also bear to be alone and can enjoy being himself in the presence of the 'other':

> The ability to be truly alone has as its basis the early experience of being alone in the presence of someone. . . . In the course of time the individual introjects the ego-supportive mother, and in this way becomes able to be alone without frequent reference to the mother as mother-symbol. (Winnicott 1970, 32)

At this point I want to return to some of Winnicott's other insights. One is that of creative reflection—a further discussion of that imaginative play and psychic nurture that develops from primary maternal preoccupation. We may examine Winnicott's psychoanalytical insights here in the context of a whole field of philosophical anthropology that is coming to parallel conclusions. See, for example, the writings of Helmuth Plessner, F. J. J. Buytendijk, and Martin Buber.[6]

Martin Buber, for example, examined the "principle of human life, that is, its beginning" and found "distance and relation" to be a relevant field of enquiry (Buber 1964, 63). Man's existence, says Buber, has a special quality that we need to recognize; it belongs to "relation." As Buber writes, "one can enter into relation only with being which has been set at a distance, more precisely, has become an independent opposite" (60). Man's 'being' can only develop and exist out of this relationship with "being which has been set at a distance"—with what Buber calls the "significant other," a phrase that existentialist psychotherapists, such as Rollo May, have used significantly.

An animal perceives only those things that concern it in the total situation available to it, and it is those things that make the animal's world. But it is perhaps not correct even to use the word *world* because the animal lives, instead, by an "image of a realm," which is nothing more than the "dynamic of the presences bound up with one another by bodily memory to the extent required by the functions of life which are to be carried out." With man, however, "with his human life, a world exists" (61).

> An animal in the realm of its perceptions is like a fruit in its skin: man is, or can be, in the world as an enormous building which is always being added to. . . . he is the creative (*Wesen*) through whose being (*Sein*) "What is" (*das Seiende*) becomes detached from him, and recognized for itself. . . . Only when a structure of being is independently over against a living being (*Seiende*), an independent opposite, does a world exist. (61)

Man is capable of what Buber calls a "synthesizing apperception," by which he means "the apperception of a being as a whole and as a unity. Such a view is won, and won again and again, only by

29

looking upon the world as a whole" (62). Here Buber emphasizes the relationship between being able to see the world in a whole and creative way and relationship—not least those primary relationships that create 'being'. As Buber says:

> Man wishes to be confirmed in his being by man, and wishes to have a presence in the being of the other. The human person needs confirmation because man as man needs it. An animal does not need to be confirmed, for it is what it is unquestionably. It is different with man: sent forth from the natural domain of species into the hazard of the solitary category, surrounded by the air of a chaos which came into being with him, secretly and bashfully he watches for a Yes which allows him to be and which can come to him only from one human being to another. It is from one man to another that the heavenly bread of Self-being is passed. (71)

Buber himself recognizes the relationship between this interpersonal basis of 'being' and imagination. He discusses a "capacity possessed to some extent by everyone":

> . . . the capacity to hold before one's soul a reality arising at this moment but not able to be directly experienced. (70)

He discusses how

> "imagining" the real means that I imagine to myself what another man is at this very moment wishing, feeling, perceiving, thinking, and not as a detached content but in his very reality, that is, as a living process in this man. (70)

We have also seen, as Masud Khan points out, that Winnicott stresses the necessity of a mother's capacity to meet imaginatively, as well as effectively, the first creative gestures of the infant-child and that this forms the basis of the child's true confidence in his evolving and crystallizing sense of self.[7] In this context, certain other papers by Winnicott are relevant, especially his essays "Transitional Objects and Transitional Phenomena" (1971a) "The Mirror-Role of Mother and Family in Child Development" (1971a). Both are developments from his study of primary maternal preoccupation and the phenomena of psychic birth.

Winnicott's essay on transitional objects originally appeared in 1951, and since then there has been considerable interest in his theories of this phenomenon. Winnicott believes that the child's use of a transitional object—a cuddly rag or a teddy bear—is a significant moment in the child's relationship with reality and in his cultural development. The transitional object is the infant's first symbol. It stands for the child's possession of the mother, in his inner life, and enables the child from thence forth both to develop inner resources (the child can be alone in the dark so long as he has the transitional object) and to feel linked with other human beings (for his cuddly rag smells of the mother and so unites the child with her even when he is alone). It is the first "not-me possession."

What Winnicott opens up here is the whole mysterious development of the human being's capacity to relate to the world of reality and to be effective in it. We take this autonomous creativity for granted, but in fact it is *the* supreme achievement of the human person. And it is given to us by the mother. What F. R. Leavis calls "the living principle" is a faculty that grows out of the responsiveness of the mother to her infant and the imaginative play between them; thus, the "reality sense" grows out of the imaginative "poetic" faculties, out of that capacity to symbolize that which grows out of body play. The implication of this emphasis is of great importance for child study and for education. Imaginative play and the arts are not mere distractions but are fundamental to those developments by which we find and deal with objective reality, as well as the subjective world. If we agree with Susanne Langer (1957) that symbolism is the basis of all thought, then our capacity to think has its origins in play with the mother.

The aspect of Winnicott's essay I will discuss here is illusion and the value of illusion. At the beginning, the mother adapts totally to her baby and "affords the infant the opportunity or the *illusion* that the breast is part of the infant."

> It is, as it were, under magical control. The same can be said in terms of the infant care in general, in the quiet times between excitements. Omnipotence is nearly a fact of experience. (Winnicott 1958, 238)

The mother's role ultimately is to "disillusion" the infant, but she cannot do this unless she has provided first the opportunity for illusion. She "allows" the baby to suppose that "the breast is created by the infant over and over again out of the infant's capacity to love or (one can say) out of need" (238).

> A subjective phenomenon develops in the baby which we call the mother's breast. [In a footnote Winnicott makes it clear he includes the whole technique of mothering; in this term, whether an infant is breast or bottle fed.] (239)

This wide meaning of the word *breast*, Winnicott says, should be kept in mind. It really means the whole world, which is the mother:

> The mother places the actual breast just there where the infant is ready to create, and at the right moment. (239)

These interactions between mother and infant lie behind the wider problem of finding reality. From birth, says Winnicott, the human being is concerned with the problem of the relationship between what is objectively perceived and what is subjectively conceived of,

> and in the solution of this problem there is no health for the human being who has not been started off well enough by the mother. (239)

The importance of transitional phenomena is that "there is no meaning for the human being in the idea of a relationship with an object that is perceived by others as external to that being" (239).

What all this has to do with is our capacity to see a *meaningful* world. It is this that the mother gives us, by fostering the illusion that we have made our world or, so to speak, made it "ours." We are subjectively involved in the things we see. As we shall see, a whole era of alienation from the world of reality is diagnosed by one psychotherapist, Karl Stern, as having its origins in the way the world was stripped of its meaning for René Descartes as the result of his mother's death when he was an infant. Out of his psyche, which was deeply disturbed by this loss, Descartes invented a way of dealing effectively with reality by splitting certain dimensions of it off from the emotional agonies and deficiencies associated with this terrible loss—experienced by the infant as rejection. This mode virtually became the mode of modern science, in which the universe is seen as an entity from which we are alienated. It has been in opposition to this kind of universe that certain important artists, such as Blake, Dickens, and Lawrence, have sought to exert the claim of 'being'. A parallel impulse lies behind Lawrence's championship of a harmony with nature and 'being' against all that he means by "will" and "industry." (Under the Cartesian influence the world is not sufficiently felt by us to be "ours.")

It is important to bear in mind that the central issue is that of meaning—the finding of a real and meaningful world. This quest has its origins in the infant's experience. The infant, in a certain setting provided by the mother, "is capable of conceiving of the idea of something which would meet the growing need which arises out of instinctual tension" (239). At first, the infant cannot be said to know what is to be created. At this point in time, the mother presents herself. Therefore, there is an "overlap between what the mother supplies and what the child might conceive of" (239). To those who look on from the outside, it seems that the infant perceives what the mother presents. But as Winnicott says:

> The infant perceives the breast only insofar as a breast could be created just there and then. There is no interchange between the mother and the infant. Psychologically the infant takes from a breast that is part of the infant, and the mother gives milk to an infant that is part of herself. In psychology, the idea of an interchange is based on an illusion. (239)

Winnicott knows these mysterious processes through his experience with babies and infants, as well as through his experience with psychotics in whom they have gone wrong. We ourselves may experience these perceptual complexities in mothers and infants. Winnicott provides two diagrams to show that the transitional object—the first symbol—emerges from this area of confused illusion. (See Winnicott 1958, 240).

It is a matter of agreement between the adult and the baby that we will never ask the question "Did you conceive of this or was it presented to you from without?" This is simply not a question one asks; it is unthinkable. Therefore, the baby believes he has made his cuddly rag, just as he believed the mother's breast to have been made by him.

The problem becomes a problem when the mother begins her next task. Having given her infant the opportunity for illusion, she then must "disillusion" the infant, so that the infant can reach the important stage of discovering that he does not in truth create his world. Winnicott states:

> This is preliminary to the task of weaning, and it also continues as the task of parents and educators. (240)

The matter of illusion is one that no individual solves for himself. The problem continues throughout our lives—in our discovery of what is real. If all goes well with the infant at this stage, "the stage is set for the frustrations that we gather together under the word weaning" (240). The process of "disillusionment" underlies weaning:

> If illusion-disillusion has gone astray the infant cannot attend to such a thing as weaning, nor to a reaction to weaning, and then it is absurd to refer to weaning at all. The mere termination of breast feeding is not a weaning. (240)

Of course, the problems of reality and illusion remain with all of us. However "good enough" the mother may be, the problems of illusion and "disillusion" are never solved. That is our human problem.

> It is assumed here that the task of reality-acceptance is never completed, that no human being is free from the strain of relating inner and outer reality, and that relief from this strain is provided by an intermediate area of experience which is not challenged (arts, religion, etc.). . . . This intermediate area is in direct continuity with the play area of the small child who is "lost" in play. (241)

In his later discussions of transitional-object phenomena, Winnicott develops his theory of the continuity between play and culture. Our absorption in cultural activity is an engagement with the perpetual problem of the reality of the world and of how much we feel it to be "our world"—that is, one which is benign, one that we may act creatively in and 'be with', while admitting its objective features that we cannot change but only subjectively adjunct to.

Another relevant paper by Winnicott discusses the mother's reflecting role. Winnicott refers to the term *mirror phase*, from a paper by the French psychoanalyst and anthropologist Jacques La-

can. A translation of Lacan's paper "Le Stadt du Miroir" was published in the *New Left Review* on October 1968 (though it was
originally written in 1949). In it Lacan refers to the moment when
the child recognizes himself in a mirror. Winnicott, however, finds
it odd that Lacan fails to notice the mother's reflecting role, and in
his essay he tries to put the mother back into the mirror phase.
Winnicott begins his paper with a reference to Lacan's:

> Jacques Lacan's paper "Le Stadt du Miroir" has certainly influenced
> me. He refers to the use of the mirror in each individual's ego-devel-
> opment. However, Lacan does not think of the mirror in terms of the
> mother's face, in the way that I wish to do here. (Winnicott 1971a,
> 111)

Winnicott finds the origins of creative perception—the capacity
to see the world and to find a meaning in it—in being seen by the
mother. He speaks of the mother's role of "giving back to the baby
the baby's own self".

> Now, at some point the baby takes a look round. Perhaps the baby at
> the breast does not look at the breast. Looking at the face is more
> likely to be a feature. . . . What does the baby see there? (112)

What the baby sees is himself or herself. In *Therapeutic Consultations in Child Psychiatry* (1971b), Winnicott writes as if the child
seeks for an imago of himself in the mother's inner psyche, as if he
has to find out what idea she has of him. It is out of such interpersonal responses that the sense of self and world develops.[8]

> In other words the mother is looking at the baby, *and what she looks
> like is related to what she sees there.* (Winnicott 1971a, 112)

Here we have the origins of many themes in poetry. Not least of
these themes is the anguished problem in the works of Shakespeare
and other writers of the difference between appearance and reality.
It is the problem posed by the natural ambivalence of the mother
who seems so radiant but may also be ill, depressed, angry, blank,
tired, or even totally rejecting. If she dies, it seems as if this beautiful face has concealed some ultimate hate. All this must be read
into the underlying problem of existence: once we were all totally
dependent—in our capacity to find ourselves—on a woman, into

35

whose face we searched for reflection. This was a dreadful situation, particularly if we consider that she, like all of us, was but weak and mortal. Winnicott describes the history of "George" (Winnicott 1971b), in which a baby looked into his mother's consciousness to see what idea she had of him and found nothing. The mother had not wanted him, and the doctors had refused an abortion, so she totally denied his existence. He was incurable.

The danger always is that a baby who is not reflected may never be able to see the world in such a way that his subjective life is involved in what he is seeing. Such a person cannot achieve apperception:

> Perception takes the place of that which might have been the beginning of a significant change with the world, a two way process in which self-enrichment alternates with the discovery of meaning in the world of seen things. (Winnicott 1971a, 113)

Winnicott, discussing failures in this process, writes:

> The baby quickly learns to make a forecast: "Just now it is safe to forget the mother's mood and to be spontaneous, but any minute the mother's face will become fixed or her mood will predominate, and my own personal needs must then be withdrawn otherwise my central self may suffer insult." (113)

If there is a precariousness about the predictability, there may be, Winnicott contends, "a threat of chaos." Evidently, Winnicott based this opinion on his experience of severely ill people.

> A baby so treated will grow up puzzled about mirrors, and what the mirror has to offer. If the mother's face is unresponsive, then a mirror is a thing to be looked at but not to be looked into. (113)[9]

It is important at this point to make it plain that I use the word *hate* in a particular way, derived from psychoanalysis. Hate is not the opposite of love, which would be indifference. In psychoanalytical thinking, hate is the inversion of love and represents a demand that the other responds in some way, where there seems to be no natural response from love. Hate belongs to the attempt to compel the 'other' to give that which should be one's by right or to destroy the 'other' in oral need.

To see it in its most positive light, the motive power of hate can be seen as a desperate attempt to secure the needed confirmation and sense of meaning when they cannot be found by love. It is a retreat to the most primitive modes, akin to the "attack" that the baby makes upon the breast and the fantasies of "emptying" that accompany it—leading ultimately to a fear of causing harm to the object. If the capacity for such fear can be achieved, then we may develop the ability for concern or the desire for reparation—the giving that restores the fantasized damage. This is seen in object-relations psychology as the basis of the moral sense: the concern we feel about the possible damage that may be done to others by our destructive fantasies and impulses, once we have found the reality of the 'other'.

Since woman is the primary focus of love and of our hungry needs, she also becomes the focus of our hate. She also can be terribly feared because, in certain circumstances, she can be felt to be likely to turn her hate against us in retaliation. We fear that if we hate her or if she is provoked into hating us, the creature who brings us into being may become the witch who can threaten to take us out of existence.

Such unconscious fears underlie many common human problems. Karl Stern's *The Flight from Woman* begins with his own experience as a therapist treating of men of restless energy but emotionally empty, in whom he found, as do other psychotherapists, "a maternal conflict and a rejection of the feminine" (Stern 1965, 1). Such individuals may combine a fear of accepting tenderness with a shrinking from all forms of passivity. Yet, deep down they betray an extraordinary need to be mothered. These men suffer from *activism* and tend to exhibit drive and ambition, which are manifestations of a "flight into work"—that is, an escape from emotional problems into intense, distracting effort. Yet, these individuals are actually in terror of dependence:

> The very possibility of being in the least dependent or protected, or even being loved, amounts to nothing less than a phantasy of mutilation or destruction. (5)

Insights from Psychoanalysis

Stern discusses two other related phenomena: the fear of being loved and the flight from falling not only into undue activism but into undue intellectualism—that is, into cold, rational abstractions. Often, Stern says, hyperactivist and hyperrationalist attitudes go together. Such people may be "successful" in the usual sense, and they tend to be great believers in the mechanics and manageability of human relations: "If individuals like these have any philosophical convictions at all, they tend to be rationalist and positivist" (9).

The female counterpart to the kind of man Stern is discussing is the woman who finds it difficult to accept her womanly role:

This is quite independent of the injustices imposed on women in many societies; it is rather an over-evaluation of masculine achievement and a debasement of values which are commonly associated with the womanly; a rejection, often unconscious, even of motherhood; an aping of man, associated with an increasing undertone of envy and resentment. (6)

The trouble is, as I was aware throughout the preparation of this book (and, I believe, Stern was throughout his), that the so-called hustler type of man and the feminine-rejecting woman are, at the moment, powerfully influential in our society. Yet, this development often is supposed to represent progress and liberation, while it may, instead, be a sign of weakness. For the truth is that "in either case, whether of the man or the woman I have just sketched, there is a *flight from the feminine*" [italics mine] (6).

To Stern, there arises the ghastly specter of a world "impoverished of womanly values," by the domination of thought and social life by the masculine modes, the one-sidedly rational and technical, and the impulse to exploit and manipulate. Stern warns us here against making sweeping generalizations, but he finds a general alarm that something of the kind is happening. To solve the problem, we need once more to go "to the hearts of men," and Stern tries to do so in the spirit of phenomenology and existential philosophy, drawing on his experience as a therapist. Stern's preliminary pages are largely an attempt to rescue the question of male and female from contemporary fashions.[10]

Woman, in the person of our mother, is the first being with whom we are in contact:

> There is no more intimate union than that which exists between the child and the mother who keeps it in the sheltering and nourishing womb. It all begins with a true *fusion* of being. (18)

That extraordinary oneness and communication continues for quite some time after birth:

> The infant is utterly dependent on the mother. . . . He would starve if he was not fed, he would become sick if he were not cleaned. He is not only dependent for physical nourishment but also for mental nourishment, for love. (18)

There exists, says Stern, a *"participation mystique, a psychic flow from child to mother and from mother to child"* (18). (Stern borrowed the French phrase from the anthropological work of Levy-Bruhl.)

Stern's account of the primitive developing relationship between mother and child is close to Winnicott's. This early drama, Stern declares, is decisive for the formation of character. Stern underpins the importance of the mother's role by referring to the work of John Bowlby (1953) on the child's tie to the mother, and to the work of H. F. Harlow and others with monkeys, which showed that monkeys deprived of their real mothers were inhibited in their emotional development. Stern also refers to another important element in the way in which we feel imbued with a sense of the mysterious in woman—that of time. As we grow older, time seems to accelerate. When we were babies, we inhabited a vast time universe, in an intimate physical and mental fusion with another being. In this realm lie the origins of human concepts of eternity.

Women manifest the *rhythm of being*: They go through the four-week period of ovulation and the nine-month period of gestation. Stern points out that it is common for women who have had an abortion to break down just when the baby would have been born.[11] This may happen despite the woman's unconsciousness of the significance of the date and despite her moral approval of her own act. It is a reaction of loss that belongs to the time of 'being'—a deep unconscious awareness of the tides of the body.

> Woman, in her being, is deeply committed to *bios*, to nature itself. The words for *mother* and *matter*, for *mater* and *materia* are etymologically related. (Stern 1965, 23)

The first few pages of Stern's chapter entitled "Womanhood" are devoted to resisting developments by which these truths are denied. Anthropologists, such as Margaret Mead, have concluded that the roles assumed by man and woman depend upon notions implanted in the child at an early age; and that, apart from the mere matter of sexual reproduction, sexual difference is an outcome of social and cultural constellations. (See Mead 1955.) Radical and progressive attitudes are still based on such views, and absurd feminist progressive groups are even trying to get books banned, on the grounds of this doubtful position.

But Stern warns us of the consequences. It is true that for centuries women have suffered atrocious forms of social and legal injustice. They have been, as Stern puts it, "victims of a kind of interior colonialism" (Stern 1965, 14). But it is disastrous that, since the French Revolution, the cry for equality has changed into a demand for sameness, so that distinctions have come to seem like discriminations.

In this, Cartesianism has played a part. The Cartesian view of the nature of the human person defines anatomical differences as nothing more than accidental, interchangeable implements of the body. (A view such as this is found and often illustrated in much sex education.) Metaphysical differences are felt to belong to superstition and are open to correction by scientific enquiry—a view that is itself a triumph of the masculinity of knowledge.

Therefore, as in the writings of Simone de Beauvoir, the idea of woman's difference is "unmasked" as a mere myth. In de Beauvoir's writings and in Sartre's (with whom she lived), there emerges, however, not a truly phenomenological or existential presentation of the nature of woman (such as in Buytendijk [1965]) but "a thesis reminiscent of scientific positivism" (15).

The final result of de Beauvoir's thesis is an extraordinary impoverishment. What began as a movement of liberation ends in a new slavery. For if "sexual characteristics" are a mere "product" of "culture," persons are reduced to fleshless ciphers, to "mere intersection points in the graph of a social structure" (15).

> That secret of freedom which lies at the depth of a man's or woman's personality would be conjured away, and would be replaced by a vastness of social entities, faceless and manageable. (16)

This is the fate D. H. Lawrence feared, under the impact of the "social idea." Stern's approach matches the warnings given by Paul Roubiczek in *Ethical Values in the Age of Science* (1969), where he discusses the effects of mere "unmasking" in the social sciences.

Traditionally, Stern points out, men have been aware of the deep differences between man and woman and their symposium to Taoism (yin and yang), the Kabbalah, and the Upanishads. The biological entities suggest a polarity of 'being':

> The sex organs and the sex cells manifest a polarity and complimentariness and morphology and in function. In the act of sexual union the male organ is convex and penetrating and the female organ is concave and receptive; the spermatozoon is torpedo-shaped and "attacks," and the ovum is a sphere "awaiting" penetration. (Stern 1965, 9)

In traditional religions and philosophies, the concept of sexual polarity did not stop at the physical or psychological. There was felt to be an antithesis at the very heart of things that strives for synthesis.

To apply the kind of veracity demanded by positivistic science limits the perspective to that of Cartesian dissociation. The traditionally recognized polarity means something, in the metaphysical sense, and it is characteristic of our time to fail to grasp this. It will not do, either, to attribute the change to the recognition of indisputable scientific facts. If we take the phenomenological perspective, which enquires into 'being' and the person as does psychotherapy, then the polarity and the essential difference of woman must be recognized, not least because woman is the creator of all consciousness.

Stern quotes a story about Tolstoy—the creator of Natasha, Marie,

Anna Karenina, and Kitty. After listening to a group of writers talking about women, Tolstoy said:

> "I am only going to tell the truth about women when I am standing with one foot in the grave—I shall say it, jump into the coffin, pull the lid and then I'll say; 'do with me what you want!' " (Told by Maxim Gorki in *Reminiscences of Tolstoy*, quoted in Stern 1965, 17)

As Stern says, it seems as if a man could not tell the truth and stay alive. This indicates the sense of awe and mystery that haunts any man who seeks to recognize the truth about woman: "the element of the veiled and hidden is associated with the very idea of womanhood" (17). And, as Stern says, this feeling of the *mysterium tremendum* associated with woman is manifest in the Gioconda smile, which is impossible to imagine in a male portrait.

Man's activity, as Stern points out, is more often than not *against* nature—that is, the impulse to master our relationship with reality and to solve our problems rationally. Woman, by contrast, "acts and reacts out of the dark, mysterious depths of the unconscious, i.e. affectively, intuitively, mysteriously" (Helene Deutsch 1929). Women don't give their secret away because they don't know it themselves. Women, however, have what Stern calls a "transrational" power, which goes beyond reason—that is, intuitive intelligence. (Yet, as Polanyi argues, all creative knowing is rooted in something of the kind.)

Woman not only has the special gift of making herself at home in the world of others; she possesses "the spirit of love" (" 'ch'avete intelletto d'amore" as Dante stated it). "Her outlines blend mysteriously with the *chtonic*" (Stern 1965, 26).

Stern criticizes Freud for giving only an essentially negative view of woman. Fortunately, therapists since Freud's time have restored the balance. There follows an interesting discussion of creativity, in which Stern implies that great creative work could never have been produced by "male" explicitness. According to Stern, in all creation there is something that may be indicated by the German word *Wurf* (something thrown), which is the word used for birth when referring to the animal kingdom. There is an element of naïveté and anonymity in the creative act that is like the act of conception and birth.

At the peak of artistic creation (and in philosophy and science as well), man approaches the level of feminine creativeness, namely motherhood. Stern then quotes two passages from Tolstoy to illustrate that woman has a special capacity to relate to the newborn child that a man does not have (that is, to use Winnicott's phrase, primary maternal preoccupation or Stern's *participation mystique*). "The experiences most decisive for our entire life," says Stern, "stem from a preverbal, preconceptual and prelogical realm" (36)—the realm of our relationship with woman 'being for' us. It is this that underlies the dread of woman's dark, mysterious powers.

The rest of Karl Stern's book is of great interest to our understanding of philosophy and its links with the problem of woman. He believes that psychoanalysis, existentialism, and phenomenology are providing a totally new perspective on problems of our knowledge of man and the world. I cannot, however, follow him myself in his religious faith. Astoundingly, he declares that "natural anthropology, presented by psychoanalysis and phenomenology in our time" seems to *confirm* the "Christian image of Man and of History" (Stern 1965, 274). On the contrary, I believe philosophical anthropology reveals how disastrously wrong the Christian church has been in its attitudes to women and sexuality, even though we may admit that in its attention to 'being' the church recognizes a dimension sadly lacking in the modern *Weltanschauung* (Worldview).

What is relevant here is Stern's emphasis that, as Coleridge declared, the mind must be androgynous. (What Coleridge actually said was "the truth is, a great mind must be androgynous"; but, as Stern declares, this holds for everybody—"in a way we cannot yet define." (39).) According to Stern, "*in the psychic budget of the individual, the two components, male and female, must be linked in harmony.*" (39).

There is a "womanly" way of experiencing and knowing; and in order to find ourselves and the world and to find meaning in existence, we must apply both. In this respect, Stern believes, there have been serious deficiencies in the Western philosophical tradition since the seventeenth century. This tradition excludes too much the capacity to know by sympathy, by "feeling with," as through union with the knowable—by intuition. Stern refers to work by Husserl on intuitive knowledge and to work by Jaspers on "understandable connections" in the knowledge of patients in therapy and others.[12] Stern links these insights with the historical process, by which the few who have become aware of the problem, such as Blake and Goethe, have resisted the nullification of man that threatens because of the masculinization of knowledge and the exclusion of female-element modes. This is

> a conflict in which everyone of us is involved. For if the scientific-technological approach succeeded in objectifying man and society, man would cease to be man and become something for which no word has yet been coined. Man as a pure object, *reified* Man, ceases to *be*. (56)

In an entirely objectified world, we would end up by *having* everything, but *being* nothing.

Behind this philosophical question of apparently academic interest, says Stern, lies a profound sense of dread. And this dread, as I have suggested, becomes attached to the problem of woman. Woman stands for, symbolizes, and *is* the focus for an awareness that we need to be in touch with 'being', and that we need to be able to find a meaning in life—in the context of a world that is menaced by a lack of meaning and the elimination of 'being'.

Among his other concerns, Stern traces the development of a modern form of nihilism from Descartes, through Schopenhauer to Sartre. The original scientific revolution actually was made possible through the intellectual achievement of Descartes, which, however, generated a serious split in consciousness. It was Descartes who substituted mathematical structures for real things and divided the *res extensa* of things from the *res mensa*, which thus became ineffectual. Despite the effectiveness of this dualism, which enabled man to manipulate the world with cold detachment, Descartes's influence, says Stern, contains a psychopathological element. Descartes lost his mother when he was a baby, and his universe tends to be one in which man is alienated from Mother Earth, because the mother is the one who brought blight to the world and rejected man in an ultimate way. In the tradition referred to above, says

44

'Being for' and Other Primary Processes

Stern, the dread and horror of the mother deepens, insofar as the universe represents "the mother," until we are plunged, with Sartre, into total nihilism and a total revulsion—symbolically speaking—from the breast. From these dissociations derives the Western failure to find the capacity for 'being-at-one-with' all things that is the goal, for example, of many Eastern religions. The normal individual who has experienced an adequate introduction to 'being' continues to seek a connection with 'being' through the mother and through woman. Through personal relationships of a close kind, the individual finds a sense of 'being-in-the-world' and thus finds meaning in existence.

In the West, under the influence of figures such as Descartes, our traditions of philosophical enquiry have lost touch with the investigation of 'being,' so that the original *telos* of Greek thought about existence has been betrayed, as Husserl alleges. Western science continues to investigate the world "out there" but has separated this exploration from the investigation of the subjective realm— the inner life of man—and from questions proper to philosophy in the widest sense. Metaphysical enquiry, as to logical positivism, seems to be only "emotional noises." In science, only that which actually can be seen or measured is considered real, and in philosophy only that which can be verified is taken seriously. These concepts represent the triumph of masculine thought over feminine modes of thinking and awareness.

Stern believes that in our era we have suffered a disastrous masculinization of thought. In Descartes's world, human beings are separated from Mother Earth. Descartes's own difficulty with woman generated a mental view of the universe in which we cannot be at home, so long as we are under the influence of his thought. In consequence, in the universe of the scientific revolution there is no place for the experiencing 'I'. At the same time there has been, from Galileo through Descartes and Schopenhauer, an increasing rejection of the world as Mother—that is, of the universe as a symbolic breast that is the source of our 'being'. The universe is seen as alien, and there seems to be no place in it for the human being and for humanity's cultural achievements. Yet, it is only the uniqueness of the 'I' and the meanings that develop from our subjective experi-

45

ence that make life worth living. The central problem is to experience the *Dasein*—that is, the personal sense of 'being there', of
having some meaning in our unique experience of acting and choos-
ing from our center in the world before we die and become nothing.
This existential experience of meaning can be achieved only if the
feminine element is alive, and if, by the experience of 'being-in-the-
world', and in relation to Mother Earth, we can feel a sense of
meaningful existence. We can apply this equally to women, of
course. Women also need to embrace the creative woman in themselves and to relate to the feminine in man, to Mother Earth, and
to the universe, in turn, as the 'other' and to find 'being'.

Stern is not the only psychoanalytical writer to take this view. It
is to be found in the writings of Harry Guntrip, who spoke of the
"pathology of science," for example, and believed that behind it
there lies a fear of woman—of woman as the focus of 'being'. There
is also throughout Western thought an undervaluing of the feminine attributes in men and women. Many have pointed this characteristic out, especially those read in existentialist philosophy,
such as Rollo May, Victor Frankl, Roger Poole, and Peter Abbs.
There is a rejection of the creative, of the intuitive, of the tacit, of
the emotionally vulnerable or receptive, and of the poetic. As Marjorie Grene (1968) points out, one can find much hostility in figures
such as Galileo to the poetic because it was thought that the poetic
"falsified."

In contrast to the vague and shadowy myths of poetry, Descartes
settled for "clear and distinct" ideas. From Galileo and the early
pioneers, the scientific revolution inherited a distrust of secondary
qualities. As a result, there qualities were banished from the realm
of truth and were assigned to the realm of unreality. Of course,
since we exist in the world and do our work in the world—even if
we are scientists—we cannot escape from secondary qualities; and
the deep predicament that Husserl examines springs from our ne-
glect of these qualities.

This, again, represents a masculinization, since in her traditional
role woman lives with secondary qualities. Real things in the world
are colored, messy, sticky, and in many ways intractable, as anyone
knows who has done domestic work, cooking, or rearing of children.

However, there are also qualities in scientific work that evade "clear and distinct" ideas. Such qualities evade the Cartesian reduction. Scientists, for example, confess that they still know very little about the structure and nature of a simple substance like water. But then, when it comes to any actual man, whether he is a scientist or not, there are subjective problems of his emotional life, his sense of identity, his unconscious life, his 'being'. Shall he not find these as real? Galileo may have relegated these problems to some "limbo of paradox and anomaly" (31), but they do not go away from the world. It is simply that science fails to take account of them and to include them in an analytical picture. But, as Grene says, we ignore these problems at our peril.

F. R. Leavis (1975, 31) saw that one must, in some way, be anti-Cartesian. Leavis's work was concerned with the restoration of wholeness to our view of life and with the restoration of those "subtle essences of humanity," of which Dickens wrote. Leavis saw that we must agree with Kierkegaard, who regarded as "blasphemy" the application of natural science to the realm of man's spirit. Scientific method, whatever breathtaking results it may have achieved in our analysis and control of the physical world, cannot be applied to questions of the origin of the world and life, the infinite variety of forms, the destiny of man, and the presence of hate and corruption and their coexistence with love and beauty. Positivists may declare emotional and metaphysical problems in the widest philosophical sense to be pseudo-problems. To most of us, however, such problems remain burning issues; and men feel that they cannot live unless they try to solve them. The processes of 'being' and 'becoming' resist the objective analysis; but even though they are not caught in the scientific net, they are real enough in our lives. Jeremy Bentham, the nineteenth-century Utilitarian, may have called poetry "push-pin," but poetry deals with problems that are primary in our lives.

As Erik Erikson suggests, it is as if we have come to the end of the possibilities of male modes. We have now reached a situation in which we are asked to believe a "scientific" explanation of how things came about, especially how life itself came about, which is, as Karl Stern declares, crazy—"not crazy in the sense of slangy

Insights from Psychoanalysis

invective but rather in the technical meaning of psychotic" (Stern 1965, 290). Although it is totally improbable, we are asked to believe that simply by accident, sun-warmed mud, lightning, and chance generated life and that these elements became—also by accident—conscious, aware human beings. We believe science has "explained" life, but it has not. "Millions of data from the cumulative sciences form a fearfully intricate net of causalities to tackle this mystery but my being and becoming are not caught in that net" (290). We are asked to believe impossible explanations, as E. W. F. Tomlin (1977 and 1979) declares, such as the scientific view that consciousness could have come into existence by chance or that evolution happened by mere chance, despite serious doubts now being raised by mathematicians who are showing that there has not been enough time for evolution to have taken place by "chance and necessity."

The philosophical problems are bound up with problems of society and politics. Here, there are some relevant papers by Winnicott that need to be borne in mind. The political implications of the unconscious fear of woman are discussed by him in his 1950 paper "Some Thoughts on the Meaning of the Word Democracy," which appears in *The Family and Individual Development* (1964b).

Psychoanalytical and allied work, Winnicott says, demonstrate that all individuals have in reserve a certain fear of woman. In a footnote Winnicott relates this fear to the individual's fear in early childhood of the parents, to the fear of a combined figure ("a woman with male potency included in her powers [the witch]"), and to the "fear of the mother who has absolute power at the beginning of the infant's existence to provide, or to fail to provide, the essentials for the early establishment of the self as an individual" (164).

Some individuals have this fear more than others, but it can be said to be universal. The unconscious fear of woman, suggests Winnicott, lies behind much unfairness to women in social and political life and is responsible for the immense amount of cruelty to women, "which can be found in customs that are accepted by almost all civilizations" (16).[13]

The root of this fear, declares Winnicott, is known. Its origin is

48

in dependence. In infancy, the mother's devotion is absolutely essential for the individual's healthy development. The fear is an acknowledgment of this debt, which is too awful to acknowledge openly. The fear exists in the form of a fantasy woman in the unconscious. This woman has no limits to her existence or power and is feared for the possibility of her domination. Individuals will even put themselves under authoritarian domination in order to avoid domination by this fantasy woman (who occasionally surfaces in art as She, Melusine, Lady Macbeth, or the strange hag who appears in Somers's dreams in D. H. Lawrence's *Kangaroo*.)

The question of domination is discussed in the postscript to *The Child and the Family* (1957a), where Winnicott makes the point that "the fear of domination does not lead groups of people to avoid being dominated; on the contrary it draws them towards a specific or chosen domination" (143). Evidently, Winnicott was pondering the phenomenon of Nazi Germany. (His radio talks to mothers were broadcast from 1940 to 1950.) However, we may apply his observations here to a writer such as D. H. Lawrence, whose work I discuss elsewhere. Clearly, as we know from *Sons and Lovers*, Lawrence suffered from a dominating mother. Underlying his work is a profound fear of woman, and much of his writing is devoted to the attempt to overcome that fear. But in the end, Lawrence's fear led him to an obsession with domination, so that in his later works he identified with the dominator who subdues woman. To this, the remarks made by Winnicott on the psychology of the dictator are relevant, which appear in the introduction to the Penguin edition of *The Child, the Family, and the Outside World* (1964a):

> He is trying to control the woman whose domination unconsciously he fears, trying to control her by accommodating her, acting for her, and in turn demanding total subjection and "love." (10)

It is these philosophical problems of our attitudes to existence that lie behind the problem of woman in Western literature of the last century or so. To be in touch with 'being' was especially difficult for the Victorian mind, in a world dominated by the masculinization of society at all levels—in industry, the economy, and thought. The adult world was a world seriously deprived of femi-

49

nine modes of thought. Resistance required a rediscovery of the condition of the child—which explains the special preoccupation with the child in Dickens, Lewis Carroll, Charles Kingsley, and George MacDonald. Of these writers, George MacDonald was most consciously aware of belonging to the romantic tradition. He believed that human beings should preserve the child within them, together with the child's poetic sense and that kind of access to the deeper levels of 'being'. The child has direct access to the unconscious. And as MacDonald made plain, the adult suffers through the loss of this faculty—as Blake and Wordsworth also knew. To keep in touch with the child within the adult and with the springs of 'being' in the unconscious means a reassessment of attitudes to woman in the modern consciousness. I believe that both Lawrence and Tolstoy were aware of this.

The quest for an adequate attitude to the feminine is crucial to the contemporary predicament. Our world and the ways in which we think about it and deal with it belong almost exclusively to the predominance of the masculinization of knowledge. Does the present excitement around feminism today arise from the sense that male modes have come to the end of their possibilities? Is there perhaps an urgency to return to a female-element 'being'? Certainly, in a world in which objectivity is dominant and male "doing" is exhausted, individuals are confronted with a deep sense of meaninglessness. There is an urgent need to ask the questions of meaning and 'being', which are the "feminine" questions of existence.

James Joyce is a characteristic figure in twentieth-century literature, where the problem of woman is concerned. He betrays a characteristic problem of our time over accepting the whole reality of woman. Writing to his wife, Nora, he said:

> One moment I see you like a virgin or madonna the next moment I see you shameless, insolent, half-naked and obscene. . . . Are you too, then, like me, one moment high as the stars, the next lower than the lowest wretches? (Ellmann 1959, 296)

Such splitting seems to have its origin in an idealization of the mother and in the attempt to make the relationship with the wife into that of mother and child:

50

> O that I could nestle in your womb, like a child born of your flesh
> and blood, be fed by your blood, sleep in the warm secret gloom of
> your body! (303, from Joyce's letter of 2 September 1909)

Thus, woman becomes the focus of the schizoid need for a rebirth
of the regressed ego. Joyce merely transferred his *Holy Mary syndrome* to Nora,[14] although his belief in her honor at least checked
his split-object sexual behavior of earlier days:

> In the figure of the Virgin he had found a mother image which he
> cherished. He had gone to prostitutes and then prayed to the Virgin.
> (304)

Both ways of behaving manifest the incapacity to engage in a
relationship with a real, complete woman. Such a man cannot find
a balance between a remote ideal and partial-object, depersonalized sex with a woman who is paid to be unrelational. (The prostitute is woman under control and in contempt by reason of her paid
role, as is woman in pornography.)

Joyce's writing was for him a "gestation":

> The sense of the soul's development is like that of an embryo not only
> helped Joyce to the book's imagery [*Portrait of the Artist as a Young
> Man*] but also encouraged him to work and rework the original ele-
> ments in the process of gestation. . . . From the start the soul is
> surrounded by liquids, urine, slime, sea water, amniotic tides. . . . In
> the last few pages of the book. . . . The soul is released from its
> confinement, its individuality is complete. (307)

In *Ulysses* we see Joyce striving to bring together his female
element (Bloom), his male element (Stephen, for whom thinking is
male "doing"), and the libidinal and ideal in Molly Bloom—who,
at the end, prefers her relational need for Bloom and his feminine
sensitivity to the brutish lust of Blazes Boylan (who represents false
male "doing" par excellence).[15] In such writing, as Richard Ellmann says:

> Joyce seems to reconstitute his family relationships, to disengage
> himself from the contradictions of his view of himself as a child and
> so to exploit them, to overcome his mother's conventionality and his
> father's rancour, to *mother and father himself*, to become, by the
> superhuman effort of the creative process, no one but James Joyce.
> (309)

But the creative gains do not solve the life problems of splitting, integration, and security of existence. To Joyce, Nora was an enemy insofar as she was not "him." If she manifested the truth that she was an independent being, he found it hard to bear:

> A few days before I left Trieste I was walking with you in the Via Stadion. . . . A priest passed us and I said to you, "Do you not find a kind of repulsion or disquiet at the sight of one of those men?" You answered a little shortly and drily said, "No, I don't." You see, I remember all these small things. Your reply hurt and silenced me. . . . Are you with me, Nora, or are you secretly against me? . . . Another night I came home to your bed from the café and began to tell you of all I hoped to do. . . . You would not listen to me. . . . It was very late and of course you were tired out after the day. But a man whose brain is on fire with hope and trust in himself *must* tell someone of what he feels. Whom should I tell but you? (314–15)

As Ellmann writes, "she [Nora] must feel *exactly as he feels;* otherwise she is an enemy." Of course, Joyce's moods were changeable—"my love for you . . . is really a kind of adoration" (315) But this adoration only too easily turned to contempt or fear in Joyce's personal life, while in his art the failure to solve the problems of identity and gender generated a flight into technique. Joyce's fascination with manipulating language seems to have even become a way of avoiding the central themes of meaning in his work. The technique becomes as much idolized as the woman for whom he writes—but who cannot bear the burden of the tribute.

I have discussed the Holy Mary syndrome in relation to Mahler. This syndrome would seem to be common to creative males whose severe problems of existence often originate with the mother and her shortcomings, leaving the man with a perpetual woman problem. Because of man's first troubled experience of woman, an ideal of the feminine is invented, that is split off from the whole being. The splitting results in intense difficulties in personal relationships, while the individual's art often represents a painful and slow progress toward sufficient integration to become able to relate, which is not always achieved.

CHAPTER 3

Male Knowing and
Female Knowing

An important theme that has emerged from philosophical anthropology is the recognition of other ways of knowing than the male
and the analytical. Psychoanalysis, which in practice is a version of
the mother's relationship to her baby—of love—depends upon the
creative use of intuitive insights and has contributed to the increasing recognition of feminine modes. Psychoanalysists have had to
struggle against the masculinization of thought, not least in the
work of the founder.

In his approach to therapy and in his phenomenological interpretation of dreams and symbols, Freud was capable of the practice of
love in this feminine way (as Ian D. Suttie [1935] made clear). But
he belonged to a society in which the male mode predominated and
to traditions of thought in science and medicine in which masculinization was predominant. As a result, he tried to reduce psychic
phenomena to an organic base, as with his theory of the death
instinct, his economic theories of psychic energy, and his whole
"organic" bias. Freud's theory, declares Suttie, is a "hate" theory,
quite at odds with the love displayed in therapy. We may say that
the theory is male, while the practice is female.[1] Incidentally, Freud

discriminated against women, particularly in the sphere of sexual fulfillment. Recent students of human nature in this field have restored the balance, notably through D. W. Winnicott, who, in the wake of Melanie Klein, has restored the female element to the center of the picture—not least by that insistence, emphasized by Harry Guntrip, that "being comes first."

The problem is, however, that although the female element of 'being' is primary, it is also the most fraught with danger. The female element is the sphere of 'being' that arouses in us the greatest dread. For her capacities to create 'being', to use her special powers of intuition, telepathy, and 'being for'; and for special cultural and imaginative powers, woman is the focus of tremendous envy. An air of mystery has always surrounded woman, as Jung and others have pointed out, while in human culture and consciousness her powers have been symbolized by female goddesses and in figures such as Minerva and Siva. However, woman is also Clytemnestra and Medea. The witch figure is the obverse of the creative mystery. In her, all the powers to create 'being' are reversed; and she manifests extraordinary powers to destroy, as in Lilith, Lady Macbeth, and the Fata Morgana.

It is not surprising, then, that open recognition of the special mysteries of the female powers of 'being' is met with hostility and denial. In our time, in the feminist movement, there seems to be an attempt to deny the problem altogether. For example, some women try to imply that woman need only become a certain kind of man to achieve equality—often, a rather nasty kind of man. In modern fashions many women dress like men or bathe naked from the waist, like men. In one sense, some of these developments represent a claim for freedom; yet, implicit in some is a manifestation of the fear and denial of woman's special importance, in consciousness and 'being'.

Even in the sphere of philosophical anthropology, the insights of the psychology of 'being' make only slow headway. Even work of Winnicott is neglected in some quarters and is allowed to go out of print. In education there seems to be a retreat from the marvelous recognition of the needs of 'being' established by such writers as

Male Knowing and Female Knowing

Susan Isaacs (1929) while psychoanalysis itself seems to be suffering from a decline in its recognition, not least in the most important areas that have been explored by such existentialist writers as Abraham Maslow, Rollo May, and Peter Lomas. Instead, there seems to be a withdrawal into more intellectual and analytical modes such as in the writings of Jacques Lacan, while the history of the influence of R. D. Laing seems to be one of great opportunities missed and spoiled. Yet insights from dynamic psychoanalysis can be applied to modern life with rich rewards in understanding, while often the more analytical and intellectual works can be read without much enlightenment. In this retreat, we must detect a fear of the needs of 'being' itself, which is, in its origin, the fear of the original dependence on the mother.

A number of complex themes are interwoven around the question of woman. There is woman's special nature itself and the modes of understanding and responding that are natural to woman, which belong to 'being' and 'being for'. There is the existence in men of feminine modes, which they take into themselves from their mothers and which belong to their 'being' side and their creativity. There is the existence of a female kind of knowing and dealing with experience. Finally, there is a kind of philosophy that may be called feminine, or which may be said to recognize the feminine, which is neglected in our era.[2]

In our era, thought itself has been largely masculinized. Karl Stern (1965) argues, as we have seen, that the scientific ethos to Mother Earth is rooted in Descartes's attempt to locate reality in terms of a mathematicized, masculine paradigm in which all elements of female-element 'being' have been eradicated. We may relate this perspective to what we have understood in Winnicott. If 'being' comes first and is the primary basis of 'being' and if our dealings with the world are based on a foundation from which female-element 'being' is excluded, the result will be a serious deficiency at the heart of our dealings with the universe. This split, I believe, led to what T. S. Eliot called the "dissociation of sensibility" after the seventeenth century. What we may call poetic modes of understanding and forms of imaginative sympathy with nature became neglected, despite the attempts of important poets like Blake, Coleridge, Keats, and Wordsworth to restore them.

Winnicott wrote a good deal about the need to have a basis both for our subjectivity and our objectivity. He brought female-element 'being' to the center of the stage; indeed, he argues that feminine modes are the basis of all other modes. Without achieving the basis of the reality sense and perception through loving communion with the mother, there is no capacity to find the real world; objectivity emerges only from subjectivity in the original primitive encounter.

These beliefs may be related to the insights of Michael Polanyi, the distinguished chemist turned philosopher of science, in his examination of the nature of thought—particularly, of thought in science—in his book *Personal Knowledge: Toward a Post-Critical Philosophy* (1962) and elsewhere. All knowledge, he tells us, is either tacit or rooted in tacit knowing (see 87–131). That is, in all knowing we rely on ineffable processes of which we are focally ignorant—and we do not know how we know. Polanyi does not say as much, but these roots in tacit knowing seem clearly female, in the sense that they are like those intuitive ways of knowing upon which the mother relies and by which she is able to draw out the capacity to be in the infant and at the same time to enable the infant to perceive and come to terms with the world of reality. Polanyi shows that even objective knowledge is rooted in the female capacity of imagination and that the "leap of the imagination" is the basis of all discovery.

This area of insight is important to our considerations of the nature of thought itself. We must not fear the feminine mode of understanding the world, despite its ineffable nature. We must live with it because it is the basis of all knowing. Polanyi and Prosch (1975) argue convincingly that "all our knowledge is inescapably indeterminate." Their statement refers not only to artistic knowledge but also to the findings of science and even that "the bearing that empirical knowledge has upon reality is unspecifiable" (61).

> There is nothing in any concept that points *objectively* or automatically to any sort of reality. That a concept relates to a reality is established only by a tacit judgement grounded in personal commit-

ments, and we are unable to specify all these personal commitments
or to show how they bring a given concept to bear upon reality and
thus enable us to trust it as knowledge. (61)

We cannot ultimately specify the grounds—metaphysical, logical, or empirical—upon which we hold our knowledge to be true.
(How absurd, if this is true even of scientific facts, that dialectical
materialism can hold it to be a valid scientific truth, that its interpretation of history and man's destiny is so demonstrable that
everything—not least millions of lives—should be sacrificed to it!
As Polanyi demonstrates in his essay "Beyond Nihilism," in *Knowing and Being* [1969], the grounds of such cold fanaticism are in
deep, passionate convictions, which the apparent rationality disguises. Thus, at the heart of "scientific" politics is a deep ambiguity
that can only be hidden by ruthless force and suppression and the
perversion of truth).

However, in philosophical anthropology the remarkable insight
is developing that even scientific exploration of reality depends—
like the novel—on feminine modes, particularly on *imagination*.
Even the exercise of scientific discovery depends upon tacit, ineffable factors of the nature of which we are ignorant; or, as I would
add, upon female-element dynamics, such as the "leap of the imagination." This means, for one thing, that that epitome of the
("doing") masculinization of thought, the "thinking machine,"
can never be a true model of the human mind:

> The very process of tacit integration, which we have found so ubiq-
> uitous, is, when we turn our attention upon it . . . also indetermi-
> nate, unspecifiable. We cannot spell this process out in explicit steps,
> and it is for this reason . . . that no "thinking" machine can ever be
> adequate as a substitute, or even as a model, for the human mind.
> Our dwelling in the particulars, the subsidiary clues, results in their
> synthesis into a focal object only by means of an act of our imagina-
> tion—a leap of a logical gap; this does not come about by means of
> specifiable, explicit, logically operative steps. (Polanyi and Prosch
> 1975, 62)

The "thinking-machine" analogy fails because all knowing depends upon processes that never can be reduced to logical steps; yet,
a "thinking machine" can only be built on such principles. The

"leap of imagination" is a product of the first stages of play and encounter between mother and baby and is a *feminine* capacity.[3] Thus, there exists a radical division between objective, analytical (positivistic) thought and poetic thought, which has its roots in whether or not the *mother*—that is, the female elements in knowing and perceiving—is recognized. Literature is, as Lawrence and F. R. Leavis knew, the *whole* way of exploring the truth of the world, which embraces the female modes. (In contrast, in much of science the female modes are denied, even though science rests ultimately upon them.)

Two other points from Polanyi and Prosch may be invoked here: another indeterminacy is that when we modify our judgments about anything, we make subsidiary use of certain new principles, "which is to say we dwell in them."

> Because of this we actually make existential changes in ourselves when we modify our judgements. For we literally dwell in different principles from the ones we have been at home in, and we thus change the character of our lives. (62)

All our knowing involves a commitment that we can never define at will. This, as the individual working in the arts and the humanities will recognize, is the creative component of our work. After listening to a piece of music or reading a novel or poem that has moved us, *we are never the same again*. And this is a female-element capacity, being able to change one's mind. The whole process, of the intentional effect of responding to literature, for example, is often subjected to hostility or denial in academic thinking about the subject. Academic approaches to the arts are often too intellectual and inhibit that openness to creativity which can bring change. To be open to change is the nature of woman and it is one of the disturbing aspects of creativity that in order to respond to it we must take the risk of a surrender to fate to a degree—even in reading a poem.

When we modify our judgments about anything, we make subsidiary use of certain new principles. Moreover, even if we could know what these new principles are to which we are committing ourselves, the consequences to our lives of adopting them must remain "indeterminate" (62). We cannot apply these principles to situations we shall meet before we actually do apply them.

> These applications will each be an act of our creative imagination pulling ourselves and our situation at that time into some sort of meaningful integration. We cannot make these "discoveries" before we do in fact make them. (63)

Again, Polanyi and Prosch are identifying a female-element capacity—in both men and women. Women have the capacity to live through an experience and to be changed by it, for this they must do by nature in pregnancy and birth. Moreover, women perform the role of showing each child the way to discover the reality of itself and the world, in such a way as to allow always a new moment in time and experience—a discovery that cannot be made before it is there to be made.[4]

For those of us in English and the humanities, this is the hope and confidence of our work. We hope that through a student's tacit possession of the arts and the indefinable readiness the arts inculcate, as well as by the existential changes our kind of knowledge brings, the student will be able to deal with totally new, unfamiliar, and unknown experiences when they appear. This is an aspect of our work that is often implicitly denied. For example, it is denied by the tendency to treat literature as a set of facts to be acquired or as a source of new and striking intellectual theories as in structuralism or as by the manner of syllabuses and examinations, which more often than not tend to confine the whole discipline to one of the explicitly known and delineated, rather than allow the "open" to exist and move into the future—into the unknown.

I come to my subject, thus, as one who has come to recognize that in the widest sense we in the humanities are dealing with forms of knowledge and ways of approaching the world, one of which is substantial literary art, such as poetry and the novel.

CHAPTER 4

The Symbolism of Woman

The problem of male and female is thus one of the deepest of all human problems and, like the problem of death, may be insoluble. But perhaps we can overcome some of the worst human tendencies if we understand the problem by looking at it in depth. This process will be painful because what is involved is our understanding of ourselves.

Whatever the so-called enlightened individuals may say, there is one inescapable and terrible fact of life that cannot and must not be denied. Look out at a busy street, on La Place de la Concorde, or Vatican Square, or Wembley Stadium, or the shanties of Calcutta. Once, *every one of those human beings was inside a woman's body.* They were once totally dependent upon a woman, and without her care they would have died. The reality is even more extraordinary and terrifying than that; all were once, so to speak, "inside" a woman's psyche.

Moreover, the essential processes were beyond any kind of male control. A woman does not rear her children and enable them to deal with the world and become autonomous selves by using a manual of babycare or even by relying on doctors' instructions—that is, male analytical knowledge. Explicit instruction or knowledge would have been useless (which is not to say that the capacity for babycare cannot be improved by intelligent awareness, of course). A woman mothers her children by applying her intuitive, creative, and natural skills; or she fails.

The mother is able to respond to the emerging infant, to *creatively reflect* him or her, by intuition—by the totally ineffable processes of 'being for'. And these capacities are beyond her conscious awareness or control. Or, she cannot provide "good-enough mothering," and so everything may be chaos for her child.

We were all once totally dependent upon a woman's mysterious capacity for 'being for'. And we could have been left as dead—psychically dead—by her failure. Without this mysterious process (which, according to Winnicott, shows up as a schizoid illness if the baby dies), we should have had no chance whatsoever. We either would not have lived or we would be mad or dissociated in some way.

It is this terrible truth that underlies both gratitude in human beings and their terror of dependence behind their idealization or hatred of woman. It is a deeply disturbing truth to bear, for it is centered both in our sexual lives and in our quest for the meaning of life. (Our sexual lives are equally beyond the beck and call of will, though we pretend otherwise.)

For those with whom this mysterious psychic birth was not successful, they must especially deny that such a process exists. Hence, the immense denial of these truths in Western culture. Some, like Simone de Beauvoir, deny that there is anything special about the woman's role. Or, like Sartre, some see psychic nurture as a process of subjection to a horror, submitting, as it were, to be sewn up in the sack of the self. To some it may seem as if the self has been imposed by some monstrous process of domination; and where the mother did exert a powerful substitute for 'being for', the whole attitude of an individual to woman may be seriously harmed and distorted.

Some individuals suffer a life-long dread of woman because of an aggressively dominating mother or because of a mother who failed them. Few today would deny the effect of such a maternal failure on an individual's psyche. What we need to study in more depth are the universal problems all human beings have with the woman they "took into themselves" as a dynamic of their personality, in infancy, from the mother (or from the mother substitute). Of course, since all mothers and children are human, they have the normal ambiguity of the emotional life. A further problem arises concerning the splits that develop between the good and the bad in each. W. R. D. Fairbairn (1952), for example, devised an impossibly complicated pattern to describe the infant's response to various facets of the mother and the infant's own attempt to deal with each facet by splitting up his own response to them.[1] The mother can be exciting but also rejecting. She can be idealized, dreaded, sensually enjoyed, not there when wanted, or too much there when not wanted. Thus, when it comes to woman, a man may not know whether to be on his knees to her as Virgin Mary or full of sensual contempt for her as prostitute. Thus, desperately in need of her presence or impelled to destroy her, he pays her the tribute of ultimate need.[2] These manifestations appear in literature, from Joyce and Swift to *L'Histoire d'O* and *Héloïse et Abélard*. No one can escape these problems, and they are the price we pay for having mothers. Yet there is no life, no autonomy, no free 'being' without the mother. Without her love, there is no meaning.

Woman's fate is to be envied and yet be the focus of an urge to control her because she creates the world—without whom nothing was made that was made. The analogy in the past between woman and God is not difficult to understand. It is also not difficult to see why D. H. Lawrence wanted woman in one sense to be God—that is, to provide meaning for our lives.

The problem of woman is thus the problem of life and its secret. Woman can create us—by reflecting us—and enable us to seek meaning in existence; or, she can leave us without a created identity and in a condition of meaninglessness. No wonder she is feared and hated, as well as respected and loved.[3]

There are also the negative elements in these problems of gender: the feared phantom woman, the malignant anima. And here lies the connection between woman—existence and nonexistence, or death—and meaning or meaninglessness.

It is difficult to separate the "truth about woman" in philosophical anthropology from the truth about what we all, and what men especially, feel about woman. These areas are full of ambiguity. For example, woman is traditionally regarded as the weaker sex. Yet, as one psychologist has pointed out, it is man who is in one sense the weaker sex, since it is he who has to perform sexually; and this potency is extremely vulnerable. In actual dealings with the world, though she may be less aggressive (women are a small minority in prison and in physical conflict, as in war), woman can be far more courageous in tests of endurance, such as single-hand sailing or exploration, because she is equipped to be courageous in giving birth. She can also be more cruel and dangerous in hate, as we know from Lady Macbeth and Irma Grese (the "Beast of Belsen").

Where literature is concerned, the connection we have to make is between the truths of philosophical anthropology—a discipline that takes into account the subjective and intentional—and the phenomena of consciousness surrounding our subject—that is, we must examine the symbolism of woman and the meanings attached to woman as a subject of poetry, fiction, and drama. In light of this, figures in fiction like She in Rider Haggard's *She*, Eustacia in Thomas Hardy's *The Return of the Native*, or Maggie Tulliver in George Eliot's *The Mill on the Floss* take on a special dimension. Examined in the same light as phenomenological analysis of dreams in psychoanalysis, such characters may be seen as dramatizations of endopsychic situations. They may be understood as attempts to express the authors' attitudes to woman and to their own female elements and thus the female component in human nature. They embody the authors' attitudes to female knowledge and other modes, particularly within the authors' themselves. The artistic success of such characters may then be estimated in light of this wider perspective.

Moreover, there are other archetypal patterns in the symbolism that may have to be taken into account, as we shall see. Faces and eyes are important because woman is associated with creative reflection. The individual who hungers for confirmation of identity (not least as a source of meaning in life) may search everywhere for the eyes that can respond to him or for the face in which can be found the confirmation of his 'being'. Such symbolism is a powerful component of Mahler's music and the poetry of Sylvia Plath. The symbolic use of faces and eyes is found in fairy tales, as well as in the fantasies of C. S. Lewis, George MacDonald, Lewis Carroll, and others. Symbolism of the mother's body, of birth, and of play may also be found—associated with existence and development. The rocking and crooning moments at the opening of Mahler's Ninth Symphony are a case in point, as are the symbolism of the wardrobe and going through the wardrobe into another world in C. S. Lewis's "The Narnia Chronicle" and the sea change as a symbol of birth in Charles Kingsley's *The Water-Babies*. Here, we need to draw not only on Freud's phenomenology but on that of many later psychoanalysts and theorists of symbolism in art, such as Gaston Bachelard, the philosopher of surrealism. (See *The Poetics of Space* [1969b].)

When problems of existence and nonexistence are part of the ambiguity, the woman-related symbolism assumes a more bizarre form. The more bizarre elements are often found in the work of those who have suffered some devastating loss of maternal reflection and care in infancy. Either the mother has died when the individual was a baby or child, or the mother weaned the individual traumatically, or there occurred the death of a sibling or the father. These point to an association of the mother with the problem of mourning. I already have invoked Karl Stern's suggestion that many of our philosophical problems have to do with Descartes's loss in infancy of his mother and his consequent alienation from Mother Earth. The unconscious element in Descartes's successful division of *res mensa* from *res extensa* (successful from the point of view of effective control of outer reality) in his feeling of the cold bleakness of the world.

As Stern (1965) says, success in the outer world may, however, disguise failure in the inner world and emotional life. The problems of the inner world are often explored in fantasies, in terms of those "secondary worlds" (as J. R. R. Tolkien has called them) that a writer creates. These fantasies often deal with the problem of woman.

In some fantasies there is often another world, such as Narnia in the fantasies of C. S. Lewis or the worlds of George MacDonald's tales, which is blighted by a witch. There is a journey, and during the journey something crucial has to be sought in the bleak world and brought back to restore meaning. This often is something shining, magical, fruitful, or potent. This quest is symbolic of the need of the individual who cannot complete mourning to find the dead mother—in the world of death—and to obtain from her the completion of reflection, thus restoring meaning to life. The loss has left the individual aware of the lack of meaning in his existence, consequent upon the insufficiency of the mother's creative reflection. Therefore, the individual must find her ("She") or her magic attributes (her eyes or her breasts) to complete the existential process. It may be, of course, that this is a universal predicament because no mother is perfect. Thus, when the mother dies, we all feel that we have not finished with her. Since her death has blighted the world, we need to find her to return meaning to the world. What we may be said to be seeking is the breast. The topography of the symbolic quest will include the mother's body and the "house of the self" (for example, the "upper storeys," symbolizing the mind in the head, from which the quest often begins).

The trouble is, of course, that we also have a number of complex feelings of a negative kind related to the mother. There is her rejecting side and our experience of her hate, or of her impingement experienced as hate. We have memories of our own moments of hate toward her—when as infants, we wanted to destroy her, or eat her, or at least wish her out of the way. When she dies it may seem these wishes have had their effect. Or, we may fear her retribution for these death wishes. Therefore, one of the problems of mourning is that we desperately need to refind the dead mother—as a source of meaning—to sustain our existence. But then, we cannot be sure that if we find her, in that other world of death, she will not be malignant. We have seen how, in the unconscious, there is the phantom woman who embodies our fears of what Freudians call the "castrating mother." Since the roots of this fear are in infancy, the "hate mother" is fantasied in body terms appropriate to the infant's body-mind existence. In response to the infant's

involvement in parental sexual excitement, which the infant con-
ceives of as a consuming oral voraciousness, the child dreads that
the mother (or combined parents) will turn on him, thus castrating
or annihilating him (eating him). It is not difficult to find symbols
of this dread in fairy tales and in nursery rhymes, such as the three
blind mice whose tails were cut off or Red Riding Hood. Such
symbols are also represented by wolves in fables and even the sun
or moon turned malevolent or tumbling out of the sky, such as in
the fantasies of C. S. Lewis.

The mother who is so desperately sought in the other world of
death for her power to reflect and give meaning through love may,
it is feared, turn out to be the castrating, or annihilating, mother—
the malignant anima—who will blight us, as she has blighted the
world, and through hate deprive us further of meaning. This is the
basis for the dread of the White Witch in the Narnia books and of
"She." It is this negative female element that is embodied by Lady
Macbeth, Goneril, Regan, Lilith, and Salome.

We shall expect to find many themes in literature having to do
with an unconscious fear of woman, with consequent feelings of
the need to attack her, to control her, to humiliate her, to murder
her, to rape or sodomize her, or to alter or correct her by various
forms of punishment or transfiguration. Or, she may be sought as a
means to further creative reflection—that is, further mothering. In
all these what we have are manifestations of both the deepest
human need—to become fully born psychically—and the deepest
human weaknesses—the fear of dependence. Thus there is an ambiguity in our feelings about woman and in the images writers have
created to define the nature of woman. Is she creative mirror or
witch? It is in this complex ambiguity that we find the association
between woman and death—that is, between 'being' and nothingness.

In turning to apply these insights to the problem of woman, I
shall begin by discussing some plays by Sir James Barrie. It was my
puzzlement about these plays that brought me to try a phenomenological approach to the problem of woman. The plays are continually performed; and audiences respond to them, without under-

standing fully what they are about. What is the unconscious material that so engages the attention of the play-going public to these extraordinary works? It was this question that generated my first attempt at phenomenological analysis of the image of woman in literature.

PART TWO

The Insights Applied:
Sir James Barrie

CHAPTER 5

Woman, Death, and Meaning in
Peter Pan and *Mary Rose*

It may seem odd for a literary critic to turn from psychoanalysis to *Peter Pan*. To most serious critics, this play might seem to be a trivial popular fantasy. To Edgell Rickword, writing on Barrie in *Scrutinies* by various writers (1928), the sentimentality was disastrous. He quotes from the film version:

PETER PAN:
When was I born?
MRS. DARLING:
At midnight, dear.
PETER PAN:
I hope I didn't wake you, Mummy.

However, as a social phenomenon alone, the work of Sir James Barrie poses a problem. The plays seem really quite mad; yet, they are enormously popular. *Peter Pan* continues to be performed. It is a remarkable success, even though—or perhaps because—it lies totally outside of rationality and is sheer fantasy. Barrie's *Mary*

71

Rose was revived in Edinburgh in 1988 and the National Theatre in London experimented recently by having a man play Peter Pan.

I was surprised to find myself discussing Barrie's *Mary Rose*, that mysterious play, in my study of Mahler. I alluded to the play in relation to the Holy Mary syndrome—that is, the impulse to impose a certain kind of idealization upon woman. Here, I pursue the matter further. Clearly, from all the biographical accounts, Barrie had a serious problem with woman. And, I believe, it is his cultural engagement with the problem of woman that makes his plays everlastingly and universally fascinating, despite their madness. They are about woman as the focus of 'being-in-existence,' 'going-out-of-existence,' and of life and death.

As is so often true, where we encounter the image of woman at the heart of a literary work (as in D. H. Lawrence, C. S. Lewis, and George MacDonald and in Coleridges's *The Rime of the Ancient Mariner* and the poetry of Sylvia Plath and the music of Mahler), what we encounter is a problem of death.

The problem of woman is often linked in some way with the problem of mourning. How do we explain this? I intend to show that the exploration of the problem of woman in literature continually returns to the association of woman with death. In this, I believe, *Peter Pan* and other works of Sir James Barrie are illuminating.

One important clue is to be found in D. W. Winnicott's insight that the mother has a mirror role—that is, she creates us by her creative reflection. If she dies or turns a blank face upon us, then we are faced with extinction. In desperation, we seek another source of confirmation of our 'being'; if we cannot find it, our life is forfeit. It is her face and eyes that connect woman with death. Of course, I am talking phenomenologically about the symbols and meaning of the unconscious mind and of the phenomena of consciousness.

Peter Pan is thought of as a play for children. But from my phenomenological perspective, it is a play about 'being-unto-death' in relation to woman and the mother. We only have to open *Peter Pan* to see the problem of 'being-unto-death' evoked in symbolism that focuses on the mother in ways related to existential meanings. The first tension in the play involves a face at the window:

(As . . . [Mrs. Darling] enters the room she is startled to see a strange little face outside the window and a hand groping as if it wanted to come in.)
MRS. DARLING:
Who are you? *(The unknown disappears; she hurries to the window.)* No one there. And yet I feel sure I saw a face. My children!

It is a moment of yearning for creative reflection and a yearning to make substantial the ghost of someone who isn't there.[1] Here we have too the presence of the dead sibling in Barrie's life. His brother David was killed suddenly in a skating accident at the age of fourteen. His mother withdrew completely and lived shut in her room, refusing food. James took it upon himself to try to bring her back to life by engaging in childish antics like standing on his head—by play. In desperation, he would count the number of times she smiled, in an attempt to relieve her deathlike depressions. His mother kept the lost child's christening robe, and it seems to have been the most important memento in her life. She would talk to the dead David as if he were there. We have in this phenomenon a terrible threat to the meaning of existence, which generated the strange phenomenology of Barrie's work. For Barrie, as a child, was deeply involved in his mother's failure to mourn, while at the same time as an adult he wrote all his books for her, in a way parallel to his attempts as a boy to lift her depressions by amusing her. The ghost of his brother, too, wanted to "come in," for his mother yearned for David to come back from the world of death to this world.

There was another problem that I shall examine further. Marietta Karpe and Richard Karpe (1957) suggest that Barrie was traumatized earlier by the birth of a sister when he was an infant. We may say, I believe, that he needed more creative reflection *to be born*. Mrs. Darling in *Peter Pan* responds immediately and wants to see the face, exclaiming "My children!" We have a similar moment in Mahler's *Kindertotenlieder* (Songs on the death of children) when the poet Friedrich Rückert seems to see his dead child come into the room with the mother (*"Dort wo würde dein lieb Gesichtchen sein"*). The reference to mothering is even more plain in *Peter Pan:*

WENDY:
Now let us pretend we have a baby.
JOHN:
(Good-naturedly.) I am happy to inform you, Mrs. Darling, that you are now a mother. *(Wendy gives way to ecstasy.)* You have missed the chief thing; you haven't asked, "boy or girl?"

At once it seems of primary importance as to whether reflection establishes that the new creature is a boy or a girl—that is, there is an underlying craving for one's gender identity and authenticity. On this theme Barrie develops the following playful exchange, where Michael pretends to want to be born:

MICHAEL:
(Expanding.) Now, John, have me.
JOHN:
We don't want any more.
MICHAEL:
(contracting.) Am I not to be born at all?
JOHN:
Two is enough.
MICHAEL:
(Wheedling.) Come, John; boy, John. *(Appalled.)* Nobody wants me!
MRS. DARLING:
I do.
MICHAEL:
(With a glimmer of hope.) Boy or girl?
MRS DARLING:
(With one of those happy thoughts of hers.) Boy.

In his essay on Barrie, Rickword (1928) points out the ineptitude of Barrie's art in dealing with adult emotions, love, and death. Rickword exposes the "infantile" element in Barrie's works. Yet; what we still have to explain is the astonishing appeal of Barrie's plays and the way people attend them and love them. His plays are popular despite their embarrassing and even rather mad episodes—

those that one really cannot give a rational account of. The plays appeal to the unconscious level and to the primitive *Dasein* need (as evidence in the previously quoted dialogue)—that is, the urgent need to come into being and to be someone for the 'other'.

Peter has lost his shadow. Whatever strictures the literary critic may make on Barrie's art, the achievement is in one sense remarkable. He managed to present quite surrealistic material in a normal domestic setting and to open up in the nursery setting strange aspects of the *Dasin* problem—that is, the fundamental problems of existence as the child dreads them. If one is real, one has a shadow. Peter has had his cut off by the window falling:

(She produces it from a drawer. They unroll and examine the flimsy thing, which is not more material than a puff of smoke, and if let go would probably float into the ceiling without discolouring it. Yet it has human shape. As they nod their heads over it they present the most satisfying picture on earth, two happy parents conspiring cosily by the fire for the good of their children.)[2]

The literary problem is that the playfulness of the language is at odds with the dreadfulness of the essential theme, which is the fear of going out of existence. Just as Coleridge, in close relationship with his sleeping baby, fears the extinction of consciousness if the flame on his fire goes out (in "Frost at Midnight") so Barrie evokes the fear of one's substance going out like "smoke." At the same time, there is the reassurance that parental love *is* a guarantee of one's identity; but this, again by the weakness of the language (which is an emotional weakness), is sentimentalized. The shadow is that of the dead sibling, and the stage direction evokes the strange evanescence of the human personality that, after death, when one becomes shadowless, *is* less substantial than a puff of smoke and "might float to the ceiling without discolouring it." The ineptitude of Barrie's capacity to deal with such an existential theme is revealed if one compares with this playful passage Mahler's funeral march on a childhood theme in the second movement of his First Symphony in which the depths of the heart are touched in relation to the death of a child.

But there is also a grim undercurrent to *Peter Pan*. Although Peter Pan is the fairy protagonist of the play, he is menacing because he is going to take the children out of this world into the world of shadowless death in which he exists (or nonexists). The mother leaves a symbol of her eyes to watch over her children because she suspects some ghostly presence is after them:

MICHAEL:
Can anything harm us, Mother, after the night-lights are lit?
MRS. DARLING:
Nothing, precious. They are the eyes a mother leaves behind to guard her children. . . . Dear night-lights that protect my sleeping babes, burn clear and steadfast tonight.

These "eyes" are a guarantee that the children will not be left to go out of existence by a failure of reflection or because of the ghost that comes from the world of death. This scene fascinates audiences because it evokes the fears we all suffered in infancy of going out of existence when mummy put out the light. Len Chaloner writes in *Feeling and Perception in Young Children* (1963) of our fears about what would happen (as in the *Kindertotenlieder*) if the mother's eyes stopped reflecting us. They go out like children:

(*They blink three times one after the other and go out, precisely as children (whom familiarity has made them resemble) fall asleep.*)

Again, we hear almost an echo of the *Kindertotenlieder* ("*Ein Lämplein verlosch in meinem Zelt!*" and "*O Augen!*"). Their light is taken over by the light of Tinker Bell.

The children are taught to fly. (The theatrical device by which they are fixed up to fly is stressed, as Barrie keeps our minds fixed on the need for a willingness to suspend disbelief.) In one sense, flying represents the growth of sexuality and adulthood (after latency), by which children, in fact, fly away from the nest. But flying is also an adventure into the world of nonexistence, into the Never Land:

(*The broken-hearted Father and Mother arrive just in time to get a nip from Tink as she too sets out for the Never Land.*)

While Barrie never allows us to feel deep adult feelings, as does Mahler in the *Kindertotenlieder*, he does offer play with the real problems. However, the disturbing quality about this play is its manic quality: it derives from antics intended to overcome the depression derived from the fear of death. Mahler tried to distract his dying brother Ernst, and this is manifest in his music. The difference in quality has to do with the capacity to find the 'other". Barrie's fairy tale has limits because it is too much in a mode that denies death. It is this denial of death that we see in Barrie that we simply do not in Mahler. In the background of Barrie's work lurks a fear of the mother: Can the mother, or the female element, be trusted to reflect and confirm us? Is she good or bad? If she is bad (hate rather than love), then we may be annihilated; if she responds to us and helps create us, she is love and goodness. Thus, these symbols may be related to the *Dasein* problem—that is, what can be set against the nothingness that death thrusts at us?

In the end, Peter Pan cannot stay (any more than the dead ghost of the dead brother could stay). Wendy cannot fly as she once did as a child, and she has to use a broomstick. (She is growing up to adult sexuality, and the broomstick represents a penis. This growth to adult sensuality divides her forever from Peter, who died as a child and must remain a child.) Mrs. Darling does what she can; but there remains for Peter "the riddle of his being," which she cannot solve because he is a ghost. (*"If he could get the hang of the thing his cry might become 'To live would be an awfully big adventure!"*) What is so fascinating about *Peter Pan* is that such unusual explorations of schizoid existence anxiety, of death, and of 'nonbeing,' should be dealt with in such a way that adults and children in the theater take it all in their stride and allow themselves (in a sense) to go mad and to perceive the play's surrealistic fantasy as quite acceptable. In trying to solve the existentialist problems in the play, the mother does what she can ("I mean to keep you"); but Peter is beyond her power. By the end, we almost feel that Mrs. Darling is a foe, as she closes and bars the windows, which surely are acts of manic denial.

The word *manic* is important in connection with the play. It is all play, and it is significant that Peter chooses never to grow up and will play on forever ("He plays on until we wake up"). In the introduction, Barrie writes: "*all the characters, whether grown-ups or babies, must wear a child's outlook on life as their only important adornment.*" To put on one's shadow is to come back from the dead and become real. But when Wendy sews on Peter's shadow, he does not become real. Barrie's mother obviously wanted her son to return from the world of death, but her hopes could not be fulfilled. He, like Peter, could remain in the world of the house only as some kind of dreadful untouchable: As a stage direction tells us, "*He [Peter] is never touched by anyone in the play.*"

Although the play is remembered for its dealings with fairies and pirates and seems a bit of fey nonsense for the children being walked round Kensington Gardens, it is persistently about death. Its play about death is child's play—about death in the home. Appropriately, the term *Wendy House* has entered the educational establishments and its vocabulary, in recognition that children, in playing mothers and fathers, are engaged in serious play with notions of sexuality, existence, and death. In *Peter Pan* we return to the earliest fears of the child, so beautifully discussed by Chaloner (1963). The boys encountered in Never Land are those children who fall out their prams: "*not that they are really worrying about their mothers, who are now as important to them as a piece of string.*"

The pirates are embodiments of the threat of death in the world. The crocodile with a clock inside it is death itself. The crocodile has "killed" Captain Hook's arm and yearns for him. When he dies, he enters "the yawning cavity . . . like one greeting a friend." (Melville's *Moby-Dick* is in the background here.) Tootles, believing Wendy to be a bird, shoots her. The woman who the lost boys hope will be a mother to them is shot. In the background, of course, is the *The Rime of the Ancient Mariner*. The reference is highly significant because in Coleridge the symbolism belongs to that of "the stage of concern." The mariner's act is a thoughtless one, like an infant directing a fantasy of hate at the source of life. He has, painfully, to dwell on the possibility of having blighted his world by his assault on life. Through the benign light of the moon shining on the stark sea, in which swim the water snakes, he is able to find a spring of love rising in his heart: "I blessed them unawares." The moon is the mother, and her light enables him to find the power of reparation.[3]

The level of the action had to be kept at the level of child's play, for Barrie could not aspire to deal with realism through the dreadfulness of the tragic. But Wendy is the child's ideal object:

TOOTLES:
When ladies used to come to me in dreams I said 'Pretty mother,' but when she really came I shot her!

A kiss has saved Wendy; and Omnes cries, "Wendy lady, be our mother!" Later, even the pirates want a mother:

SMEE:
(*Not usually a man of ideas.*) Captain, could we not kidnap these boys' mother and make her our mother?

But then the female is dangerous, and even the fairy Tinker Bell gets up to some vengeful tricks. The mermaids try to pull you under the water to drown you. And behind this fear of the dangerous woman lurks the problem of sex. Tiger Lily wants to be "something else" to Peter Pan, not his mother. Peter Pan wants Wendy so much that he shuts the window at the end so she cannot return to her mother. Mrs. Darling is heard moaning, "Wendy, Wendy, Wendy." Peter says,

She wants me to unbar the window. I won't. She is awfully fond of Wendy. I am fond of her too. We can't both have her, lady! (*A funny feeling comes over him.*) Come on, Tink; we don't want any silly mothers.

The "funny feeling" is a recognition that begins to dawn on him, of feeling a need that belongs to "something else." Peter, however, does not want to grow up: "I just want always to be a little boy and to have fun." When the water is rising, he says, "To die will be an awfully big adventure." And reality is again dissolved in play. At the end, Barrie writes:

(*If he could get the hand of the thing his cry might become "To live would be an awfully big adventure!" but he can never quite get the hang of it, and no one is as gay as he.*)

Peter Pan tells us why Barrie could "never get the hang of it" —woman is too dangerous. We may interpret the phrase "get the hang of it" in a sexual sense. While most of the play is play with death, there is also play with sexuality, as there is when children play mothers and fathers. The danger in Barrie's life was that his mother yearned to bring her dead son back into the world, as Mrs. Darling yearns to bring her lost children back: "When they call I stretch out my arms to them, but they never come, they never come!" The lost boys come with them. The maid Liza immediately becomes the mother of Slightly; they are born at this very moment, so to speak.

But how could one bear to approach woman if (like Barrie's mother) she is capable of exercising with such poignant intensity evocative powers over life and death? How could one bear sexuality with her, to enter her body, and to create from there new life? Such a mother was terribly dangerous; thus as one can see from Peter, any suggestion of love intimacy with woman in the sexual sense must be playfully avoided because for him it is impossible.

Toward the end of the play, Wendy is inclined, like a teenage girl, to want to fly away to Peter, while Peter wants to keep her for himself, like any young suitor, rejecting the mother's claims. Wendy's inclination to fly into Peter's world horrifies Mrs. Darling. But Peter cannot accept the challenge of sexual commitment:

WENDY:
(*Making a last attempt.*) You don't feel you would like to say anything to my parents, Peter, about a very sweet subject?
PETER:
No, Wendy

Mrs. Darling offers to adopt Peter as well as the lost boys. Would she send him to school and to an office? "I suppose so" So, Peter would be threatened with becoming like Mr. Darling, who is a nonentity and at last retires into the dog kennel. Peter, who larks with the fairies, still needs a mother. But Wendy will be released to him, for "spring cleaning."

"Spring cleaning" may be read as a euphemism for the kind of duties a wife performs for her husband. We see Never Land a year hence. The little Wendy House appears; Wendy looks a year older but Peter looks the same. As I have pointed out earlier, Wendy "flies so badly now that she has to use a broomstick." Instead of the magical, playful love of the latency period, Wendy now has libidinal urges for a phallus. It is the instrument with which you do the "spring cleaning."

WENDY:

When you come for me next year, Peter—you will come, won't you?

And then she becomes worried:

If another little girl—if one younger than I am— (*She can't go on.*) Oh, Peter, how I wish I could take you up and squdge you! (*He draws back.*) Yes, I know. (*She gets astride her broomstick.*) Home! (*It carries her from him over the treetops.*)

Wendy's maturing sexuality carries her away from Peter Pan, who is impotent.

(*In a sort of way he understands what she means by "Yes, I know," but in most sorts of ways he doesn't. It has something to do with the riddle of his being.*)

The appeal of *Peter Pan* lies in the way it plays upon this "riddle of being." For what the play says is that Barrie himself had become mystified by the strange psychic state of his mother, in her unrelievable grief of bereavement and that he was possessed by such a fear of woman that he could never advance beyond the state of childishness in relation to woman. If a woman wanted to "squdge" him, he could only draw back; and then her broomstick would carry her away from him over the treetops.[4]

The Insights Applied: Sir James Barrie

There are two remarkable essays from the psychoanalytical point of view that have been of considerable use to me in developing a phenomenological approach to the work of Sir James Barrie and, indeed, to the works of other fantasists. One is an essay by P. Lionel Goitein, entitled "A New Approach to Analysis of 'Mary Rose,'" published in 1926. This is an oddly old-fashioned account that finds Barrie's play to be a religious analogy, yet also brings to it some remarkable intuitive insights. The other is by Marietta Karpe and Richard Karpe, entitled "The Meaning of Barrie's 'Mary Rose,'" published in 1957. The latter provides many insights into the connections between motherhood and the problem of death. The implied connections among mothering, death, and images of woman in these essays have helped me in my studies of C. S. Lewis, Sylvia Plath, George MacDonald, Gustav Mahler, and D. H. Lawrence.

Before I discuss the play *Mary Rose*, I should like to pursue further certain clues from these essays and elsewhere to Barrie's uncanny preoccupation with woman as a focus of the problem of life and death, and the mystery that surrounds her. I hope to show how some of D. W. Winnicott's concepts illuminate the problems outlined in these essays. One of these is primary maternal preoccupation and the mysterious state into which a woman goes when she is giving psychic parturition to her infant—especially the concept of the mother's reflecting role as creative mirror. In these processes, the mother draws out the potentialities of the infant—his 'soul', his 'being'. What happens if this process is disastrously disturbed, either by death or by the effects of death, as when a sibling dies? I believe that with Barrie, as with Dylan Thomas, Mahler, MacDonald, Lewis, and Lawrence, the death of a sibling so disturbed the psychic processes between mother and infant that the result was catastrophic in one sense but was the mainspring of a creative drive in another.

One of the chapters in Barrie's book about his mother, *Margaret Ogilvie, by Her Son* (1896), is called "How My Mother Got Her Soft Face." Among other things, his book deals with the crisis provoked in Barrie when his mother became severely traumatized by the sudden death of his brother at the age of fourteen, in a skating accident. As we shall see, Barrie's mother withdrew completely; and the boy Barrie took it upon himself to try to draw her back into the world, into reality. In a similar spirit he wrote all his books for her, and so we can see that his creative effort has to do with the problem of life and death in the woman and in consequence in himself, insofar as he was totally dependent upon the woman. Yet, at the same time, in complex with this urge was a drive to deny reality altogether. In Barrie's shadow plays there is, of course, a massive dynamic of denial of reality, of the need to grow up and find one's adult reality—that is, one's mortality. To accept one's mortality also means, incidentally, finding and accepting one's sexuality. The mother's sexuality, which produced the offspring to which she should have conveyed reflection, is seen, in the background, as being part of the problem.

Out of these problems, a troubled mind can devise an ideal woman, a woman who has none of the difficulties and dangers of being mortal or sexual. Barrie evidently picked up from his mother the impulse to deny reality, in favor of manic denial. As we shall see, although Barrie wrote all of his books for her and they were a deeply significant element in her life, there was one story to which she needed always to be blind. The story is "Dead These Twenty Years," in which Barrie wrote of a death similar to his brother's. Such a denial of the reality of death and such a failure of the processes of mourning can only be achieved by a kind of magic—by the invention of a mother-woman who is perfect, beautiful, gentle, eternal, never suffers from depression, never hates or rejects, is magically nonmortal, is never weak, and never threatens rejection. We may, I believe, relate Peter Pan's failure to grow up and Mary Rose's uncannily nonhuman presence to this fantasy of a magical woman of the *Geist* (spirit).

Margaret Ogilvie, for whom Barrie wrote his books, is such an immortal magical woman. She is eternally manic:

> Her face beamed and ripped with mirth as before, and her laugh that I had tried so hard to force came running home again. I have heard no such laugh as hers save from merry children; the laughter of most of us ages, and wears out with the body, but hers remained gleeful to

the last, as if it were born afresh every morning. There was always something of the child in her, and her laugh was its voice, as eloquent of the past to me as was the christening robe to her. (Barrie 1896, 18)

As a child Barrie strove to transform the actual mortal, ailing, threatening, depressed mother into this idolized woman.

Of course, there were other lesser psychic conditions that affected Barrie. Family life must have been difficult enough, as was the problem of adjusting to new siblings. The Karpes write:

> Barrie was born at Kirriemuir, a small Scottish town, the ninth of the children and the third son in the family of a poor weaver. When he was three and two months old, the last child, his youngest sister was born. In his autobiographical book *Margaret Ogilvie* Barrie tells us that he has a complete amnesia for the first six years of his life. . . . We thus have no direct description of little James's reaction to his sister's birth, but we can guess from the unusually intensive relationship which later developed with his mother that he must have felt very deeply her preoccupation with her new baby. (Karpe and Karpe 1957, 409)

But then the normal difficulties were exacerbated by his brother's death:

> At the age of six a tragic event occurred which had a deep and lasting influence on Barrie's whole life. He then had two older brothers, the oldest Alexander, already grown up, and an adolescent brother David . . . much loved by the mother. When David was killed in an accident on the eve of his fourteenth birthday . . . the mother went into a deep depression. For many days she stayed in bed in a darkened room, her face to the wall, refusing food and paying no attention to her children, until little six-year-old James *succeeded in arousing her interest in him again* [italics mine]. From then on James took it upon himself to cheer his bereaved mother, and these attempts provide his first childhood memories. (408)

Perhaps in such a large family, Barrie had experienced already a deficiency of creative reflection. There was perhaps a deficiency in his earliest infant life, of that telepathic experience of total identification in which the child's emerging identity has its basis. Thus, he may have known the sense of being totally threatened in his existence by a lack of confirmation, which we find in his plays. Perhaps even before his mother's withdrawal he had experienced that the mother could disappear into "another world" and thus virtually go out of existence, leaving him in existlessness, while yet obviously physically still alive and growing. Certainly, what we find in Barrie's work is an intense need to try to find the mother who can give him more reflection. He cannot grow up psychically unless he finds her; and finding her seems to involve an immense effort to get into another world, back in time, and back into the primal relationship. Yet, there is a poignant sense that the time is gone.

As we have seen, there is a good deal of childish magic in this; and this may be seen in connection with the mother's magic, of trying to bring the dead sibling back to life:

> But I had not made her forget the bit of her that was dead; in those nine-and twenty years he was not removed one day farther from her. Many a time she fell asleep speaking to him, and even while she slept her lips moved and she smiled as if he had come back to her, and when she woke he might vanish so suddenly that she started up bewildered and looked about her, and then said slowly "My David's dead!" or perhaps he remained long enough to whisper why he must leave her now, and then she lay silent with filmy eyes. When I became a man and he was still a boy of thirteen, I wrote a little paper called "Dead this Twenty Years," which was about a similar tragedy in another woman's life, and it is the only thing I have written that she never spoke about, not even to that daughter she loved the best. No one ever spoke of it to her, or asked her if she had read it: one does not ask a mother if she knows that there is a little coffin in the house. She read many times the book in which it is printed, but when she came to that chapter she would put her hands to her heart or even over her ears. (Barrie 1896, 18)

The conflict in Barrie's work is thus between the ghost that persists in existence, like Mary Rose in his play of that name, and those who seek to put it to rest. The conflict is between those who cannot become real or perhaps do not want to become real, like Peter Pan, and those who mourn the loss of their shadows, who have fallen out of their prams and have never been convinced by the mother that they were real. As Peter Coveney writes in *Poor Monkey* (1957), there is one central image in Barrie's works. It is not the "central image of Barrie's neurosis"; it is an image of an existence problem:

But the window was closed, and there were iron bars on it, and peering inside he saw his mother sleeping peacefully with her arm round another little boy. Peter called "Mother! Mother!" but she heard him not; in vain he beat his little limbs against the iron bars. He had to fly back, sobbing, to the Gardens, and he never saw his dear again. (Barrie, 1902, 186)

Peter cannot be confirmed in his existence because the mother is given over to another. This seems like a final catastrophe. There is no second chance:

Ah Peter! we who have made the great mistake, how differently we should all act at the second chance. But Solomon was right—there is no second chance, not for most of us. When we reach the window it is Lock-out Time. The iron bars are up for life. (187)

For Barrie, "the iron bars were up" because his mother remained forever in a state of primary maternal preoccupation for the ghost of his sibling and not for him. For Barrie, because the time of psychic parturition is over forever, it is too late; and in both plays we have a poignant sense that the time that could have brought fulfillment is gone forever. Even at the end:

All this time there seemed to be something that she wanted, but the one was dead who always knew what she wanted, and they produced many things at which she shook her head. They did not know then that she was dying, but they followed her through the house in some apprehension, and after she returned to bed they say that she was becoming very weak. Once she said eagerly, "Is that you, David?" and again she thought she heard her father knocking the snow off his boots. Her desire for that which she could not name came back to her, and at last they saw that what she wanted was the old christening robe. It was brought to her, and she unfolded it with trembling exultant hands, and when she had made sure that it was still of virgin fairness her old arms went round it adoringly, and upon her face there was the ineffable mysterious glow of motherhood. (Barrie 1896, 200)

This mysterious state of the mother belongs to the same *participation mystique* by which Tolstoy's Kitty in *Anna Karenina* feels that her baby needs her:

It was not a mere guess—the bond between herself and the baby had not yet been severed—and she knew surely by the flow of milk within

86

herself that he was wanting food. She knew he was screaming before she reached the nursery. And so he was. She heard his voice and increased her speed. (Tolstoy 1878; part 8, sec. 6)

But for Margaret Ogilvie, this mysterious state was for a dead child; and its magic power was terrible because it spelled everlasting immaturity for Barrie. Over him she exerted an obliterating possessiveness. Since all he wrote was for her, it was necessarily manic and in it was always the denial of death. Just as Barrie's mother had scotomized the death of her son forever and had kept him as a baby, she kept herself in a state of permanent 'being for' that baby. Caught in such psychic toils, Barrie could achieve nothing of the *Dasein*— nothing that is, to set in terms of 'being there' against death and 'being-unto-death'. He could never find the true path toward separateness, out of union, so that he could exist alone and become a man with his shadow attached but also with life and freedom. Thus, as Coveney writes, Barrie's fixation on his mother meant his exclusion from creative fulfillment. We may add to this the possibility that because of her state of mind, this meant exclusion for Barrie from an adequate relationship with reality—in truth, "disillusionment." By "dissolutionment" Winnicott means the process by which the mother gradually enables her child to find the real world as painful as this may be for him (and for her). Barrie, like Peter Pan, withdraws from reality; his woman fades into evanescence like Mary Rose, who periodically slips out of this world.

In view of the problems I am discussing of the mother and her role in the formation of identity as they are explored in psychoanalysis, it should be no surprise to find chapters in Sir James Barrie's *Margaret Ogilvie* headed "What I Should Be" and "How My Mother Got Her Soft Face." Coveney quotes Barrie as saying, "the love of mother and son has written everything of mine that is of any worth" (Coveney 1957, 204).

Barrie's books, he said, were written to "please one woman who is now dead." But there is an element in his urgent activity that make his reparation incapable of really restoring his object and the world, thus establishing a "living principle" between him and the world. His is a manic reparation, directed at trying to keep alive what cannot be kept alive and to make the woman perfect in a

The Insights Applied: Sir James Barrie

magical way, so that she has no ambivalence and no unreliability
—no human qualities, indeed. Barrie thus made his mother his
heroine and put himself entirely in her hands, becoming whatever
she wanted him to be. It is this sacrifice of authenticity that both
fascinates and appalls his readers. It is also what makes a critic like
Rickword so scathing, since such a denial of adult freedom seems to
involve us in an emotional "mess"—that is, a forfeiture of appropriate responses. In chapter 8 of *Margaret Ogilvie*, Barrie reports
with affection his mother's dominance of his work:

> We had read somewhere that a novelist is better equipped than most
> of his trade if he knows himself and one woman, my mother said,
> "You know yourself, for everybody must know himself" (there never
> was a woman who knew less about herself than she), and she would
> add dolefully, "but I doubt I'm the only woman you know well."
> "Then I must make you my heroine," I said lightly.
> "A gey auld-farrant-like heroine!" she said, and we both laughed
> at the notion—so little did we read the future. (Barrie 1896, 60)

And in the following chapter he writes:

> My Heroine

> When it was known that I had begun another story my mother might
> ask what it was to be about this time.
> "Fine we can guess who it is about," my sister would say point-
> edly.
> "Maybe you can guess, but it is beyond me," says my mother, with
> the meekness of one who knows that she is a dull person.
> My sister scorned her at such time. "What woman is in all books?"
> she would demand.
> "I'm sure I canna say," replies my mother determinedly. "I thought
> the women were different every time."
> "Mother, I wonder you can be so audacious! Fine you know what
> woman I mean." (163)

On her part, Barrie's mother identified closely with Barrie's struggle
to become a writer:

> After her death I found that she had preserved in a little box, with a
> photograph of me as a child, the envelopes which had contained my
> first cheques. There was a little ribbon round them. (82)

88

Woman, Death, and Meaning in *Peter Pan* and *Mary Rose*

On the last day, my mother insisted on rising from bed and going through the house. The arms that had so often helped her on that journey were now cold in death, but there were others only less loving, and she went slowly from room to room like one bidding goodbye, and in mine she said, "The beautiful rows upon rows of books, and he said every one of them was mine, all mine!"

If creative work is to be judged by the degree to which it is successful in establishing existential authenticity and freedom, Barrie seems to have made few gains in the way of genuine creativity. He never found his freedom because his view of self, world, and others never escaped from the confines of his mother's need to preserve her denial of time, death, and growth (rather like Miss Havisham in Dickens's *Great Expectations*).

As Coveney points out, Barrie himself came to see in the end that he had been unable to escape from this "flight from life." Later in his life he wrote, "It is as if long after writing *Peter Pan*, its true meaning came to me. Desperate attempts to grow up but can't" (Coveney 1957, 209).

However, the phrase "unable to grow up" masks the deeper problem. Coveney concludes his discussion of Barrie with a moralizing tone of discrimination, by which he conveys that it is somehow reprehensible and "uncreative" to "fail to grow up," despite heroic efforts to solve the problem of one's existential self.

Coveney recounts how Elizabeth Bergner[5] was able to coax Barrie's talents into life with the suggestion that he write a drama based upon the legend of David and Goliath, in which "the main and eccentric dramatic point of the whole play should reside in David's obsession with acquiring Goliath's spear" (209).

After the battle the boy trails the stage disconsolately, because he cannot raise the treasured possession onto his shoulder. In the final scene he confides to Jonathan that he can at last raise it, and the final curtain finds the boy on the highest rock on the stage with the spear shaft as wide as a "weaver's beam" mounted on his shoulder. From anyone who would deny the phallic character of the symbol (it is to be remembered that Barrie's father was in fact a weaver) it would be interesting to have an explanation of the dramatic point of *The Boy David*. (209–10)

The Insights Applied: Sir James Barrie

Barrie's work often is based on fantasies of stealing the father's penis and using it to possess the mother: "For the rest of the night he lay on me and across me. . . . He always retained possession of my finger" (Barrie 1902, 232). But this approach seems both too Freudian and deterministic, as if the work can be explained in terms of such oedipal material. This leads to "oedipal morbidities," says Coveney.

An approach based on phenomenology, however, acknowledges that the symbolism has a deeper meaning. The struggle of David against Goliath can be interpreted as the struggle to discover and assert against impossible odds (the weight of the mother's sickness and dread) a certain male-element strength of identity. The symbolism of phallic sexual desire for the mother can rather be interpreted as a yearning to find sustenance, to receive more reflection from her, and even to receive "disillusionment" from her in order to discover one's own independent strength of identity—so that, in adulthood, one could, in turn, support the mother against nothingness and loss of meaning. When the Boy David holds the mother's finger, it is possible that what he wants of her is something from her male element (*her* penis) that will enable him as an adult to deal with a "difficult and sometimes dangerous" world. But because of her need to depend so manically on Barrie, Margaret Ogilvie disarmed her son for such creative dealings with reality. What Coveney calls "oedipal morbidities" may thus be interpreted as a quest for genuine creative potentialities in an impossible situation—and so are not so blameworthy as they appear from Coveney's somewhat moralizing approach. If we hold back for the moment from moralizing discrimination, we may understand better and see that what we are dealing with is magic. (Of course, the trouble is that magic doesn't work in the real world.)

But the recognition of the element of magic will help us to understand such things as the mysterious way in which Mary Rose, in the play of that name, disappears periodically into another world while her son grows up.[6] At the end of the play, Mary Rose's son takes her on his lap like a child. What the author himself seeks is to be released from his problem of identity. This Barrie achieves in

90

Mary Rose by inverting the problem, so that Harry's aim is to release Mary Rose:

HARRY:

All I know about them for certain is that they are unhappy because they can't find something, and then once they've got the thing they want, they go away happy and never come back.

MARY ROSE:

Oh, nice.

HARRY:

The one thing clear to me is that you have got that thing at last, but you are too dog-tired to know or care. What you need now is to get back to the place you say is lovely, lovely.

MARY ROSE:

Yes, yes.

From the Freudian way of looking at the problem, it might seem, as it does to Goitein, as if the creator of Mary Rose is "keeping her for his sexual pleasure":

This means the author of her being, the father creator, has kept her for himself and his pleasure, has drawn her back into his mind and ultimately suppressed her from consciousness, even as he did years before, when she became the object of sexual desire in the fullness of his youth—lost her in the mists of the unconscious.[7] (Goitein 1926, 196)

But if we look at the problem in light of Winnicott's exploration of the origins of existence in the experience of total identification with the mother, as a problem of existence, we can penetrate beneath the sexual pattern (which is undeniably there) and see a schizoid pattern. That is, what Barrie is seeking is existential rebirth of the regressed ego—the rebirth of 'being' in the experience of the female element. Goitein sees that there is a theme of rebirth:

What is the problem Mary Rose really endeavours to settle when she comes to earth? It is stated in the play as the question of eternity which is of course, "How can man live forever, how reclaim his lost youth, and be born again, how come to be a little child once more to

91

enter the Kingdom of Heaven?" Or, expressed in the "projected" form, "What is it Mary is ever searching for and longing for, and returned for?—a baby." Indeed she goes through a *"nightly travail that can never be completed"* till this Harry is here *"to provide the end."* (187)

But the "baby" is Barrie's own regressed libidinal ego—that is, the unborn infant self in himself.

Barrie wants to re-create the mother who can give him (psychic) birth as his real mother never did. Thus, he creates a dream mother who is forever anguished by her need to complete her baby, so that he can "enter the kingdom of heaven" of integration. Goitein continues:

> Now the latest content of this question is the personal heart-searching: "How can a man tear himself away from the mother, and yet be at one with her. . . ?" Mary herself is eternal, always virgin, ever young. (187)

Mary is the "ideal object" who is not prone to the threats to her survival inherent in becoming an adult. An adult is capable of libidinal sexual creativity and in this is at one with his mortality. Mary may not have this. She must be kept in pseudoinnocence. (Goitein says that Mary Rose is a virgin throughout the play and that the marriage is never consummated.) A mother kept magically in this state is not susceptible, of course, to one's own dangerous envy. Therefore, she cannot then—as castrating mother—turn jealously against one's oedipal involvement in parental sex. She will always be there to reflect one in a totally controllable manner and will never threaten withdrawal or rejection, as a mother does when she mourns, attends to a new sibling, belongs to her husband, or recovers her self-interest. This mother is kept in a state of perpetual primary maternal preoccupation; and she lives, therefore, is a magical world:

> She has solved the problem, but she is from another world, for which "the loch" and the "vale of the shadow" separate us. ("There was a door for which I had no key. There was a veil past which I could not see.") (187)

This other world is the world where the dead mother is. There, if one can find her, she will prove to be the creatively reflecting mother who was not adequately experienced. The new world—the spirit world—is a world in which one may experience psychic birth as one never could before (as in George MacDonald's other world or the world at the end of Charles Kingsley's *The Water-Babies*). It is the inheritance of love and encounter that one has never had as a neonate. The problem for, us, of course, is to estimate the value the re-creation of the world may have for us: How much rebirth do we need? "How is it with us?" asks Goitein.

> We cannot be Peter Pans, that is certain: reverie and dream are not enough, if as men we would live again we must recreate ourselves: go back to the womb from whence we came—and this must mean reunion with the mother. Or man may create himself by 'being one with' his own grandchild—by union with his daughter. Of course, this is but deep, unconscious reasoning; in life it is but metaphor, it satisfied the mind's censor in the guise of religious drama; and on the stage it is but the enacting of a dream: and so again may pass the world's censorship. (187)

Goitein discusses the play in Freudian terms of sexual impulses expressed in Christian symbolism:

> His [Harry's] answer to the immortality problem is "Through the creation of a daughter" . . . the union of the Father with the daughter and the rise of the immortal Son and Lord. . . . He makes love to her: the sparks of the fire he has made "leap up as often as they are trampled down," but as he approaches her, "an unholy organ" of another "increasing in volume" rakes the bushes for her. . . . The Father has drawn her in unto Himself; she is no more. (188)

Goitein also discusses problems of identity:

> He [Harry] returns to the "old home," the fabric of the mother, and dandles on his knee a little girl spirit; whose childish patter and babyish ways show best what age Mary Rose has reached. (188)

As Goitein sees, Mary Rose is "*the beautiful youthful maiden form the mother is unconsciously ever thought to be.*" (188) Perhaps Mary Rose is the mother who is remembered as having allowed her baby to make her the subjective object. She is re-created now as still being able to allow him to make use of her in primary maternal preoccupation, yet she is made into a controllable little toy girl.

Thus, at the end of the play we have the disturbing image of a man holding on his lap the mother—who has become so identified with her baby that she now is the baby, while the adult writer is a man.

According to Goitein, the implication is that "the problem of the ages can only be settled on earth as it is in heaven," and "in reality the solution is a poor one as far as the human race is concerned":

> It is an ideal of a kind, harboured by many desperate minds who would fly in the face of conventions of racial evolution, and eventually be their own unwitting slayers. It may hold for the phantasy [sic] of the family in heaven; it must fail for the families on earth. (189)

Isn't the point, instead, that what we have here is a symbolism of schizoid suicide—that is, a weariness with life, in the absence of an inward confirming possession of the female element of the mother, that tends to lead to withdrawal into death, into a ghostly world. There may be in this a hope of rebirth, but could it prove to be a negative path of ultimate regression? An underlying feeling of the lure of death permeates the play. It is the malevolent call to which Mary Rose herself gives such ecstatic assent.[8]

But at the same time, a real need is being expressed—the intense need for reexperiencing that confirmation of identity that the mother reflection should originally have provided. The problem with *Mary Rose* is that the solution to the problem of the need to have one's existence confirmed *is* simply magical; it belongs not to heaven but to the preservation of an attitude of magical infantile omnipotence. Harry retains an ability such as a child believes in, even to defy God, to manipulate the universe, and to restore the object to heavenly perfection by sheer manic necromancy:

HARRY:
. . . If there was any way of getting you to that glory place!
MARY ROSE:
Tell me.
HARRY:
(*Desperate*.) He would surely send for you if he wanted you.
MARY ROSE:
(*Crushed*.) Yes.
HARRY:

It's like as if He had forgotten you.

MARY ROSE:

Yes.

HARRY:

It's as if nobody wanted you, either there or here.

MARY ROSE:

Yes. (*She rises.*) Bad man.

HARRY:

It's easy to call me names, but the thing fair beats me. There is nothing I wouldn't do for you, but a mere man is so helpless.

From Barrie's childhood experience we can recognize the origins of this combination of feelings of hopelessness and the urge to restore the object:

> From then on (from the moment when he managed to "arouse her interest in him again") James took it upon himself to cheer his bereaved mother, and these attempts provide his first childhood memories. He recalls in his autobiography how he sat in his mother's room, trying to entertain her by standing on his head or by similar childish tricks and counting how often she laughed. He devoted a great deal of his boyish efforts and energies to cheering his mother by letting her talk about herself, and, almost like a psychotherapist, encouraged her to talk of her own childhood, her father whom she had adored, and her early hopes and experiences. This intensive relationship continued for the next *twenty-eight years* until her death, even though James never completely succeeded in making her forget David, *to whom she was always talking in whispers as if he were constantly with her* [italics mine]. Barrie's mother also remained on intimate terms with other dead persons, a fact which must have been of great importance to him. When one of his sisters, after the death of her fiancé, decided to marry the dead man's brother, her mother begged the dead man's forgiveness, asking him to understand how sad and lonely is the life of a friendless girl. (Karpe and Karpe 1957, 409)

As Marietta Karpe and Richard Karpe write, "the tragic loss of a love object seems able to become a stimulating factor for an artist's or a child's creativity, and the revival in fantasy of a lost object is one way of mastering that loss" (408). The problem, I believe, is deeper than one of loss and mastering loss. Loss presents the problem of existential despair, which in turn presents the question "What

95

is the point of life?" This question then requires engagement with the *Dasein* problem.

It is interesting at this point to note that, as the Karpes point out, the basic idea of *Mary Rose* first occurs in a story book, *The Little White Bird* (1902). Among the episodes are fantastic answers to the question "Where do I come from?" One chapter, "A Nightpiece," deals with the birth of David.

> The author tells David, a little boy of five, what happened on the night of his birth. He tells how he, the author, walked the streets all night with David's father waiting for David's mother to have her baby, and surprisingly enough their thoughts turn to death and to ghosts. "The only ghosts, I believe," he writes, "who creep into this world, are dead young mothers: returned to see how their children fare. There is no other inducement great enough to bring the departed back. . . . But what is saddest about these ghosts is that they may not know their child. They expect him to be just as he was when they left him, and they are easily bewildered, and search for him from room to room, and hate the *unknown boy he has become.*" (Karpe and Karpe 1957, 409)

It is true, as the Karpes say, that in this we have the synopsis of *Mary Rose*; but within in it, we also can see several important themes that address existence anxiety. In talking to David, who is five years old, the author is talking to the boy who died in 1867 at the age of fourteen, when Barrie was six. The Karpes suggest that the fantasy of death associated with birth may have had its origin in Barrie's experience of the birth of his younger sister. But isn't it better explained in terms of a failure in early babyhood to be confirmed as alive and real? Barrie may well have sensed that the birth of David (as well as his sister) meant even a greater lessening of his mother's capacity to confirm him, while David's birth becomes merged with his death, by the consequences of which all confirmation and hope of confirmation seemed lost. Barrie's young mother was to him a "dead young mother" because she did not make him feel alive, while the ghosts' bewilderment ("they may not know their child") springs from the terrible experience of being unconfirmed by a dissociated mother and then being confused by her with the ghosts of a dead sibling by being put on the same existential plane.

Surely, the relationship of Barrie's mother to dead persons manifests a form of dissociation from reality that gives the reader a clue to Barrie's own existence problem. A mother who confused real persons and ghosts in this way would obviously prove less than dependable in the formation of the child's identity, since the child could never be sure whether he was being treated as a real person or as a ghost.

Barrie's attachment to his mother can thus be seen as an attempt to help her become real and alive because she had not enabled *him* to feel real and alive. However, the attachment involved him in accepting her dissociation, so that the problem of integration comes into conflict with the magic by which he sought to preserve her. When these manic processes broke down he would be subject to one of his own "periods of deep depression in which he refused to see anyone and cut himself off from all contacts" (409).

Thus, even Harry seeks to persuade Mary Rose that in being indifferent to her God is being cruel—a paranoid attitude that often accompanies an inability to tolerate and accept one's mortal reality.[9] In Barrie's writings, we often find such resentment expressed in terms that surely derive from his own puzzlement over his brother's death—a death that the mother herself seems to have been unable to accept. At the end of *Mary Rose*, Harry says:

I wonder if what it means is that you broke some law.
If it was that, it's surely time He overlooked it.

Here surely is the attitude of a bemused child who feels that the woman's suffering must be a consequence of some guilt and that what is needed to overcome this is a mollifying and propitiation of some persecutor. Lifting his mother's depression was also sharing her paranoia and so trying to propitiate her persecutors.

Mary Rose, Harry supposes, may have broken some law, "just to come back for the sake of—of that Harry?" The recognition that the mother is dead and inaccessible as a source of rebirth is impossible; therefore, the law that has been broken is the law of the need to accept reality. For breaking this law, Mary Rose has alienated herself from God. She is stuck unhappily in existence, although really out of existence, just as David, although really out of existence, became stuck in existence because Barrie's mother continually recognized the presence of his ghost and refused to recognize his death.

Thus, we can see the infantile logic of those twenty-eight years: My brother is dead, but my mother continues to confirm his (nonexistent) existence as a person. What does my core of feeling of nonexistence mean, since I am living? Why do I not feel confirmed even so? The answer was to change the *malevolent call* that called the mother out of confirming existence, which is what caused the damage in the first place, into a *benign call*. Yet, this transformation happens only by magic. At first, the stars of the actual universe seem indifferent. Harry says, "You are too small a thing to get a helping hand from them"

But then, as God's hard heart is softened by Harry's remonstrances, comes the celestial music that is "the only sound in the world." The stage direction is intensely sentimental and is imbued with a force of tremendous magical desire that things should not be as they are and never have been:

> (*The call is heard again, but there is in it now no unholy sound. It is a celestial music that is calling for Mary Rose, Mary Rose. . . . As it wraps her round, the wearly little ghost knows that her long day is done. Her face is shining. The smallest star shoots down as if it were her star sent for her, and with her arms stretched forth to it trustingly she walks though the window into the empyrean. The music passes with her.* HARRY *hears nothing, but he knows that somehow a prayer has been answered.*)

THE END

This is the epitome of manic reparation. The problems of existence anxiety and identity are solved by the capacity of the infant to move a star out of heaven, to make his object good enough for him to "begin." This is cosmic infant monism indeed—to make the stars into the mother's eyes! Strangely enough, after *Mary Rose* Barrie was able to produce nothing more that was creative. He had somehow re-created and magically assuaged his anguish for the female element of 'being'. Significantly, perhaps, his next attempts at plays were called *Shall We Join the Ladies?*, *Farewell Miss Julie Cogan*, and, his last, *Boy David*. As the Karpes write, "The free flow of his creativity seemed cut off after the writing of *Mary Rose*" (Karpe and Karpe 1957, 408).

These writers argue that *Mary Rose* fulfilled an important "dynamic function" in Barrie's life. However, "dynamic function" seems a positive term for a strangely negative process. For example, it seems likely that one of the motives for writing the play was an attempt at reconciliation with his former wife, Mary. In fact, she was later hospitalized with a paranoid condition; and *Mary Rose*, as the Karpes say, "helped him to reject the idea of marriage." They go on to say that writing the play "liberated him temporarily from his lifelong struggle with his mother's youthful image" (411). The word "liberated" seems strange here, when, in fact, Barrie seems to have solved the problem of his turmoil over Mary's reappearance on the scene at the time by making Lady Cynthia Asquith his "private secretary" and forming a close relationship both with her mother Lady Wemyss and Lady Cynthia's two little boys. (Barrie "always loved little boys and needed their proximity"—presumably because they fulfilled the intense need in his own relationship with his mother to resurrect David). Lady Cynthia simply provided the mother relationship:

> Lady Cynthia describes the days of depression and gloom when nothing could cheer him, with one exception; if she presented him with some trouble of her own, he immediately became interested in her problem and forgot his own sadness, obviously a repetition of his old tendency to cheer his grieving mother. (410)

Barrie's sense of identity depended upon having a mother object whose confirming regard he gained by seeking to lift her grief, but this was no solution. Nor did it lead him to mature engagement with existential problems (as he would have had to had he rejoined his former wife). Barrie merely became a child again who was faced with an impossible task. Therefore, like a child, he asks existential questions but; he cannot answer them except in childish terms:

The Insights Applied: Sir James Barrie

His attempt to free himself from the ghosts of his childhood proved unsuccessful. Should the dead come back from their graves? Where are the children before they are born?—the eternal questions of life and death. Barrie's gallant attempt at solving them in his magical, illogical and philosophical way did not succeed, and he died discouraged, a lonely old man, in spite of many friendships. (411)

Barrie's play may have begun as a "parable of life," but even the terms in which he phrases his philosophical questions are not philosophically mature or "disillusioned" enough. He is too content with the terms and concepts of a Victorian nursery and a Sunday-school Christian cosmology—little stars, heavenly voices, the dear dead, and the innocent souls of children. One existential question is "Where do they go when they die?"—for the essential question is "How do I know I exist, especially when others (who should confirm my existence) go out of existence?" It is rather like Alice and the Red King. However, instead of waking up and ceasing to dream of her, so that Alice ceases to exist, the Red King dies—and where would Alice be then?[10]

Barrie speaks of the "narrow loch" that separates us from nonexistence, but his nonexistence remains a dream. He cannot accept utter loss. He stays in the metaphysical state of childhood, in which the child cannot accept nonexistence but must believe in another world of easily available ghosts. Thus, Barrie's method of expressing loss is merely childish:

MARY ROSE:
The last time of anything is sad, don't you think, Simon?
MARY ROSE:
Simon, if one of us had to—to go—and we could choose which one . . .

Barrie's world is disturbing because we are never allowed, and the characters are never allowed, to develop an adult's self-interest. The characters and the readers always must go over into the state of confirming the existence of another or letting another confirm their identity in terms of total identification. In other words, all are subjective objects. We are involved in striving to bring Mary Rose out of the world beyond existence, and we yearn for others to do this for us—from Mary Rose herself, to the voices of the spheres at the end, to Harry. In responding to the play, we hear a shriek in our ears that means "let me never be confounded!"

To avoid going out of existence in truth, a mystic and magical power *is* needed. In reality, that power is the uncanny state of the mother—that is, primary maternal preoccupation, her schizoid extension of identity in creative reflection that establishes our sanity, a kind of telepathy. When this power cannot be found, we have a desperate quest for all kind of magic to take its place. Goitein says of Barrie in relation to *Mary Rose*:

> He is not only anxious, but troubled, for the essential incident seems to worry him; and he, therefore, seeks as many outlets of expression as possible. For no discovery in science is left untried that can be enlisted to throw light on his theme and support his inmost contention. "Haunting", Hallucinations, Sublimation, Brain Waves, "telepathy," and Wireless Waves, are in turn offered as explanations to justify the pet delusion. (Goitein 1926, 181)

As Goitein writes, all these preoccupations enabled Barrie to combine nearness to truth and "probability of genuine occurrence" with a "quasi-scientific attitude" and phenomena of "abnormal psychology." In truth, *Mary Rose* is a mad play, with all the madness of primal existence anxiety, when the uncanny state of primary maternal preoccupation has gone "wrong":

> . . . its power of skipping over time, and leaving some of its images uninfluenced by time; its logic, its confusion of the characters, its sudden appearance, and its fading away. (181)

There are images of *as-if:* "As if . . . as if a cold finger has touched my Mary Rose." There are also hallucinations: "the old woman on the stairs" seen by Mary and the baby waving his bib seen from the island ("you needn't pretend you can see him"). Mary Rose has been seen "talking to some person who wasn't there and listening as it were for some sound that never came." She herself is like a "collective hallucination," says Goitein, "we cannot see her quite so clearly." The whole play is a "beautiful illusion." Goitein writes "that in going back to the "Home" and its "little room" we are going back to the Mother" (183).

The Insights Applied: Sir James Barrie

Thus, the play is an act of symbolic magical regression. As Goitein points out, the imagery of the anatomy of the "Home" is full of imagery of being "inside" the mother. This is an expanded metaphor for the reconstructed memory of intrauterine life. (From my point of view, this is symbolism of being inside the *psychic* uterus):

> For the house and its rooms, more especially the Mother's Room, . . . is the mother of the family. It wears "her disturbing smile,", "the smiles that she has left about";[11] and its aspect "takes on a semblance of herself"; even as every room is "full of herself, hanging on nails and folded away in drawers." We are privileged to see a Vision of life "in the old manner" (old manor) in the confines of the old-time mother. Small wonder they "whimper and thrill at his coming." Our attention is focused first on the garden external to her, with a blossoming tree as the open window, whose foliage scrapes the glass. This leads to a big room and (with-) drawingroom, where the baby first learnt to swim; and by a "fearsome narrow dark passage" into a single room—the baby's room "where he used to sleep"—the oldest part of the mother. It has two windows of stone and spanned above with wooden rafters: the door is never locked, it is often held, but the key is lost (only the grim blade—"the visiting card"—is to be thrust against its door). It is here that the ghost-mother pauses, hunting still for her child. Down below is the kitchen with its well-known smells (and rat holes) and the front door. Over our head and "so near us" is the Apple-room so called (?) from the large apples pressing against its walls. It is gloomy within—a chamber from which the *thumping* cry now and then to be answered by a thump quicker and happier from the big room below "when things are getting on, and going well." As we trace our way outward we observe a picture of a "waterfall" on the wall of the (with-)drawingroom; its "window opens outward" and it was down the parent trunk of the foliaged tree that her baby "slipped away" into the garden. (184)

(Incidentally, this is a superb piece of phenomenological analysis.) Harry unwittingly hurls his knife (= penis) at the door of her chamber, "the oldest room" in the fabric of the mother. As Goitein points out, Mr. Morland, on "calling" Mary to himself, is thinking of Mary Rose rather as "the old lady with wrinkles" and of the name on the island trunk which forever stops at MAR. (Barrie's mother's name was Margaret.) The knife breaks in the middle of her. The knife, Goitein believes, is a symbol of the dangers of incestuous desire for the mother. Perhaps the knife symbolizes instead the unconscious hatred that is directed against the mother's failure in psychic parturition. Here, the existence problems meet the oedipal problems. The consequence of both is the need for splitting to preserve existence because hate must be kept apart from love and goodness; hence, the "Holy Mary syndrome". Goitein's analysis of the religious elements in the play (with Freudian interpretations he does not quite make explicit) is fascinating:

> As a woman she is certainly not of this world, "she is different from other girls," "a little odd" with that peculiar "attribute of her that never plays with them." Like the Madonna, she is likened to a flower, *"a rare and lovely flower,"* and her parents were never anxious *"to take the bloom off her."* Like the Virgin [likened to a blood red rose] Mary-the-Rose is her name. Her little calyx (bassinette) holds the Babe; but that flower has inherited eternal youth by the cold finger of fate—a "cold finger had once touched my Mary Rose," as "frost may stop the *growth* of a plant and yet leave it *blooming."* . . . her saint-like purity is hinted at in many places. *"What you are worrying about is just her innocence—which seems a holy thing to me."* . . . "Marriage . . . it is so fearfully solemn." "We'll try to be good, won't we?" says Mary Rose: and while Simon is craving for her hand, Mary is sitting in the cold room above *"thinking holy things"* about love; and in her simple way, says Barrie, is worlds above the average "secret women" so much less innocent than she. Her island, which embodies herself (her soul) is a bird *sanctuary:* silent and "still as an empty *church":* and when in the shadow of a church she is buried, that site is a "holy spot." That is the dust, but her spirit rises "to the stars" of "the empyrean," when the "celestial music" calls her to her Father. . . . Mary is a virgin throughout the play (virgin-mother), but we may spare references to what the reader will detect for himself (e.g. How her child is adopted . . . "some baby you had borrowed . . ." "I sometimes think so still . . ." It was a phantom pregnancy and an imaginary delivery when Simon was sent away to Plymouth—an artifice suggested to the author's mind by the recently prominent case of Mrs. Slingsby and almost identical; the *ear* rather than a tuft of hair that being stressed in the imagined likeness to the father. The "holding of her tongue," her being told "to dry up" at the end of the scene of making love, both of these metaphorically and in fact, she does. For her, the reflection that she is an island, a garden enclosed, whose whins [whims] have first to be torn down to get through to her

and win her—even at the risk of bleeding limbs. And finally, when the "call" does come, is the "attempt to beat them back and put a girdle of *safety* round her"—all these point to her successful guarding of her virginity).

> Finally, she is Maria Stellarum when the "smallest star shoots down from heaven for her." ("My star" as Simon calls her;) and the little thing ascends at the divine call (the music of the spheres) into a "night of stars." Then surely she *"hid her head amid a crown of stars,"* and the moment was the Ascension of the Virgin. (189–90)

Such a split-off, pure, ideal object (deprived of all bodily sensibility) can exist ultimately only in "the land where the dead dreams go," since Mary Rose is so much divided from any real libidinal and ambivalent woman. Such a splitting must also accompany a division within the subject. Since to keep the subject's goodness unspoiled by hate requires an equal feat of internal splitting and projection, there is necessarily paranoia; hence, the "unseen devils" and Harry's remark:

> As if in a way there were two kinds of dogs out hunting you, the good and the bad.

—while the call is malevolent:

> A storm and whistling winds, increasing in volume till the mere loudness is horrible.

There are two observations to be made here: One is that the splitting prevents the acceptance of ambivalence in experience—our mixture of love and hate. The other is that the call which removes Mary is the libidinal power of "the Father," which is felt to be bad, even malevolent. Again, both symbolize a failure to embrace humanness in a whole way. This may be associated with the barrenness of Barrie's play, about which Goitein notes:

> One fact must surely emerge from the study of *Mary Rose*, and one of which the author is consciously unaware, and that is the hopeless barrenness of every character in the play. (207)

Simon never married again; Cameron will remain a bachelor "until . . ." and does so; Harry is unattached; and so on. As Goitein suggests, they are all waiting

> for the hand of Mary Rose—a creature who is the perfection ideal of their dreams—*an unreal phantasy* [sic] *that cannot be*—a woman that cannot be. (207)

Thus, the infant gravely unconfirmed in his identity, in the aspect that should have been confirmed by the female element of "being', needs to invent a hallucinatory split-off female element that will confirm him, although he has no capacity in himself to realize feminineness. Desperately the infant tries, but the image remains too good to be true, too heavenly, too pure, too ideal to be anything but barren and sterile. It remains (as Goitein says) the "image of a child," and its only place is among the cold, dead stars. The implicit impossibility is paralleled in Barrie's own relationships with women.

Mary Rose, too, is about woman and death, about 'being-in-existence' and 'going-out-of-existence'. As the Karpes and Goitein point out, at the time of the play's first appearance there was much discussion of the meaning of *Mary Rose*. The play was puzzling not only to audiences but to the author himself. It was also virtually the last creative work Barrie wrote. "According to the Karpes, the free flow of his creativity seemed cut off after *Mary Rose*" (Karpe and Karpe 1957, 408). It ended a period of twenty-nine years of intensive productivity, during which Barrie wrote twenty-seven plays. His secretary, Lady Cynthia Asquith, reports that he asked her, "I wish you could tell me what it means and settle the matter for once and for all" (Asquith 1954, quoted in Karpe and Karpe 1957, 408) But she could not tell, and she says in her book, *Portrait of Barrie*, that she preferred to leave the play unexplained.

The Karpes see that the play is about "the loss by death of a loved one we were not ready to give up" (408). Goitein points to the symbolism in the play: The apple tree that grows up toward the dining room, from whose branches we first hear the voice of Mary Rose, is the tree of life. The Island is "life," divided by a narrow channel from eternity. We arrive on it, have experiences there, as

Mary does with her lover-husband, and then disappear. Goitein also examines in detail the complex time sequence of the play.

As will be seen, the play relates to the very question of woman as the *mysterium tremendum*; and I have tried to show how the play is illuminated by Winnicott's concepts. In the response of the mother—the *participation mystique*—the new human being finds his own sense of 'being'. There are various ways in which this process can be broken, and one is death—the death of the mother or the death of a sibling (which can leave the mother in a schizoid state). As the Karpes say, a loss by death is often the mainspring for that existential anguish by which a creative writer is driven to try to find a sense of meaning in existence. In Barrie's plays, while their meaning is not evident at the explicit level, it is clear from their very mysteriousness and ghostliness that they have to do with 'being-unto-death'. As Mary Rose, "the last of anything is always sad." In *Peter Pan*, the clock ticks away inside the voracious crocodile, while in *Mary Rose* there is the "wheezy smith in the corner" who hammers out the time.

There does seem to be a problem of time, in relation to the mother's capacity to reflect the infant. Perhaps this is so because there is a certain period during which the formative psychic processes take place. If these are not completed in this period, then serious consequences follow. George MacDonald, the Victorian fantasist, kept in his drawer a lock of his mother's hair and a letter she wrote about his sudden weaning. (In a poem in *Phantastes* (1858), he wrote:

> Alas, how easily things go wrong!
> A sigh too much, or a kiss too long,
> And there follows a mist and a weeping rain,
> And life is never the same again.
> (MacDonald, "Sir Aglovaile")

The chance of 'reflection' can be missed, and then the individual may spend his life looking for the opportunity to make it up. But then profound problems arise: the child, by degrees, becomes another person; and the child is lost forever. In *Mary Rose*, Mary as a ghost at the end is looking for her baby; but the person in the house,

Woman, Death, and Meaning in *Peter Pan* and *Mary Rose*

Harry, is now a man, come back from Australia. Harry ran away at the age of twelve, and Mary disappeared when he was two and a bit. Now, twenty-five years later, he is twenty-seven years old. The solution to her problem seems to involve her sitting on his lap like a baby. In this, we can see the intense bafflement that is felt about experience and time. Where is the mother? She exists only in the child's memory. Can she be put together again, so that the process of mothering can be reexperienced? If she is in the world of death, might she not, when she comes back, be malevolent—a mother capable of such rejection again as she was once culpable of? These perplexities are worked out in fantasy again and again by George MacDonald and by Barrie in *Mary Rose*.

As well as time, there is the puzzle of place. A central theme is that of "talking to some person who wasn't there and listening as it were for some sound that never came." David is "there": "To whom she [the mother] was always talking in whispers as if he were constantly with her." Barrie's mother, the Karpes point out, also remained on intimate terms with other dead persons. She must be suspected, therefore, of mystifying the young Barrie (who worked so hard to relieve her grief), so that he became doubtful as to whether people were really there or not. His house must have been full of ghosts. And he himself was powerfully involved in her quest. His mother, like Mary Rose, was one of those who "are unhappy because they can't find something, and then once they've got the thing they want, they go away happy and never come back." Such a statement sounds as if it emerged from a fear that the mother was so preoccupied with the (dead) rival sibling that her withdrawal in this respect threatened Barrie's very existence.

The only ghosts . . . who creep into this world are dead young mothers, returned to see how their children fare. . . . What is saddest about these ghosts is that they may not know their child. They expect him to be just as he was when they left him, and they are easily bewildered, and search for him from room to room, and hate the unknown boy he has become. (Barrie 1902, 40–41)

Behind this theme we can sense the child's most terrible dread that his own existence is threatened by the mother's failure, when he needed more maternal reflection, to respond to him and to con-

107

firm his identity. She threatens him with eternal nonexistence. As Goitein says, Barrie has identified himself with his characters and silhouetted himself in his shadow plays; and his more mysterious plays are clearly about the problem of woman being the key to staying in existence. Yet Mary Rose, of course, spends much of her time in the play in a trance and becomes increasingly evasive ("*perhaps a little indistinct*"; "*we cannot see her quite so clearly*"), as if she were a mother the child is trying to hold together in his memory but cannot hold in focus as the mirror to his emerging identity.

It is perhaps worth adding that, even though I have been thinking about *Mary Rose* for years, there are still many aspects of it I cannot fathom. This is worth admitting of any work of literature. In my experience, it cheers undergraduates to find that one is still in perplexity about a work such as *Antony and Cleopatra*—so they are quite in order if they continue to be baffled. And, indeed, how much less interesting art would be if we could understand or explain its meaning. It is satisfying because it is ineffable.

My perplexities remain concerning the symbolism of sexuality in *Mary Rose* and also concerning the uncanny theme of "the last time." I am also puzzled by the religious element—what Barrie meant exactly about the good and bad days, about "the Father," and about the end, when Mary goes to heaven. When I say "exactly meant," I am of course asking too much. It seems clear that Barrie had an explicit meaning for himself, as did MacDonald about his fantasies. It is also clear, however, that much of the unconscious meaning was not clear to Barrie himself.

I cannot agree with Goitein that Mary remains a virgin throughout. How could she give birth to a baby if she were? I suppose the Christian answer would be that the Spirit of the Lord came upon her, but that doesn't seem to fit the play. What is extraordinary is that Barrie writes like one who does not have experience of sexual play and sexual love. He seems to be childishly ignorant, as if he were in the latency period.

The way Mary and Simon talk about "making love" seems to belong to such ignorance. We have seen how in *Peter Pan* there are dark hints about love, but now there seems to be a shrinking from it. Here the absence of sexuality seems to be cold and deathly: "a cold finger had once touched my Mary Rose." Simon replies, "her innocence which seems a holy thing to me." But her "holiness" seems to go with her uncanniness, as if she were bewitched or a changeling. If we take the "finger" in the spirit of the symbolism of the passage discussed above and see it by the displacement of imagery as a penis, it seems a dead penis, while Mary is swept away on the Island by an "unholy organ" that is "raking every bush." Behind these images is a sense that sexuality is dangerous and liable to bring annihilation.

Mary discusses making love with her lover, and there seems to lie behind her questioning a deep dread of sexuality. There is some discussion of play. We have seen how play is an aspect of *Peter Pan*. In light of Winnicott's insights, play is part of that imaginative exchange between mother and infant that brings out in the child a sense of his own reality and that of the world. It is also the beginning of symbolism and culture and so of the quest for meaning. Sexual play has qualities that develop out of infant play; and it, too, has to do with meaning. When the quest for meaning through sexual play becomes desperate, we have perversions. These are often found to be related to the problems of 'being' and 'nonbeing'— sometimes even linking sex and death.

Simon and Mary talk about being "us":

SIMON:
. . .Do you like it?

MARY ROSE:
It is so fearfully solemn.

SIMON:
You are not frightened are you? (*She nods.*)

Then Mary suddenly says, "Simon, after we are married you will sometimes let me play, won't you?" He replies, "Lots of married people play games."

A little later she says, "I may be wrong, but I think I'll sometimes love you to kiss me, and sometimes it will be better not." I am puzzled by these uncertainties, but I link them with her special characteristics. Peter Pan is not touched by anyone in the play; in

Mary Rose, it would seem, there will be times when Mary Rose is not real enough to be kissed, or there is some special danger in close contact with her. Just after the above exchanges, Simon and Mary Rose discuss their wedding day and honeymoon, and she proposes they go for their honeymoon to the Island, thus connecting the dangers of disappearing with sexual intimacy.

As one often finds in fairy stories and fantasies for children, there is play on the infant belief that sex is a form of eating. There is, therefore, an inherent danger of going out of existence as a result of close sexual contact, because when things are eaten they disappear. Mary Rose is a creature who is more than usually liable to disappear. For example, when her father rows her back from the Island (after she has reappeared), he sits facing her so he can see her all the time. There is also much play throughout on keeping an eye on Mary to make sure she stays in existence. Being looked at should be a way of being confirmed in one's reality ("Thou God seest me"), but Mary Rose is terrifyingly likely to slip away under one's eyes all the same and becomes increasingly difficult to see.

I have suggested that this is like a child trying to hold his mother together in his memory, so she can reflect him. In light of the autobiographical details of Barrie's life, I think we can put the matter in a different way. There could have been times in Barrie's life when it seemed as if the mother had stopped seeing him—seeing him, that is, in the way he needed. Barrie's mother talked to a ghost as if it were real, while ostracizing the real child who needed her, turning to him a blank, depressed face. It would seem, then, that there was a terrible possibility—that there might be a last chance, a last time for confirming exchanges. If one needed love, there was always the problem of this last time, it therefore, would perhaps be better never to allow oneself this mortal reality at all.

Thus, Mary says, "Some day, Simon, you will kiss me for the last time":

SIMON:
That wasn't the last time, at any rate. (*To prove it he kisses her again, sportively, little thinking that this may be the last time. She quivers.*) What is it?

Woman, Death, and Meaning in *Peter Pan* and *Mary Rose*

MARY ROSE:

I don't know; something seemed to pass over me.

This moment seems to indicate quite clearly that Barrie felt that sexuality was dangerous and that any physical contact could prove to be the "last time": the Island is jealous; or, God the Father is jealous; or, the good or bad dogs are jealous.

And there is a last time of seeing a baby. Immediately, Simon says:

You and your last time. Let me tell you, Mistress Blake, there will be a last time of seeing your baby.

and he refers to the fact that children disappear and become adults. Mary Rose then declares, that it will be lovely when her baby can take her on his lap, as she now puts him on hers. It is this that happens at the end of the play, but the truly terrifying thing is that Mary Rose disappears out of the life of her baby for twenty-five years.

If there can be a last kiss, there can also be a last act of sexual intercourse. I interpret the tuft of hair on Simon's head to be a displacement image of a penis. Mary says the "loveliest thing on Lieutenant Simon Sobersides is the little tuft of hair which will keep standing up at the back of his head," and she immediately talks about how "I—have—got—a baby!" In the conversation about "last times," Mary says:

There must be a last time I shall see you, Simon (*playing with his hair*). Some day I shall flatten this tuft for the thousandth time, and then never do it again.

SIMON:

Sometime I shall look for it and it won't be there. That day I shall say, "good riddance."

MARY:

I shall cry.

In other words, she will be sad that he has become impotent.

If the tuft is a penis, then the butter dish is the woman's genital. It is as close to the reality of woman's sexuality as we get. When Mary Rose becomes pregnant, she throws the butter dish at Simon.

SIMON:

I had always understood that when a young wife—that when she took her husband aside and went red, or white, and her head on his bosom, and whispered the rest, I admit I was hoping for that; but all I got was the butter dish.

But Barrie cannot give us the reality of birth. Mary plays a "dastard trick" on Simon; she doesn't tell him she has had a baby. She asks him what that funny thing was in the bassinette, and he thinks, "it was some baby you had borrowed." Although Barrie shrinks in his Peter Pan way from the reality of months of pregnancy and the pain of birth, he can allow his lovers to discuss which of them will die first. And he makes Simon speak of how the mother's polarity must be for her child—the one who must be reflected.

SIMON:

If I did go, I know your first thought would be "The happiness of Harry must not be interfered with for a moment." *You would blot me out for ever*, Mary Rose, rather than he should lose one of his hundred laughs a day [italics mine].

Behind this we surely see the child Barrie who felt "blotted out" by his mother's devotion to her dead son. We also see his attempt to give her a "hundred laughs," so that he could be reflected. This discussion occurs only moments before Mary disappears for twenty-five years.

The strangest aspect of the final relationship between Harry and his mother (he never calls her mother) is that the love play with the tuft of hair is transferred to him:

HARRY:
I like your hair.
MARY ROSE:
Pretty hair.
HARRY:
Do you mind the tuft that used to stand up at the back of—of Simon's head?
MARY ROSE: (*Merrily.*) Naughty tuft.
HARRY:

I have one like that.

MARY ROSE:

(*Smoothing it down.*) Oh dear, oh dear, what a naughty tuft.

It is at this moment he tells her his name is Harry. He has taken the father's place. He adds, "But you don't know what Harry I am." He goes on trying to instruct his mother on how she can be freed as a ghost. He wants to get her to that "Glory place." Mary can go to heaven because she has found her baby at last, even though she never recognizes him as such. She even suspects him at one point of having stolen her baby, which, in a sense, he has since the child Harry has been absorbed into the adult.

However, the end, or the solution, is magical and manic. But what is the religious significance of Mary's departure? When she is carried away on the Island, it seems to be by a horrible force: "in a fury as of storm and whistling winds that might seem an unholy organ." It seems like a hostile male force, "raking the bushes". Perhaps it is a spirit like Heathcliff. The loudness of the sounds is "horrible."

But there is opposition: "They are not without an opponent. Struggling through them, and also calling her name, is to be heard music of an unearthly sweetness that is seeking perhaps to beat them back and put a girdle of safety round her." Later, there are references to the good and bad days. But the call at the end has "now no unholy sound." Indeed, "a prayer has been answered."

I find myself baffled by these good and bad forces, and I cannot accept Goitein's explanation that the father wants her for himself. I believe the play is a gesture at the completion of mourning, so that the burden of the ghost of the dead mother can be released. The development can be seen as analogous to the resolution of a destructive dynamic (hate) by the power of love, as in Mahler's later works.

Is it the powers of evil (like Macbeth's witches which are bubbles of the earth) that have taken Mary away? And what has happened at the end, to release her only to the powers of love?

Harry has penetrated to the womblike room in the house and has used his knife to find the ghost of his mother. She sits on his lap, like a child, to be instructed in the secret of her haunted and ever-questing state. Can he tell her what only the dead know? Actually, she exits having seemingly learned nothing of the reality of her predicament—that is, she seeks what time has changed out of all recognition and what can never be refound. All that can be accepted is the reality of her son as an adult; but she doesn't come to terms with that either, and so the end is a magical piece of manic denial.

Yet, the ending still leaves me baffled as to what its meaning might be, except that it seems no solution to turn the mother, who is the focus of perplexity about 'being', into a little girl child who needs playful elucidation as to the nature of existence—which is what one never got from her.

The strangest thing of all is that the end is virtually an act of sexual intimacy with the mother. This seems to lead in a totally false direction, if one supposes the goal to be a grasp of adult reality and meaningful existence. But men with an intense fixation on their mothers do seem to seek a relationship with woman as a mother, even though this is ultimately sterile and deadly. Behind *Mary Rose* is a cold air of loss, sterility, and death—which the ending does not alleviate.

The strange case of J. M. Barrie and his plays shows that the public can enjoy literary works, recognizing intuitively that, though they make no explicit sense at all, they relate to the deepest problems of 'being-in-existence' and 'going-out-of-existence'. Upon examination, Barrie's works also show that they are bound up with problems of woman and that we cannot explain or understand these works at all unless we draw on the insights of dynamic psychoanalysis. Even so, when we apply these insights, we encounter immense difficulties, as demonstrated by this brief study of Barrie. When we turn to a major writer such as Shakespeare, these difficulties become even more acute.

PART THREE

The Insights Applied: Shakespeare's Anguish Over Woman

I returned to teach undergraduates in 1980 after a long time as an independent writer. Women were then being admitted to my college, and a powerful feature of the scene was enquiry into the attitudes of male writers to woman. For example, John Donne as a poet writing about love came in for a great deal of reexamination. (See Andrew Brink's *Creativity as Repair* [1977a].)

When my students and I penetrated to the depths of a play such as *Antony and Cleopatra*, we found deep disturbances beneath the surface, centering, we thought, around sexuality. There seemed to be a fear that the beautiful and dynamic woman could also be a threat to man, exhausting him and unmanning him as Cleopatra does Antony: "I wore his sword Phillipan." Was this fear something that Shakespeare was "placing" as a manifestation of a manic impulse to live in a larger-than-life way? Or was he expressing his own fears? For the most part, we felt that Shakespeare brought the underlying fears into the context of his art. However, there are still moments that stand out as manifestations of a dread that has no source in the plays themselves, such as Timon's outbursts when there is no woman or sexual corruption in the background. And what about Lear's outburst about the "sulphurous pit"? How does that fit into the theme of that tragedy?

This is not only a question of Shakespeare's attitudes to marriage or love. (And I do not share the attitudes of the students' organization in Victoria State, Australia, which banned the film of *The Taming of the Shrew* because it was "sexist.") It is rather a question of the unconscious factors and of Shakespeare's grappling with the themes that emerged as he plunged deeply into the darker realms of the human soul. I do not intend to psychoanalyze Shakespeare but rather to show that when he sought insight, he inevitably found the witch and had to deal with her. And, as I hope to show, he found the capacity to embrace the darker aspects of femininity in the human soul.

CHAPTER 6

Hamlet's Sexual Obsessions

Throughout Shakespeare's work we find a predominant theme—that he seemed not always able to control—which has to do with trust in relation to woman. At a deeper level, this theme relates the sense of security to 'being' and meaningful relationship to the world to the enigma of woman. That enigma is her outward fairness—her bewitching quality—in contrast to her unseen animal capacity for lust—her libidinal aspect, which has a rapacious, if not vulpine, quality.

For Shakespeare, love was the focus of a deep sense of meaning:

> Oh, no, it is an ever-fixèd mark
> That looks on tempests and is never shaken; . . .

Some believe it is possible to read this sonnet (116) as an expression of bitter irony, but I find it hard to accept such a reading. Certainly, there is in Shakespeare a deep anxiety—that the very source of meaning, the one-object experience that seems to offer the possibility of overcoming time, may be simply a delusion and even a source of the deepest and most destructive betrayal. It can "betray me to the very heart of loss." What seems, then, to give ontological strength also threatens to generate the possibilities of complete disintegration.

This is exactly what the archetypal woman is capable of doing. She can bring you into fulfillment by her 'being for'; but if she withdraws her love, she can condemn you to everlasting unfulfillment—that is, to annihilation or 'nonbeing'.

To our insights into the psychological themes we must add the religious dimension, which is today so difficult for us to grasp. Sexual fulfillment in marriage was to the Puritans of the seventeenth century a glimpse of heaven. But sexual relations outside of marriage were, in the morality of the medieval church, literally a gateway to hell. Fornication was a deadly sin; therefore, lust, used for expedient ends as in court intrigue, was a deathly game, in the spiritual as well as in the political sense. Of course, with many, there was a profound division between how they actually behaved and the official doctrine of the Church. Many priests had concubines, for instance. But in the pattern of beliefs during the Middle Ages and of the Church of Christian Protestantism, fornication was a deadly sin. Besides destroying souls, in many ways it menaced the fabric of society. Fornication could generate false loyalties, break up marriages, lead to uncertainties of inheritance, or even promote murder.[1] Moreover, the arrival of syphilis brought another horror to the scene, whereby what was sinful seemed to have a concomitant in a hideous form of divine punishment.

It is the awareness of dangers inherent in sexual love that underlies *Hamlet*. It was absurd for D. H. Lawrence to suggest that *Hamlet* represents some dynamic of self-loathing in the prince. (Some reaction was set off, no doubt, in Lawrence by Hamlet's obsession with his mother's sexuality, for Lawrence was deeply guilty about sexuality.)

The roots of Hamlet's obsession are not in self-loathing. There are two underlying pressures beneath Hamlet's problems: One is that the fabric of the kingdom is threatened by Claudius's impatient sexual possession of Hamlet's mother. Hamlet fears the possibility that his mother is implicated in his father's murder, her all-too-quick marriage to Claudius being a sign of failure in a woman of integrity because of sexual appetite. The other is that almost certainly Hamlet has had secret sexual relations with Ophelia and that Ophelia has become a pawn in a dangerous political intrigue. Ophelia may even be pregnant by Hamlet, and this compromises him seriously. Later, Hamlet becomes aware that Ophelia is being used as a plant and that the king, Polonius, and Hamlet's old student colleagues Rosencrantz and Guildenstern are now watching for him to reveal himself as sexually implicated with Ophelia. If it were found that he actually had committed fornication with her, he could perhaps even be arrested and tried, like Claudio in *Measure for Measure*, to the ruin of his life and Ophelia's. In any case, in that she is drawn into the plot against him, her actual or possible pregnancy is fatal.

Sexual love thus becomes for Hamlet the focus of the collapse of all social bonds and the system of rule, as well as a collapse of all values, trust, and security of 'being.' I should add that this is a central theme for Shakespeare: given the capacity of sexual love to alter men's and women's allegiances and to shift the whole polarity of their worlds—their *Lebenswelt*—how can we ever hope to have a system of stable relationships upon which to conduct the organization and government of society?

This was not only Shakespeare's theme, of course. We may pursue this perplexity in Wyatt's poetry; and it is a central preoccupation of art throughout the centuries, becoming a focus of desperate cynicism in Jacobean tragedy. But Shakespeare seems to have had a particular concern with the problem and with wider and more universal concerns. Shakespeare is not concerned merely with political reliability, treachery, betrayal, and ambitious manipulation. He is concerned with the power that passion has to corrupt human social organization and to corrupt the world—that is, passion can lead to a general disintegration of all human relationships with the world of nature.

In Marlowe's *Edward II*, we have an earlier and somewhat coarse exploration of the effects of an unmodified passion (the king's homosexual passion for Gaveston). But the verse of that play does not involve us in such a wide and pervading sense of the effects on the world, such as we have in Shakespeare's *Antony and Cleopatra*, in *Troilus and Cressida*, or in *King Lear*. The images of serpent and slime in *Antony and Cleopatra*, of disease in *Troilus and Cressida*, and of the voracious animal and denaturing in *King Lear* belong to a greater and more complex art, in which there is a deep and troubled sense of the effects of sexual voraciousness upon consciousness and so upon the fundamental relationship between man and reality. Shakespeare is preoccupied with the possibilities of breakdown in the complex relationship between appearance and reality around sexuality. As I have suggested (and as I hope to show), in these works the problem of woman is not always under control and is not always reconciled or absorbed.

Good order, the sustaining of values and meaningful belief, and reliable relationships between human beings are, Shakespeare recognizes, only matters of bodily gestures, smiles, things said, agreements, and interpersonal encounters. All this, as Falstaff knew, could be seen merely as "a breath" ("What is honor? A breath"). In this web of interrelationships, the worst flaw was perhaps woman's beauty and her bewitching qualities. For here was a seeming ideal, a manifestation of something transcendent, which yet could become the focus for every form of debasement that threatened all values and truth:

> Behold yond simp'ring dame, whose face between her forks
> presages snow, . . . The fitchew nor the soilèd horse, goes to't
> With a more riotous appetite.

What I will look at later is the special energy in Shakespeare's verse at such moments. There is, for instance, an obsession with gross bodily contents. The face between the forks of the wimple, an image in which the chaste whiteness of the fabric echoes the modest pallor of the face, turns in our inward vision into its opposite: the "face" between the fork of the legs is the bearded vagina (compare with "poor bare forked animal"). This vision becomes one of a brute ("fitchew" or "soilèd horse") grossly gulping in sexual activity. It is an appetite that threatens riot—that is, the abandonment of all civilized values, modes, and restraint.

Female sexuality seemed to pose a dreadful threat to Shakespeare, and this is especially evident in *Hamlet*. Evidently, the theme has something to do with father and mother, for the ghost of

Hamlet's father has come to tell him that his uncle has murdered his father in a horrible way, to win "to his shameful lust / The will of my most seeming-virtuous queen." Freud was surely correct to indicate the serious oedipal problems underlying *Hamlet*, since Claudius has done that which the son unconsciously wishes to do.[2] But the oedipal element is not the main feature of *Hamlet*; it is, rather, a sexual fear and disgust associated with death.

More significant is the mystery of Hamlet's relationship to Ophelia. Psychologically speaking, Hamlet ought to be transferring his sexual polarity to her, away from his mother. Yet, his attention later becomes transfixed on his mother's sexuality, and he becomes obsessed with it. Ophelia's tragedy is that she becomes a pawn in the intrigue between Claudius (and her father) and Hamlet, who has become a dangerous avenger. Outwardly, as to Laertes, she is pure and unsullied. Earlier exchanges, however, must surely make us doubt her innocence.

In act 1, scene 3, Shakespeare has Laertes warn Ophelia of the danger of giving way to the young prince's importuning. It is a very important exchange, in which the language is reminiscent of the sonnets:

LAERTES:
For Hamlet, and the trifling of his favor,
Hold it a fashion, and a toy in blood.
A violet in the youth of primy nature,
Forward, not permanent, sweet, not lasting,[3]
The perfume and suppliance of a minute;
No more.
OPHELIA:
No more but so?

(Later, Laertes cries, "from her fair and unpolluted flesh shall violets spring"—an image of innocent brevity.)

Laertes emphasizes that for Hamlet emotional relationships are integral with the body politic:

LAERTES:
He may not, as unvalued persons do,

The Insights Applied: Shakespeare's Anguish Over Woman

Carve for himself, for on his choice depends
The safety and health of this whole state,
And therefore must his choice be circumscribed
Unto the voice and yielding of that body
Whereof he is the head.

Although, in a sense, Laertes's advice is commonplace, we glimpse in its verse the sense Shakespeare had that sexual dynamics in such a prince were in complex with the political body, so that "voice and yielding" vis-à-vis the woman are bound up with the "voice" and "yielding" of the kingdom.

If Ophelia were to succumb to Hamlet's lust in fornication, says Laertes, "or your chaste treasure open / To his unmastered importunity," a kind of infection could spread throughout the body politic. Ophelia would be tainted:

LAERTES:
The canker galls the infants of the spring
Too oft before their buttons be disclosed,
And in the morn and liquid dew of youth
Contagious blastments are most important.

Again, it is not insignificant that the verse echoes the sonnets (especially their rhythm), while the imagery is of a disease that strikes most formidably where there is innocence (by contrast, compare Laertes's "violets" springing from "unpolluted" flesh.) Shakespeare surely is recollecting his own painful experiences of betrayal and invokes the feeling he often expresses in the sonnets that youth, because of its innocence, is most vulnerable to blight, while "lilies that fester smell far worse than weeds."

Throughout the scene, however, Ophelia is defensively evasive, both to Laertes and to Polonius. She warns Laertes not to point her to the thorny path, while he himself the primrose path of dalliance treads. When Laertes demands that Ophelia remember his warnings, she retorts:

'Tis in my memory locked,
And you yourself shall keep the key of it.

Ophelia's reply perhaps implies that in his conduct Laertes will justify her right conduct. To Polonius she says evasively:

I do not know, my lord, what I should think.

In these early scenes, there are clear hints that in their actual behavior youth (as we know) is often at considerable odds with paternal injunctions. At the beginning of act 2, we see Polonius officiously commissioning Reynaldo to spy on his son in Paris. Polonius is muddled and confused, both in his language and his morality, urging him

With windlasses and with assays of bias,
By indirections find directions out.

Polonius has forbidden Ophelia to have anything to do with Hamlet, but now she comes in to report that Hamlet has come to her in an antic disposition. He has studied her face—evidently, in an anguish of mind as to how woman can be fair in appearance but also essentially untrustworthy:

He falls to such perusal of my face
As' a would draw it.

Polonius believes that "this is the very ecstasy of love" and that Ophelia's denial of access to Hamlet, at her father's advice, has made Hamlet mad.

I feared he did but trifle
And meant to wrack thee.

So, they go to the king:

This must be known.

If we read the early part of the play closely, we must see that Hamlet almost certainly has seduced Ophelia. He is, evidently, powerfully drawn to her and is said to have made only honorable approaches to her. However, the way he looks at her face, his later coarseness to her, and his tender murmur "Nymph, in thy orisons . . . Be all my sins remembered" suggests that they have lapsed. Now, however, Ophelia represents the temptation of that sexuality

that, in his mother, is under the shadow of murder and incest. Her
sexuality evokes in him a dreadful distrust of woman's bewitching
capacities, of her beauty, and of the disintegrative effect of his
passion for her.

This distrust in turn engages with Hamlet's distressed feelings
about himself in relation to the whole world. Out of his distress
about the mother (*Mater*), Hamlet develops a distrust of the matter
of the whole earth and himself in it. The king is aware of changes
in Hamlet, as he declares to Rosencrantz and Guildenstern at the
beginning of the important act 2, scene 2. They have been sent for
because of their closeness to Hamlet. Gertrude says:

> And sure I am two men there are not living
> To whom he more adheres.

When Polonius confides in the king, they agree to "release" Ophelia
to Hamlet, while Polonius and the king hide behind the arras to
observe him. Later in this scene, two developments appall Hamlet:
one is that Ophelia has become a spy; the other is that two dear
friends of his also have been enlisted to watch him and to work on
him. Hamlet is under the duress and dread of supposing he is dealing
with the guilty murderer of the king, his father. His life is seriously
at risk, even as he cannot be fully sure of his evidence for revenge.
And now he sees all his relationships being poisoned by politiciza-
tion, in the sense of being penetrated and perverted by politicians—
that is, intelligencers and spies.

Hamlet is caustic and bitter and develops this mood under the
guise of being mad. He calls Polonius a fishmonger who is out to
trade his daughter. He further accuses Polonius of being one who
exposes his daughter to risk like someone who puts her like a dead
dog in the sun—a situation he links with conception. Behind Hamlet's antic remarks, we may trace two themes: For Hamlet to fall
now for the trap of being exposed as the lover of Ophelia would be
deathly. For the King and Polonius to expose Ophelia in the task of
trapping Hamlet, by drawing his secrets out of him, is to reduce
Ophelia from being a beautiful object of admiration to the level of
corrupt meat. Such a plot exposes Polonius's talk of honor and other
values; for in using Ophelia as a lure, they coarsely expose her as a

sexual object in a way that reduces all human relationships to nothing, to a deathly insignificance. The misuse of Ophelia's beauty of appearance is bitterly associated in a characteristically Shakespearean way with corruption and death.

A parallel corruption sours Hamlet's relationship with Rosencrantz and Guildenstern. Outwardly, the friends maintain their bantering, courtly relationship, trying to outdo one another in concerts and euphemisms. But there is an edge to Hamlet's quips:

GUILDENSTERN:
On Fortune's cap we are not the very button.
HAMLET:
Nor the soles of her shoe?

In other words, have circumstances brought you to be trampled on even by fortune? Are you at the very bottom of prostration before ambition?

Hamlet tests his friends by seeing what response they make to his contention that Denmark is a prison; he refers to his own "bad dreams." But in all this he gets through to no real intimacy. All is wordplay, and they are manifestly in some false position. Perhaps at the moment Hamlet spies the king watching. He asks, "Were you not sent for?"

Hamlet, however, persists in his ideals. He wants to believe that there is still among them the true value of friendship:

But let me conjure you by the rights of our fellowship, by the consonancy of our youth, by the obligation of our ever-preserved love, and by what more dear a better proposer could charge you withal, be even and direct with me, whether you were sent for, or no.

Note Hamlet's invocation of the "rights" of fellowship, the reference to what they have shared in youth, the "obligation" of love, and the hint at a better purpose. He still hopes it is possible to invoke these genuine meanings of friendship. Yet he knows, too, that events already have moved too far for there to be any such possibility. To his horror, his relationship with Ophelia is one focus of the decay ("no, nor woman neither, though by your smiling you seem to say so").

The collapse of virtually all of Hamlet's relationships lies behind his disintegrating relationship with Mother Earth and mankind:

HAMLET:

. . . this goodly frame the earth seems to me a sterile promontory; this most excellent canopy, the air, look you, this brave o'erhanging firmament, this majestical roof fretted with golden fire—why, it appears no other thing to me than a foul and pestilent congregation of vapors.

The earth has become to Hamlet what it becomes to Timon in *Timon of Athens*: an evil, witch-like object. Or, if you like, it has become the bleak world of the philosopher Democritus: "only atoms and the void." The annihilation of Hamlet's love for Ophelia, because of her involvement in intelligence manipulations, and the undermining of his fellowship with the two courtiers by the same treacheries have, together with his honor at the queen's fickleness, destroyed his relationship with the whole of reality.

If love and friendship cannot be relied upon and if woman, in her most trustworthy role as mother, is tainted, then the world must lose all meaning and significance. This is Hamlet's problem. Thus, Claudius, just as he and Polonius are exposing Ophelia to spy on Hamlet, speaks of his own problem of appearance and reality in characteristic terms—terms that relate to Hamlet's later address to Yorick's skull and other similar poetic themes in the play:

KING: [*aside*]
The harlot's cheek, beautied with plast'ring art,
Is not more ugly to the thing that helps it
Than is my deed to my most painted word.

Significantly, this moment is followed by Hamlet's contemplation of suicide, for he believes that a world in which it is impossible to distinguish the reality from the painted appearance is one which cannot be borne. Only religious belief in the sinfulness of self-destruction, declares Hamlet, obliges one to bear it. Yet, ever here

the native hue of resolution
Is sicklied o'er with the pale cast of thought.

But is resolution the healthy reaction to a doubtful ghost's promptings or even to an unproven regicide? Hamlet's perplexity here runs parallel to Claudius's attempts to hide his deed under "plastering art." In both instances, the deception and obfuscation are "sickly." There is no escape either into the exercise of reason (as a trained intelligence of the Renaissance) or into the exercise of religious faith (the ghost is perplexing and, we may say, in that his intervention leads to universal death and chaos, hardly an instrument of Divine love and justice). And so Hamlet comes upon Ophelia, exclaiming tenderly (for she is innocent) the revealing lines

Nymph, in thy orisons
Be all my sins remembered.

In Hamlet's response to Ophelia, which becomes so cruel, he is perplexed by two things: first, by her becoming involved in the net of Claudius's machinations; and second, by his own horror of his mother's treacherous lustfulness:

I could accuse me of such things that it were better my
mother had not borne me.

Hamlet is not, as D. H. a Lawrence seemed to think, a manifestation of Renaissance self-loathing or of a loathing of sexuality. Rather, Hamlet feels corrupted by the nature of his mother's sin and her involvement in Claudius's offence. The ghost has spoken, as we have seen, of how Claudius

won to his shameful lust
The will of my most seeming-virtuous queen.

and of how

lust, though to a radiant angel linked,
Will sate itself in a celestial bed
And prey on garbage.

The Insights Applied: Shakespeare's Anguish Over Woman

Hamlet becomes cruel to Ophelia because his desire for her seems to threaten to draw him into a parallel chaos.

Again, one must speak of Shakespeare's problems. All his writing life, one might say, was given to the pursuit of a sense of meaning in life; of a capacity, despite a profound understanding of man and his weaknesses, to believe in the future—in the creative future of man. In the end Shakespeare achieves a feeling of confidence in human nature, as exemplified by Ferdinand and Miranda, Florizel and Perdita, and Marina and Imogen—especially in the symbolic young woman. However, there are times when, in his imaginative explorations, the fallibility of woman seems to him intolerable because of woman's very power and mystery. Woman is a "radiant angel" and yet capable of destroying the world (as Cleopatra, Goneril, Regan, and Lady Macbeth destroy their worlds). The deepest fault of woman is her impulse to "sate"—that is, her voracious sexual appetite (to "go to it" like a "fitchew" or "soilèd horse"). In the words "garbage" and "soilèd" we have the indication that Shakespeare is troubled deeply by a feeling that sexual libidinousness is filthy, unless sanctified by grace.

In the psychoanalytical sense, Shakespeare is projecting. He cannot bear the sensual witch in himself, besides the celestial element ("What a piece of work is man"). Shakespeare's quest is to accept his whole human nature—to accept ambivalence—but there are times when it almost drives him mad to do so. Thus, Hamlet expresses the intolerable perplexity of woman as a focus of appearance and reality:

> God hath given you one face, and you make yourselves another: you jig, you amble, and you lisp; and nickname God's creatures and make your wantonness your ignorance. Go to, I'll no more on't; it hath made me mad.

This is a puzzling speech. Behind it is the same horror of women being an animal, when she ought to be an angel, and the horror of woman's pretending in play that she is childishly innocent, when, in fact, she is full of lust—so open to lust that she can sate herself on "garbage."

The scene of Ophelia's exposure to Hamlet is a fascinating one (act 3, scene 1) because in it Hamlet is aware, I believe, that he is being spied on by the king and Polonius. Hamlet asks, "Where's your father?" But what speaks to Claudius from Hamlet's deranged speech is a clear disturbance due to an awareness of Claudius's and Gertrude's sinful sexuality ("Now the time gives it proof"). It should be clear that by the end of the scene Hamlet's life is in immediate danger, from the now fully alerted murderer king. What Ophelia focuses is the deepest anguish a man may suffer if all of the creative, harmonious, and celestial qualities he associates with woman are corrupted by her capacity for lust. Hamlet is cruel to Ophelia and rejects her because he can never again believe in love because woman is so weak and vile. I believe we may say that there is in this a good deal of Shakespeare's own torment over woman (which is but a manifestation of the problem every man has with woman at the unconscious level).

In discussing Shakespeare's problem with woman, we are discussing it within a historical context. By the time we come to Tourneur's *The Revenger's Tragedy* (1607), we find an atmosphere in which there seem almost no positive values left—that is, little or no trust in the reliability of human relationships. I find that today's undergraduates are deeply disturbed by such plays, by their apparently bottomless cynicism. Yet, of course, the medieval concept of sin is powerfully there in the plays; and, as Leo Salingar (1955) has pointed out, the plays are strongly moral. The characters pass over the stage like the seven deadly sins, variously called Lussorio, Ambilioso, and so on. In Thomas Middleton and William Rowley's *The Changeling* (c. 1623), we have the tragedy of a woman, Beatrice Joanna, who is prepared to yield herself to a man she loathes and despises in return for his murder of a suitor she is repelled by. Thus, she becomes compromised in her real love relationship, and her subsequent marriage is devastated in a chaos of cruelty and despair. In this play, there seems to be no hope of placing trust in human relationships, while there seems no hope of any virtue triumphing in the world, least of all in woman. Every hope seems beaten down. The intense mood of distrust and despair of the time must have been bearing down with all its force on Shakespeare. Yet, of course, even in his most tormented plays, he never gives way to the bleak hopelessness of Tourneur and Middleton and Rowley.

The fashion for the revenge play is related, I am sure, to the political manifestations of the unconscious fear of woman, as discussed by Winnicott. The fashion came at the end of the reign of Elizabeth, whose promise as a woman leader trailed off into chaos. Her successor, James, was a homosexual whose court was intensely corrupt. The forces of social change that threatened stability, which are discussed by L. C. Knights in *Drama and Society in the Age of Jonson* (1937), now menaced society with such fragmentation and disintegration that it seemed a moment to invoke a stern retrenchment and to take up again the severe morality of the Middle Ages. At the center of the emotional feelings about the decline was a feeling that woman—the woman in power who had been expected to act for the phantom woman of the unconscious—had failed. As a result, a mood of intense disillusionment set in. It was time for the male protagonist to take his revenge for woman's frailty, and something like this seems to have been going on in the collective unconscious of the time. Shakespeare's distrust of woman is thus not merely misogyny but is the result of a profound pondering of the problems of human nature and rule. In this, the problem of woman was predominant, particularly because England had been under a woman ruler for most of Shakespeare's working life; and the problems of marriage, succession, and intrigue had been critical throughout the era.

Hamlet's speech to Horatio, in act 3, scene 2, is thus of great importance:

> Nay, do not think I flatter
> For what advancement may I hope from thee,
> That no revenue hast but thy good spirits
> To feed and clothe thee? Why should the poor be flattered?
> No, let the candied tongue lick absurd pomp,
> And crook the pregnant hinges of the knee
> Where thrift may follow fawning.[4]

The energy of the verse expresses a contempt for those physical bodily gestures that express a calculating servitude and are, therefore, false because they belong to what Marx called the icy waters of egotistical calculation. By contrast, Hamlet speaks of true self awareness of genuineness in relation; and it is interesting that he attributes femininity to his soul, as anima:

> Since my dear soul was mistress of her choice
> And could of men distinguish, her election,
> H'ath sealed thee for herself, for thou hast been
> As one in suff'ring all that suffers nothing.

It would be absurd to declare Hamlet homosexual. We may, however, see in the energy of this poetry a record of some deep distress in Shakespeare's own experience that meant that he was able to be much more sure of men than of women and that he was most deeply repelled by those who used sexual modes for advancement and gain. Surely, the pipe-stopping image has sexual undertones:

> and blest are those
> Whose blood and judgment are so well commingled
> That they are not a pipe for Fortune's finger
> To sound what stop she please.

(We have seen previously an exchange about Rosencrantz and Guildenstern being "Fortune's privates.") Hamlet goes on:

> Give me that man
> That is not passion's slave, and I will wear him
> In my heart's core, ay, in my heart of heart,
> As I do thee. Something too much of this. . . .

The phrase "something too much of this" suggests that Hamlet is somewhat overcome here by feeling. Who is "passion's slave" in his experience? Claudius, of course; while Rosencrantz and Guildenstern seem willing to sacrifice their integrity for advancement and gain. On the whole, however, there is not much in the action in which men or women are corrupted or allow themselves to be played upon, for passion or for gain. There is, of course, the deep shock to Hamlet when he finds his own affections played upon by the use of the innocent Ophelia as a plant, to tempt him into revealing more than it would be politic for him to reveal. But the underlying sentiments in the speech relate rather to Shakespeare's general feelings about human nature—in his continual pondering of the problem of whether there is any hope for man and perhaps more especially for woman. In the remainder of the scene, Hamlet is "idle"; but the madness he affects is also a poetic-dramatic device, like Lear's and Edgar's forms of madness.

It seems that Hamlet is trying to force some response from Claudius in order to confirm the allegations of his father's ghost, for the ghost could be a diabolical one. In the end, although the king's response is enough to confirm his suspicions, Hamlet does not sweep to his revenge. Rather, he dwells in dangerous obsession on his mother's sexual shortcomings. Many of his intentions seem to be thwarted by intense emotions into which he has no insights. But had Shakespeare? Hamlet's procrastination, I believe, is related to Shakespeare's own obsession, which he could not solve.

There are many strong unconscious undercurrents in this part of the play, and their power is as difficult to explain as is Lear's outburst about how "down from the waist they are Centaurs" and about the "sulphurous pit," the scalding and stench in women's bodies. The theme of this unconscious material is the nothingness that the corruption of relationships through sexual lapses may bring. Hamlet often dwells on nothingness, and clearly there is a schizoid element in his mind. The king asks:

How fares our cousin Hamlet?
HAMLET:
Excellent, i' faith, of the chameeon's dish.
I eat the air, promise-crammed. You cannot
feed capons so.

The air is full of an intensity for Hamlet in the expectation of the play and the document. The king puts forward the intentionality of office ("What wouldst thou have, Laertes?"); but, to Hamlet, these promises are nothing. His view too is, "What is honor? A breath." All is nothing because, as the king himself admits in an aside, the outward forms are annihilated by the hidden crime. A capon is a neutered bird fattened for the table; you can't feed those on air. Hamlet is a vigorous, active, entire male; he does not propose to be slaughtered in passive indolence. He hungrily gulps the air because he is devoted to nothingness and regards his words as nothing:

KING:
I have nothing with this answer, Hamlet. These words are not mine.
HAMLET:
No, nor mine now.

Like Falstaff's ironic shafts, the quips tend in a schizoid way to dissolve all meanings and values (like much else in Hamlet's verse; for example, the soliloquy about the self wanting to "thaw and resolve itself like a dew"). The nothingness of words is related to the nothingness of sex:

HAMLET:
Lady, shall I like in your lap?
OPHELIA:
No, my lord.
HAMLET:
I mean, my head upon your lap?
OPHELIA:
Ay, my lord.
HAMLET:
Do you think I meant country matters?
OPHELIA:
I think nothing, my lord.
HAMLET:
That's a fair thought to lie between maids' legs.
OPHELIA:
What is, my lord?
HAMLET:
Nothing.

Hamlet is not only brutally obscene—the "nothing" being the "O" between a maid's legs, the subject of *cuntry* matters—he is also expressing the destructive attitude that sexuality is nothing. Ophelia, poor girl, tries hard to be polite and to avoid his savage hostil-

135

ity, only to provoke the comments savagely directed at her very politeness:

O God, your only jig-maker. . . .

From his contemptuous expression of disdain for the feminine, Hamlet goes on to link his offensiveness to Ophelia with his abhorrence of his mother's eagerness to marry his father's brother. A great man who does not build churches is as easily forgotten as the hobbyhorse—the reference to the hobbyhorse itself having beneath the surface a grotesque caricature of sexual play. This "idle" wit plays over the underlying horror of what sexual intercourse can lead to—a nothingness that infects all, from personal trust to the will to live. All this mischief leads up to the greater mischief of the dumb show and play:

HAMLET:
. . . this is miching mallecho; it means mischief.
The Poisoner woos the Queen with gifts; she seems loath and unwilling awhile, but in the end accepts his love.

Hamlet drives home his bitterness to Ophelia:

Ay, or any show that you'll show him. Be not you ashamed to show, he'll not shame to tell you what it means.
OPHELIA:
You are naught, you are naught.[5]

To understand the meaning and force of this exchange, as well as the sense of the whole play, it makes more sense to believe that Hamlet has seduced Ophelia and that she is pregnant. A "show" is the discharge that signals the approach of labor; and while the above lines can be read as referring to sexual display (and so a bitter reference to Ophelia's use as a decoy), they make more sense (and more cruel sense) if they are read as a cruel sneer at Ophelia's predicament. Thus, when Ophelia later comes in mad, singing

Let in the maid, that out a maid
Never departed more.

she is making a clear reference to her relationship with Hamlet. Although her grief for her father's death plays a part in her loss of reason, a more powerful effect is the recognition that her father has been killed by the now-alienated father of her child: "It is the false steward, that stole his master's daughter."

The "nothing" that Hamlet speaks of as being between a maid's legs is a focus of death. The richly evocative graveyard scene in *Hamlet* is the scene of Ophelia's burial, and Ophelia has been killed by sexuality:

QUEEN:
Therewith fantastic garlands did she come
Of crowflowers, nettles, daisies, and long purples,
That liberal shepherds give a grosser name,
But our cold maids do dead men's fingers call them.

The symbolism is clear: Ophelia has known Hamlet sexually, and his sexuality has meant her death. Her father, joining with the king in spying on Hamlet, in suspicion that he might find out about the murder and so about his mother's offence, is killed by her lover. All is in turmoil and chaos caused by passion.

In *Hamlet* there is thus a close and intense link between sexuality and death. As Ophelia's grave is prepared, Hamlet recollects the delights of sitting on Yorick's knee, when his skull—now reduced to a stinking relic—was covered with living flesh. Hamlet declares, "Now get you to my lady's chamber, and tell her, let her paint an inch thick, to this favor she must come." Why turn such animus on woman at this moment? Because to Shakespeare the flesh of woman seems but a painted covering that disguises the reality of her mortal deathliness and gives her the mysterious lure that attracts men to their doom. She is the Fata Morgana that exacerbates and torments men with the reality of death.

It only remains now to look at the intensity of Shakespeare's verse when Hamlet goes to his mother. He offers to

set you up a glass
Where you may see the inmost part of you.

It is at this moment that Hamlet kills Polonius. Hamlet's action might be interpreted by the psychoanalyst as a substitute for the oedipal act; and, indeed, Hamlet cries out his hope: "Is it the king?" Our fascination with this oedipal element may disguise another feature. Hamlet achieves nothing by his assault on his mother, nor could he have expected to achieve anything. All that happens is that Claudius resolves all the more expediently to send Hamlet to England and to his death. Afterward, Gertrude herself still regards Hamlet as mad, not least because she sees Hamlet talking to a ghost who is not there but also because she remains loyal to Claudius (as we see at the beginning of the next scene). It is true that at one point she cries:

> O, Hamlet, speak no more.
> Thou turn'st mine eyes into my very soul,
> And there I see such black and grainèd spots
> As will not leave their tinct.

If this self-awareness is genuine, it has no effect on Gertrude's later conduct. She protects Hamlet to a degree, as her son; but she does not "go over" to Hamlet.

Clearly, Gertrude has not been a conspirator against her former husband. She remains defensively resistant to Hamlet's catalogue of her sins. The impact of Hamlet's assault is that Claudius is a much lesser man than the former king. Claudius is "a king of shreds and patches." But all Hamlet's eloquence cannot hide the fact that whether the former king was handsome and more noble than Claudius or not has nothing really to do with the case—no reason certainly for being so cruelly recriminatory. Of course, Gertrude could be blamed for marrying a "murderer and a villain," but there is no evidence that she knew, or knows now from Hamlet, that Claudius is such a one.

I do not find Freud's oedipal interpretation very insightful here, though there is no doubt some disturbance, due to the fact that Claudius has done what the son unconsciously wished to do—kill the father and possess the mother. We also can see that psychologically Hamlet would hate his stepparent, as many characters in literature hate theirs (for example, Molly Gibson in Elizabeth Gaskell's *Wives and Daughters* [1864–66]).

The energy of the verse is so intense, however, that we must seek the real motive. What Shakespeare expresses here is his dread that, because of woman's libidinal capacities, a fine and noble love (such as one finds ideally in the father and mother) can be replaced by a love that is coarse and commonplace. Since this is so, any such act must lead to confusion and an undermining of all relationships, values, meanings, and concepts. It threatens the very reliability of the reality sense:

> Such an act
> That blurs the grace and blush of modesty,
> Calls virtue hypocrite, takes off the rose
> From the fair forehead of an innocent love,
> And sets a blister there, makes marriage vows
> As false as dicers' oaths. O, such a deed
> As from the body of contraction plucks
> The very soul, and sweet religion makes
> A rhapsody of words!

The struggle in the texture and meaning of the verse is in trying to relate the ideal in woman with her libidinal reality. The "body of contraction" echoes "with my body I thee worship" and conveys the embodied nature of marriage vows. Gross libidinal acts can draw the soul out of these sacred bonds and so reduce religion to mere vows. The effect of Gertrude's sexual crime is to threaten to undermine matter itself:

> Yea, this solidity and compound mass,
> With tristful visage, as against the doom,
> Is thought-sick at the act.

Hamlet often feels he is dissolving or would like to dissolve. Here, the whole world seems mournful and "sicklied o'er with the pale cast of thought" and likely to become ill, at the very thought of Gertrude's sexual conjunction with her husband's murderer. Not only is the stability of the earth threatened; reason is threatened with it:

> Rebellious hell,
> If thou canst mutine in a matron's bones,
> To flaming youth let virtue be as wax
> And melt in her own fire.

Here Shakespeare's dread breaks out—that lust in the mature and responsible older woman will teach youth to overthrow all good values:

> Proclaim no shame
> When the compulsive ardor gives the charge,
> Since frost itself as actively doth burn,
> And reason pandars will.

We are on the way to the vision of appetite in *King Lear* and *Trolius and Cressida*, a "universal wolf" so overwhelming values that there can only be anarchy: "none does offend"; no one need feel shame; sexual ardour takes hold; frost will burn; and the voracious will make a pandar of reason.

Hamlet is mad, in earnest as well as in pretence. He is also extravagant and rhetorical—manifestations of the free intellect. His vision of a world in which order and restraint have been lost is akin to the vision glimpsed in *King Lear*, where lust has such deadly effects on social life and relationships. But now Hamlet becomes obsessed and torments himself, as does Leontes in *The Winter's Tale*, with fervid imaginings of his mother's sexuality:

> Nay, but to live
> In the rank sweat of an enseamèd bed,
> Stewed in corruption, honeying and making love
> Over the nasty sty.

In this vision, man and woman become grunting pigs, and the exhudations of their sexual acts become rank and greasy. Here we touch that sense of loathing and dread of sex that we often glimpse in Shakespeare—a dread that far exceeds any appropriate element in the dramatic poem as a whole. The focus of the excitement is woman and the dangerous proclivities of her sexuality. The intensity of disgust evidently applies to both lust, which has been the cause of murder, and to normal sexuality, as the nasty qualities are not specifically linked to the crime.

In trying to persuade his mother not to go to Claudius's bed, Hamlet expresses Shakespeare's own unconscious dread of the terrible danger of parental sexuality. If Gertrude cannot hear him bringing this truth to her, then she may seal up the evil in herself:

> Let not that flattering unction to your soul,
> That not your trespass but my madness speaks.
> It will but skin and film the ulcerous place
> Whiles rank corruption, mining all within,
> Infects unseen.

There is a religious impulse in Hamlet's attempt to "save" Gertrude ("Confess yourself to heaven, / Repent"). But the predominant ("unconscious") intention is to save woman from her own libidinousness and from her acceptance of it. (It is significant that there are two references, such as to "blister" previously and to syphilis here.) In this, I believe we can say that Shakespeare is projecting. Through Hamlet, Shakespeare is, in a sense, denouncing the "bad" half of woman in himself that he fears may corrupt him and make him diseased. That half of woman must be thrown away:

> O, throw away the worser part of it,
> And live the purer with the other half.
> Good night—but go not to my uncle's bed.

Thus, Hamlet continues to speak to the theme of abstinence.

The question one must ask from a psychoanalytical point of view is "Why dwell so on the sexuality?" If Hamlet had been able to convince Gertrude that Claudius had murdered her husband, she would surely decide to have nothing to do with him at all, sexually or otherwise? The inflamed attention to sex indicates that in Hamlet's speech in this scene, Shakespeare has encountered the problem of his own attitude to woman, which he cannot easily bring into the harmony of a poetic-dramatic resolution. And so Hamlet's moralizing excuses for his action smack of the self-deceptions of projection:

The Insights Applied: Shakespeare's Anguish Over Woman

I must be cruel only to be kind.

If we speak of Hamlet's projections, I believe we must speak of Shakespeare's because Shakespeare does not "place" Hamlet's obsession—that is, he cannot see it in its proper perspective but is involved in it himself:

Not this, by no means, that I bid you do:
Let the bloat king tempt you again to bed,
Pinch wanton on your cheek, call you his mouse,
And let him, for a pair of reechy kisses,
Or paddling in your neck with his damned fingers,
Make you to ravel all this matter out.

The main emphasis here is meant to be on political dangers, on loyalties, and on the queen's need not to say anything to reveal Hamlet's knowledge of the murder. But the energy of the words (like the word "bloat") paints a revolting image of *all* sexuality— such as between the parents—being dangerous because it is liable to undermine trust. The language evokes disgust for all sexual behavior. For example, Hamlet uses the phrase "paddling in your neck" as an image of the sexual caress.[6] Besides being a manifestation of Hamlet's self-exacerbating obsession, the language also has the effect of making all (heterosexual) love play seem repulsive and seem the occupation of a "paddock, from a bat, a gib"—that is, a reversion to animality, liable to cause disaster, to

Unpeg the basket on the house's top,
Let the birds fly, and like the famous ape,
To try conclusions, in the basket creep
And break your own neck down.

In this scene we hear echoes of the child's fear of parental intercourse. Throughout *Hamlet* we hear the dread that sexuality may lead to terrible dangers—to nothingness and death—not least because woman, who ought to be the noble matron or the innocent violet, is also an animal with bodily appetite and a breeding creature.

The fascination of *Hamlet* is, of course, in the persistent procrastination of the protagonist; we are aware intuitively that this is due to unconscious factors. A psychotherapist must surely be alert to the phenomenological meaning of the scene between Hamlet and his mother. Having declared once more that he will soon proceed to his revenge, Hamlet urges the queen to gradually wean herself from his uncle's bed. What would be the point, if Claudius is to die in the next day or so, perhaps even in his incestuous bed, as Hamlet has just declared? It doesn't make sense; but nor does it that the assault on his mother is completely futile and accomplishes nothing, except to make Hamlet's situation more dangerous and to hasten his doom. It is all a characteristic piece of inappropriate behavior, with complex, unconscious impulses behind it.

There was a problem of the time, of course, as appears in drama of the period. Consider, for example, Vendice's distress in Tourneur's *The Revenger's Tragedy* (1607), when he tempts the mother of Castiza and finds her wanting. Again, if there is sexual mutiny in a matron's bones, disorder is likely to spread throughout society. As we learn from Jacobean tragedy, estates were sold to maintain mistresses; and the extravagant excesses of sexual intrigue were putting at risk the old procedures of primogeniture. How could the commonwealth stand such chaos and fluidity of relationships when ambition had become so ruthless and even murderous?

But while *Hamlet* dwells on this theme—something being rotten in the state of Denmark—the dissociation that lies beneath Hamlet's procrastination seems to be expressed most powerfully in the scene with Hamlet's mother. In this scene, Shakespeare himself becomes intensely involved in the unconscious problem of coming to terms with the reality of woman. That reality is the mother's sexual libidinousness and her participation in that dangerous and troubling activity, sexual intercourse, in which, reduced to the level of animal gratification, the human being becomes inaccessible to grace and liable to breakneck.[7]

CHAPTER 7

King Lear's
Intemperate Outburst

It is difficult to say anything illuminating about *King Lear*, which is a great cathedral of a play. We must simply experience it and suffer with it. However, undoubtedly in this most terrible exploration of the worst humanity is capable of, Shakespeare's attitude to the nature of man and woman is crucial. It would seem to me that, by a thread, Shakespeare's belief in humanity survives. Yet, even so, there are moments in the play when all hope seems gone.

What we can say is that Shakespeare knows that woman is capable of the most appalling cruelty and that this cruelty is associated in her with lust and ambition. Edmund has had sexual relations with both Regan and Goneril:

EDMUND:
I was contracted to them both. All three
Now marry in an instant.

Since the two sisters are married, the word "contracted" here can only mean devoted as a lover. Edmund's earnest of being loved is characteristic:

> Yet Edmund was beloved.
> The one the other poisoned for my sake,
> And after slew herself.

In this, the cycle culminates that had begun with Gloucester's lust:

KENT:
I cannot conceive you.

GLOUCESTER:
Sir, this young fellow's mother could; whereupon she grew round-wombed, and had indeed, sir, a son for her cradle ere she had a husband for her bed. Do you smell a fault?

The word "smell" is important. Later, Lear smells his own hand and cries, "Pah! It smells of mortality"; while in his most intemperate outburst, he speaks of the "stench" of woman's lower body. Gloucester plays dearly for his "fault":

> The dark and vicious play where thee he got
> Cost him his eyes.

Many polite interpretations of the play fail to note this terrible obsession with woman's sexual body in lust as stinking, vicious, and deadly.

Of course, *King Lear* is among other things about inheritance; thus, the sexual theme is related to social order. Lear divides his realm, and Gloucester is tormented between his legitimate and illegitimate sons. From the same loins spring the loving Cordelia and the calculating and hateful Regan and Goneril, and from the same loins are generated loving and faithful Edgar and the Machiavellian Edmund. To these themes are related the themes of nature: in which of these offspring do we find the realization of a true nature? Edmund declares, "Thou Nature art my goddess." While Albany declares:

> O, Goneril,
> You are not worth the dust which the rude wind
> Blows in your face. I fear your disposition:

That nature which condemns it origin
Cannot be borderèd certain in itself.
She that herself will sliver and disbranch
From her material sap, perforce must wither
And come to deadly use.

GONERIL:
No more; the text is foolish.

ALBANY:
Wisdom and goodness to the vile seem vile;
Filths savor but themselves.

And at the end of this speech, Albany warns that if the heavens
do not intervene

Humanity must perforce prey on itself,
Like monsters of the deep.

The enigmatic question arises, of course: What is man's true
nature? Is it to be "natural man," like Edmund who substitutes a
ruthless functionalism for grace and goodness? Or is it the "material
sap" of a human being, perhaps especially of a woman, to be good
and life promoting? (The latter links the problem of woman in
Shakespeare with the witch archetype, which I shall discuss later
in reference to *Timon of Athens*.)

Woman is, or should be, naturally life-giving; but we have to
admit the possibility of that creative power being "slivered" and
"disbranched" by the creature herself. Lady Macbeth, evidently a
witch, deliberately chooses to "unsex" herself and to deny the
greatest tenderness in herself by declaring that, to keep to her sworn
purpose, she would have been prepared to pluck her nipple from the
boneless gums of her baby and to dash its brains out.

With psychoanalytical and phenomenological insights in mind,
we may say that Shakespeare was considering here the ultimate
rejection, of which the human consciousness is all too aware but
largely consigns to the unconscious. It is our deepest dread that
woman, who has the power and mystery to create us and give us
life, could be capable of destroying us if she were to turn evil.

In contemplating these possibilities, Shakespeare even shows us a glimpse of the dreadful logic that we now know to be a condition of the schizoid mind. Since love has proved unreliable or inaccessible, the schizoid individual may give himself up to hatred and get what satisfaction he can out of that—declaring not only "evil be thou my good!" but "good be thou my evil." There are elements of this perverse schizoid logic in Edmund, and it appears in Albany's declaration that "wisdom and goodness to the vile seem vile; / Filths savor but themselves."[1] Shakespeare also sees, unconsciously, that there is an intense oral element in schizoid hate. Albany says, "Tigers, not daughters" and that the hate-driven impulse "cannot be bordered certain in itself." Moral inversions of the intense inversionist, voracious kind inevitably spread out and infect human society. In the end, unless a solution is sound, humanity will consume itself and destroy the world by appetite.

We may recall Ulysses' speech in *Troilus and Cressida*:

And appetite, an universal wolf,
So doubly seconded with will and power,
Must make perforce an universal prey
And last eat up himself.

At the political level, such lines indicate Shakespeare's fear that voracious ambition would cause chaos in the order of society.

But there is a deeper fear expressed by the symbolism, which is influenced by the medieval sense of sexual indulgence as sin. For example, to Lear in his madness, the woman's sexual organ is a "sulphurous pit"—hell itself. But there is also the Renaissance element in the sense that with all his reason and so like an angel, glorious man—and woman—cannot avoid being an animal with sexual hunger, treacherous impulses, and the proclivity for disease and death. The greater the awareness of man's potentialities, the more awful does his mortal grossness seem.

I have discussed earlier the association, which psychoanalysis has made clear, between woman and death. And as we explore Shakespeare's problem with woman, it is this association that lies at the foundation of his dread. I was going to say "extraordinary dread"; but it is not, of course, extraordinary at all but universal.

147

The Insights Applied: Shakespeare's Anguish Over Woman

What is extraordinary is Shakespeare's expression of this dread; though it also comes out clearly in myths, folktales and fairy tales.

All this leads me to Lear's most terrible outburst, when he is confronted with the blind Gloucester ("Ha! Goneril with a white beard?"):

GLOUSTER:

Is't not the King!

LEAR:

Ay, every inch a king.
When I do stare, see how the subject quakes.
I pardon that man's life. What was thy cause?
Adultery?
Thou shalt not die. Die for adultery? No.
The wren goes to't, and the small gilded fly
Does lecher in my sight.
Let copulation thrive; for Gloucester's bastard son
Was kinder to his father than my daughters
Got 'tween the lawful sheets.
To't, luxury, pell-mell, for I lack soldiers.
Behold yond simp'ring dame,
Whose face between her forks presages snow,
That minces virtue, and does shake the head
To hear of pleasure's name.
The fitchew nor the soilèd horse goes to't
With a more riotous appetite.
Down from the waist they are Centaurs,
Though women all above.
But to the girdle to the gods inherit,
Beneath is all the fiend's.
There's hell, there's darkness, there is the sulphurous pit; burning, scalding, stench, consumption. Fie, fie, fie! pah, pah! Give me an ounce of civet; good apothecary, sweeten my imagination! There's money for thee.

GLOUCESTER:

O, let me kiss that hand.

King Lear's Intemperate Outburst

LEAR:
Let me wipe it first; it smells of mortality.

Lear is mad, of course. But in Shakespeare, and especially in this play, madness—real or assumed, in Lear, Edgar, and the Fool—is a way of extending the poetic range, often into surrealistic or phantasmagoric modes. But in Lear, everything, if we tease at it, will yield a meaning that fits into the whole.

What is the point of this intemperate outburst? (This, I find, in teaching *King Lear* to students, is perhaps the most difficult passage in the play to account for and to relate to the play's central themes.) Lear is aware it is Gloucester he is dealing with, and Gloucester is known to have begotten Edmund by fornication. Thus, there is a medieval sense of sin in the air. Lear, in his anarchic denunciation of all values, declares that the imaginary culprit shall not die for adultery—the animals do it, so it is natural. But we take it that some have been condemned to death for adultery. Sexual lust can lead, therefore, to death in this world and to spiritual death—to hell.

Lear becomes anarchic as a result of his anguished loss of faith in human values and refers bitterly to the conventional morality of finding connections between lawful issue and good social behavior. As far as Lear knows, Edmund has been better to his father than have his own lawful daughters. Why not do away with all lawful bars on sexual indulgence—at least it provides gunfodder.

But then Lear takes off on the theme of appearance and reality. If we take a realistic view, we know that even the most chaste-seeming, puritanical woman can give way, in sex, to the indulgence of an animal appetite. As I pointed out previously, the imagery in Lear's speech is powerfully sexual: the pure female visage is turned upside down and becomes a bearded genital in her fork.

The vision is at one extreme of the ideal object—the pure, non-libidinal woman. As with so many poets, Shakespeare cannot bring her together with the libidinal woman. And that is the problem Shakespeare is addressing at the unconscious level.

The witch, of course, is often filthy; for example, in Spenser's

The Faerie Queene, Duessa has a dirty tail. In his most terrible moments when writing about the bad aspects of woman, Shakespeare describes her as dirty: "Lilies that fester smell far worse than weeds." In Lear's speech, "soiled" means overfed, but to soil cattle is to feed them on fresh-cut green fodder, originally used for purging. The word here (as the *Oxford English Dictionary* makes clear) is related to the word *soil* in *night soil*. Thus, the phrase "soilèd horse" changes the image of the innocent-seeming female face between its white wimples into a bearded genital that is like a copulating horse, so richly fed on laxative fodder that it is excreting.[2] The very texture of the word "fitchew" conveys, onomatopoeically, the coarse sound of sensual bodily movement and squelch.

The woman's genital, then, is a dark and vicious place where filth and stink—bad inner body contents—are encountered. "Burning, scalding, stench, consumption" suggest venereal disease. It is as if, through Lear's madness, Shakespeare is expressing a horror of entering woman's body and there experiencing hurt, pain, filth, disease, damnation and death. Lear immediately seeks to sweeten his imagination and to clean his hand. It is as if, even in his own impulses toward sexuality, Lear encounters his own mortality in the most disturbing way, for now the stench of woman's genital, the stench of the copulating, overfed horse purging, and the stench of his own hand all seem to evoke the most terrible feelings of death.

And yet, of course, this fundament is where we are born.[3] A few lines later Lear says:

> Thou know'st, the first time that we smell the air
> We wawl and cry.

Thus, we may say that Shakespeare, through Lear's mad outburst, is exploring at the unconscious level the universal dread of woman's mysterious power of parturition and the terrible mystery of birth out of her bowels—out of her menstruation.

This is the connection between woman and death—between copulation and mortality. Out of the conjunction of soiled animality and darkness, life begins. And all the uncontrollable, enigmatic, animal dynamics that lie in this dark world below the girdle threaten

every value and appearance upon which we rely for human organization. This is the mystery of woman, and why she is feared. But
though she is feared, and is shown in this play to be capable of
being hateful, she is not hated. Woman is redeemed by the devotion
and love of Cordelia, for whose devotion and love (as so often
happens in life) the only reward is death, as the ripples of evil
spread.

The triumph of acceptance of woman over hate comes, as does so
much of the play, in a moment of extreme simplicity—a moment
in which all the tormented horror becomes, like the noise of the
world, insignificant. Having found one another, Lear and Cordelia
are in the condition of 'being-unto-death':

LEAR:
We two alone will sing like birds i' th' cage.
When thou dost ask me blessing, I'll kneel down
And ask of thee forgiveness. So we'll live,
And pray, and sing, and tell old tales, and laugh
At gilded butterflies, and hear poor rogues
Talk of court news; and we'll talk with them too—
Who loses and who wins; who's in, who's out—
And take upon 's the mystery of things
As if we were God's spies; and we'll wear out,
In a walled prison, packs and sects of great ones
That ebb and flow by th' moon.

In the *Four Quartets* (1944), T. S. Eliot spoke of "a condition of
complete simplicity / Costing not less than everything"[4] and that is
what Lear and Cordelia achieve by reverting to childhood. While
hate must continue on its course (as Edmund orders their deaths),
they become translated into another sphere. And by recapturing the
transcendence of the mother-infant relationship—a love that is
indifferent to the world and "oceanic" in that sense—Lear and
Cordelia rise to a plane above cruelty, lust, and power:

Wipe thine eyes.
The goodyears shall devour them, flesh and fell,
Ere they shall make us weep!

The Insights Applied: Shakespeare's Anguish Over Woman

It is this re-creation of the ever unbreakable bond of love, as between mother and infant (though here it is between daughter and father), with its total indifference to the world, that redeems woman in Shakespeare's soul.

LEAR:
Upon such sacrifices, my Cordelia,
The Gods themselves throw incense. Have I caught thee?
He that parts us shall bring a brand from heaven
And fire us hence like foxes.

As well as all that belongs to mortality, mankind also is capable through love of rising above mere fate. This is the other lesson to be learned from woman.

As in Mahler, it is the rediscovery of the "oceanic" quality of relationship (such as we first experienced with the mother), of primary love, and of the creative power of 'being for' that enables the artist to solve the terrible torment of his perplexities—in a resolution of peace and harmony that takes us beyond this world.

The end of *King Lear* is terrible, and we can only understand it by suffering it. It even seems that Lear ends his life under a delusion, as to whether Cordelia is really dead or not. Yet, his lines

Why should a dog, a horse, a rat, have life,
And thou no breath at all? Thou'lt come no more,
Never, never, never, never, never.

are so unremitting that they are in our minds whenever we are grieving or bereaved, so absolutely do they express the dreadfulness of the fact that once we are dead we are dead forever. Yet, it must be recognized that once the dynamic of destructive hate is set in motion in human affairs, it moves relentlessly on, destroying the good as well as the bad (as throughout the tragedies). There is no natural justice in the world, as even Dr. Johnson admits in his protest against the death of Cordelia as contrary to the natural ideas of justice.[5]

But my own experience of the end of the play leaves me with the feeling that Lear and Cordelia have at least had that moment, in which they feel a new kind of invulnerability and move on to a different plane—from which the mere suffering of the world of reality no longer affects them. They have gone through that marvelous scene of mutual recognition and have found one another again (act 4, scene 7). This kind of scene obviously had great significance for Shakespeare—as did the recognition and refinding scene between Marina and her father in *Pericles* and all that is meant by the name Perdita.

The phrase "I am" is repeated many times throughout the scene. Lear's language is reduced to absolute simplicity, by complete contrast with his earlier verbosity, which goes with his tendency to see himself as a "dragon," or whatever. Here he is aware that he is only a man:

> Pray, do not mock me.
> I am a very foolish fond old man,
> Fourscore and upward, not an hour more nor less;
> And, to deal plainly,
> I fear I am not in my perfect mind.
> Methinks I should know you.

Yet he does know her, if only momentarily:

> For, as I am a man, I think this lady
> To be my child Cordelia.

The scene is so powerful I find it almost impossible to read without tears. Sometimes, indeed, one's voice falters completely because the breakthrough to "finding" Cordelia is so mysteriously potent. Cordelia's

> And so I am! I am!

clinches the exchange; and both have penetrated at this moment to the absolute 'core of being', in mutual love. The power of the scene is in the sense we have that here there is a completely authentic relationship again, in the existentialist sense, which is completely at the other pole from the one Lear has originally demanded, in his offence to love: "Which of us, shall we say, doth love us most?"

It is too late. The dangers are all around them; Lear is mad; Cordelia is defeated. All their prowess in the world is over. But this

153

is tragedy: There will come a time for all of us, when at last the world must be relinquished, and it will be unbearable. What then shall we say of our being, and its meaning? In finding one another, Lear and Cordelia find that meaning—in the absolute recognition of one unique being by another that is love, which exists in quite a different dimension from all worldly concerns and attachments. From now on, these no longer matter, for Lear and Cordelia have taken upon them the mystery of things, as if they were God's spies. (The latter phrase conveys the perspective, as if up a sacred mountain, from which the world is seen through new eyes.)

And the moment of recognition is so moving because it is something that woman can do for us, in her Cordelia-like modes. Again, we refind the mode of the *participation mystique*—of the woman as mother:

LEAR:

> Her voice was ever soft,
> Gentle, and low—an excellent thing in woman.

This moment resembles those in Mahler's Ninth Symphony when the lullaby voice of the mother expresses a reconciliation to Mother Earth, so that what must be is accepted as what must be. Lear dies saying, "Look there, look there." Although this is a dreadful delusion, that Cordelia is still alive, the final "looking" between them is a version of the original "looking" between mother and infant. For in that refinding by "looking," Lear finds that redeeming capacity to say "I am" and thus to discover the essense of his being. In this most awful exploration of the absoluteness of death, Cordelia symbolizes the power of woman to give meaningful existence through the strange powers of love—such as Lear disastrously offended against at the beginning of the play.

CHAPTER 8

Timon of Athens
and the Witch Archetype

This study began when I was working on Shakespeare's tragedies with students. We had been reading *Macbeth* and *King Lear*, discussing the particular nature of Lady Macbeth in relation to the witches in that play and Lear's strange outburst about the corrupt interior of woman.

How exactly did this vision of the sexual nature of woman, horrifying as it is, fit into *King Lear* as a whole? Then we came to *Timon of Athens*, and I found I could at first make very little sense of a great deal of that play. I could understand, of course, what might be called the Jonsonian development of the play—the way Timon's sycophantic friends turn against him when he falls into difficulties and his ensuing bitterness. But what has this to do with the themes of sexual corruption, of Timon's actual wish for the defilement of innocence? And what is the poetic or metaphorical connection between the excessive "giving" at the beginning, Timon's rejection by the courtiers, and the developing theme of enmity—of even the earth and nature itself being so corrupt as to be "takers," in the manifestations of a universal hate or voracious incorporative hate?

The Insights Applied: Shakespeare's Anguish Over Woman

At the time we were contemplating these questions, a paper on the archetype of the witch arrived, written by the American therapist and teacher Ann Belford Ulanov. This paper, "The Witch Archetype" (1977), seemed most illuminating, and so I want to invoke it here, to help in the illumination of Shakespeare's text. It is generally supposed that *Timon of Athens* is a play that is only in part by Shakespeare; or is a play that was patched up by him; or, if it is by him, it is "unsatisfactory." But I find that if I examine the poetic themes in the play, they seem to be indubitably Shakespearean. If the play is "unsatisfactory," it is in the way that *Hamlet* is —because the deeper unconscious themes prove to be too intractable and unresolvable for a wholly successful work of art.

It will be said, of course, that I am trying to psychoanalyze Shakespeare; in a sense, this is true. There are aspects of Shakespeare, particularly in his greatest work, that remain perplexing and call for some kind of deep psychological comment: Hamlet's obsession with his mother's sexuality; Lear's outbursts against corruption in woman; Timon's extravagant madness directed against all nature; and the bitterness of the other so-called dark, late plays. With such a genius, his very courage in exploiting the darker aspects of human makeup and of the world's reality must have presented him with problems that he found difficult to resolve. Such problems would have had their roots in disturbances of his own psyche. Since what drives such a creative artist is the impulse to try to find out what meaning there may be in life, this turmoil with the darker regions of the psyche also becomes a tormented engagement with the problem of existence.[1] Of course, such a writer's genius transcends his own limitations; but these remain to perplex us. I believe even Shakespeare could not always solve the problems he raised for himself.

I do not propose to discuss whether or not Shakespeare was homosexual, though we know from the sonnets that he was in love with a man. Recent psychoanalytical theory puts the problem in quite a different light—that of a man's feelings about his female element and about woman, which represent wider questions of gender. Quite clearly, Shakespeare had problems—universal problems in a sense but also particular personal problems—about woman's sexuality in relation to appearance and reality.

One problem here is a difficult one for us. The problem I want to discuss focuses on the theme of the witch. It is difficult to know exactly to what degree the Elizabethan audience believed in witches—literally, as agents of diabolical forces. However, they probably did. Certainly, the contemporary reader will find it hard to share these beliefs, however much we may suspend our disbelief for the purposes of art. But we may suppose that Shakespeare's original audience never questioned their beliefs in the way we do, since we are on this side of seventeenth-century skepticism while their thinking was much more concrete and embodied. The Elizabethan mode of thinking belongs to the age before the "dissociation of sensibility." They could live with a metaphor, believing in it as a path to knowledge. What we can do is to try to examine the theme and symbolism of witches in the Jungian way, as having a phenomenological significance. Witches belong to the exploration of ranges of consciousness, of psychic life, of living existence, and our perception of the nature of the world—especially its dark side, from which, as psychoanalysis has made clear to us, subjective factors can never be excluded.

First, let me summarize in my own way and for the present purposes Ann Belford Ulanov's paper on the subject of the witch as symbol. Why do witches turn up at all? And what makes them so fascinating? The witch seems to have special capacities: secret knowledge, powerful spells, and exceptional powers. The witch is often associated with magic.

The fascination we have from childhood for the witch reveals that we all have elements in ourselves that she symbolizes: "a cluster of images, emotional and behavioral potentialities of response that operate unconsciously . . . well beyond the immediate control of ego-consciousness" (Ulanov 1977, 3). In a Jungian way, Ulanov seems to believe that these images belong to something called "the objective psyche." For myself, though I recognize common elements in the human psyche, I cannot locate the existence of these images in something "outside" the individual human mind, which has, as it were, an autonomous and impersonal dynamic in some entity "out there"—that is, in the "collective unconscious." However, there does seem to be an embodiment of a shared culture, which consists of the common aspects of our consciousness in the common atmosphere of the human community. These common aspects are expressed through archetypes, such as the idea of the witches, which does represent a "dimension of unconscious process" abroad in human life, which affects us often without our being aware of it or being able to resist it.

Ulanov invokes Edmund Husserl[2] and his concept of "bracketing": Let us approach the phenomenon with open receptivity; let us be phenomenological about witches; let us allow the theme to disclose itself to us as it will. Let the unconscious exist in us *as* the unconscious:

> Jung stresses the fact that the unconscious is not some wastebasket to be emptied by consciousness, nor a reservoir totally at the service of our conscious thirst, nor yet a honey pot into which we dip our hands to get sweet tastes. (4)

The unconscious *is:* "It is an unmistakable aspect of human life existing in its own right, demanding to be respected as such" (4). The witch belongs to this unconscious world.

Some of the primary themes to be found in fairy tales or in works such as Goethe's *Walpurgisnacht* (Walpurgis Night)[3] are the witch's tremendous appetite and her keen interest in sex and power. We enjoy these themes, and so do children, in fairy tales; but they are terrible if they are ever acted out, as they are occasionally in psychopathic murders. When we are confronted with these themes in play or in art, we experience a deep sense of relief—no doubt because what is "there" in every unconscious mind is being recognized in a tacit way. Therefore, we may come to terms with it as an inescapable aspect of the reality of our experience, like death. Indeed, one might say that our fascination with the witch is a fascination with hate. Cultural manifestations of the witch problem represent an engagement with ambivalence—the admixture of love and hate that we all experience within ourselves and must deal with. There is also, of course, the destructiveness in the world that seems to be an *objective correlative* to the subjective witch, such as thunderstorms, sharks, and piranhas. These are objective correlatives of the voraciousness of the inner, subjective dynamics of the oral phase. (Later, I shall discuss the psychology of early infancy, which is the area of experience in which all that is symbolized by the witch has its origins. But for the moment, I will continue to summarize And Belford Ulanov's essay.)

A witch's appetite craves to feed on the human—its blood, its flesh, its soul. There are gods in various religions that resemble witches in this way. In Hindu mythology, the goddess Kali is depicted as being dressed in blood red. She stands in a boat floating on a sea of blood, a hideous blood-drenched female with the blood of her victories dripping from her fang-toothed mouth. Similarly malevolent figures, of course, are found in familiar tales, such as *Snow White*, *The Sleeping Beauty*, or in vampire tales.

This major theme, of sucking human blood, associates the witch with what seems, in our conscious perspective, a reversal of the usual flow of our life energies. A student, of somewhat subversive inclinations, recently told me that he thought Lady Macbeth represented "a positive moral energy." She does, if we reverse our conception of all normal life energies. We think of blood nourishing our bodies; the witch takes blood out of human bodies to feed her own. In some rituals and stories, she even demands the human heart, the center of our energies and the central symbol of human feeling.

The witch's demand for blood merges, states Ulanov, with her insatiable taste for human flesh, especially the flesh of children, as in *Hansel and Gretel*. These stories have their basis in maternal experience. Ulanov points out that many mothers experience a secret desire to "eat" their babies. They want to nibble at them, "taking unexpected pleasure in their edible fingers and plump cheeks" (5). She points out that we often play games with children in which we pretend to be threatening to "eat them up." These impulses spring from unconscious preoccupations, the origins of which I shall examine later.[4]

In normal circumstances, we expect the mother, altruistically, to deny herself and to feed her baby. However, the witchlike mother sacrifices the children to feed herself. In stories like *Frau Trude* in

Grimm's, a child puts herself in trustful dependency on a witch, only to be seized and burned in the fire to warm the old creature's bones.

The reversal of order extends to the spiritual realm. In folklore, witches have consuming appetites for human souls. Instead of celebrating the Mass, they perform a black mass to the devil. Witches were supposed to enjoy sexual orgies of a perverted kind and to bear on their bodies not the holy stigmata but the marks of the devil. Covens were supposed to consist of thirteen members, in mockery of Christ and his twelve apostles. Yet, the witch is also in myth a lonely figure, often set apart like Macbeth's witches in a wild place far removed from human habitation.

The witch lives on the "rim of existence," so to speak, says Ulanov. She lives in the forest or in the mountains. Her house is surrounded by skulls mounted on fence posts or grasping tendrils hanging from stunted trees. Body wastes, bloody refuse, decaying carcasses, fetid smells, and noxious gases surround her, while nothing grows near her. Yet from this poisonous remoteness she exerts her powerful bewitchment, her spells. From this state of alienation, she invades human consciousness, sometimes exerting an anaesthetizing effect, affecting us like the Sleeping Beauty. Or, we may be turned to stone, like Faithful John. She spoils health with fatal sickness and friendship with malice and hatred.

The witch is portrayed in myth as having ferocious sexual energy, using other than genital body openings. She is impelled by sexual envy, and she seeks power. She takes the treasure all to herself and hoards it, giving out nothing to anyone else. She stands for all the worst of the feminine, her extreme receptivity pulling inward, whirling downward, absorbing into primordial unconscious depths all that is conscious and human. The witch drinks our blood, eats our flesh, devours our souls, and draws into herself our sexual energies. In psychotherapy,

> she stands for that sucking intellect associated with women of undeveloped minds, who drain answers out of their teachers or their books, consuming others' ideas and never putting forward any thoughts of their own. She stands for that sucking sexuality that seduces a man

to give himself over entirely into her hands . . . that clinging, cloying sexuality that saps the last ounce of her partner's emotions. (10)

Yet, we may take a positive phenomenological view and see that the witch's positive value as a symbol may be found in this negative sucking action: "She pulls them towards the unconscious to forge a link between the two mental systems" (10). All the same, the witch reverses the normal order of things. To the mother's nurturing womb, the witch shows a devouring maw; to the mother's feeding breast, the witch brings her own insatiable hunger. Where the mother gives out, the witch takes in. Where mothers are feeders, the witch is an eater. Where mothers support and hold others, the witch drops them into a pit. Where a mother brings life, the witch faces us with death and decay. (It is important to note, for the purposes of looking at the meaning of *Timon of Athens*, this symbolism of emptiness and taking.)

Yet, says Ulanov, this provides a rest from the ego-world. With the witch, we enter what Bachelard called the world of the anima, a world of reverie, toward "the great silences, at the edge of being" (Bachelard 1969a, 62–67).

To the Jungian therapist, a "right relation to the witch archetype may have a healing effect upon us" (Ulanov 1977, 12). The darkness we might have feared shows its other face—a haven for our world-weary souls—and provides an "atmosphere of possibility and growth." If we have insight into the witch aspect of existence,

> we do not infect those we love with the regressive pull of our unconscious, nor do we feel wasted by the insatiable demands of others' unconscious needs because we turn directly toward our unconscious, we accept, as it were, the pull of witch forces within our psyche. . . . The witch archetype makes visible to us the very depths of what is humanly possible. (12)

We may gaze upon the flow of life with all its attendant horrors, says Ulanov, neither avoiding it by sentimentality nor denying it by detachment and coldness. Life is full of badness, pain, destructiveness, meanness, and death. The witch lives in the place where nothing grows, and "the energies the witch symbolizes give us the strength to combine our conscious human feelings with the tough implacability of life she represents" (13).

One especial area where the witch's reversal of the usual order appears is the sexual. "She pulls sexuality out of the human realm" (13), and she stands in contrast to the kind of sexual partner most of us would like to have. She engages in cold, inhuman, impersonal, and power-driven sex, without sharing or human feeling. She sucks her victims dry, in a ruttish instinct without shame.

Such witches are glamorized in pornography and are the subject of considerable attention in the schizoid art of our era. (The reality, of course, is that those caught up in witchlike perversions, as in black magic, are those who are giving themselves up desperately to hate because they cannot achieve satisfaction in love.)

However, the witch cannot really be seen as a liberating force. Under the spell of the witch, female sexuality cannot emerge at all but goes into a deathlike sleep (as in *Snow White* or *The Sleeping Beauty*). Another theme associated with the witch is the abandonment to a sexual passion that must lead to death. There is a powerful attraction in this kind of fantasy, when in our kind of suburban society sex has become domesticated and without passion. The witch conveys an image of demonic sexuality that can break through the old forms. She thus becomes a focus of the blasphemy that is a form of protest against the meaninglessness of modern life. Yet, Ulanov points out, this kind of "black sexuality is in fact a delusion. . . . Rousing orgies are pretty cold stuff compared with the fire of human love" (15). Thus the witch revolution (like the revolutionary orgies of Otto Gross[5]) is a false solution that merely deepens oral voraciousness and does little to allay the hunger for meaning. (There is, of course, an element of witch sexuality in Cleopatra, in Shakespeare's *Antony and Cleopatra*, which leads to death.)

Yet, Ulanov takes a very positive view of the witch archetype:

The witch arouses our imaginations to new visions of the nature of the psyche. She personifies energies that connect us with unsuspected unconscious potentialities. She typifies a kind of primordial, feminine unconscious intellect and aggression that would compensate for the highly developed conscious intellect and aggression that have gotten out of balance with human relatedness. The witch challenges us to bring unconscious "order" and "rationality" into their own light. (21)

Ulanov writes from a phenomenological understanding of a particular modern American problem—of how women may come to find true equality in a society dominated by male modes and a tradition of consciousness dominated by the masculinization of knowledge. It is not enough, Ulanov declares, simply to add women to the male organizations of society or to make references to persons gender neutral as the language of the "equal-opportunities" movement. What is needed is a rediscovery of female attributes at a deeper level—the level of the unconscious and of 'being'.

Professor Ulanov's interest is in using in therapy the phenomenology of the witch. My direction is different: I want to use these insights in the interpretation of literature. What I want to do here is to use these insights to try to understand one of Shakespeare's most perplexing plays and to understand one perplexing theme that runs throughout his works. It seems to me to be a theme that emerged from some disturbance in his own psyche—a problem of fear of woman and the feminine—and one that belongs to the Renaissance—and to Renaissance humanism of a disillusionment about woman. It is a theme that also belongs to Christianity, to a particular problem of a Christian civilization—that is, the association of woman with sin, darkness, and death and all that belongs to the "abyss" to which the witch leads us.

I have looked at King Lear's outburst against the "sulphurous pit" in woman's body. We may recall again the lines from the same play, addressed to Gloucester:

The dark and vicious place where thee he got
Cost him his eyes.

This "place," of course, is the vagina of the mother of Edmund—or perhaps her womb. Why is the source of human life "dark and vicious"? Or, to put it bluntly, why is woman's cunt equated with hell? (See also James Joyce's truly Anglo-Saxon-Puritan reference in *Ulysses* to "the grey sunken cunt of the world.") It may be said, of course, that Edmund was begot in sin—in fornication —and so, in vice. But Lear, as we have seen, goes further: The woman's lower body is hell, to be regarded with energetic loathing. Down there, she is possessed by the fiends; everything is darkness, sulphurous stench, and corruption. This is the world of the witch; and yet, it is attributed to all women, to all sexuality, with a vibration of sexual disgust taking over the energy of the verse.

One historical feature is relevant here and that is the spread of syphilis throughout Europe during the Renaissance. This terrible disease must have seemed as if it marred the new sense of men's potentialities, a humanistic sense of sexual freedom, and delight in the joys of the body. The many jokes about "the French disease," as in Shakespeare's almost obsessional references to "French crowns," would seem to indicate a deep distress and dread. (It is possible, I suppose, that Shakespeare himself had syphilis.)

But their historical spread of syphilis in Europe does not alone explain the powerful and repulsive quality that Shakespeare's verse takes on at certain key moments in his great tragedies, when he is contemplating human corruption, as in Hamlet's reference to the "bloat king:"

Or paddling in your neck with his damned fingers. . . .

And just previous to this

And either curb the devil or throw him out
With wondrous potency.

—sexual intercourse in adulterous habit, as between Gertrude and Claudius, is more than sin. It is actually a possessing devil; and behind this, again, I believe are feelings about the witch and bewitchment. To make this plain, I propose to make a detailed analysis of *Timon of Athens* in light of Ulanov's analysis of the phenomenology of the witch as a symbol of the darker—unconscious bodily—aspects of woman.

In light of Ulanov's analysis of the witch archetype, I believe we can say that in *Macbeth* and *King Lear* we have a sense that certain aspects of femininity—the witch elements or the voracious elements, such as we direct in infancy toward the mother's body and which, by way of talion revenge, we fear might be directed by her at ourselves—are latent in all creativity. These are threats every man still fears, when he experiences a woman close to him, abandoned in sexual excitement. And since woman has created us and the earth is a great creative monster, these forms of hungry abandonment are to be found even in Mother Earth. The witches in *Macbeth* are actually spoken of as bubbles of the earth:

> The earth hath bubbles as the water has,
> And these are of them.

In Lady Macbeth we have the embodiment of the witch woman, a woman of tremendous appetite with a great hunger for power. These witchlike elements are also found in Goneril and Regan in *King Lear*. These women are like witches, cruel and bloody, denying all the normal claims of affection. They display (as Bad Breast) an intense inversion of all those qualities that are normally associated with woman and mother (Good Breast). And since we were once dependent on a woman, the fact that these witch dynamics are found in woman raises the question as to whether man can go on existing, since it is possible for this woman, who is the key to existence, to so denature herself:

LADY MACBETH:
> I have given suck, and know
> How tender 'tis to love the babe that milks me:
> I would, while it was smiling in my face,
> Have plucked my nipple from his boneless gums
> And dashed the brains out, had I so sworn as you
> Have done to this.

This is either the witch speaking or a woman who has been *bewitched*. This is Bad Breast speaking, indeed, as from the most terrible fears of the infant and from the levels of consciousness where we still fear the woman turned against us in our dependence. In such women, this is seen by Shakespeare to be a denaturing, such as Albany finds in Goneril. The self-denaturing impulse of the witch, or of those bewitched by the witch's evil influence, inevitably brings desolation to the world, which they threaten to destroy, as once we (in our fantasies of Bad Breast) feared to destroy. Macbeth says to the witches:

Though you untie the winds and let them fight
Against the churches, though the yesty waves
Confound and swallow navigation up
Though bladed corn be lodged and trees blown down
Though castles topple on their warders' heads,
Though palaces and pyramids do slope
Their heads to their foundations, though the treasure
Of Nature's germens tumble all together
Even till destruction sicken,—answer me
To what I ask you.

In the uncontrollable fantasies of ultimate oral fantasy, the infant fears that he will eat up the world or that a similar voraciousness may be directed against him (not least by the combined parents if the infant becomes involved in their sex). Thus, these dynamics, projected to the witch, threaten to destroy the very fabric and germination ("germens") of life itself.

Timon of Athens raises a further question: suppose that nature, as susceptible to witch-influenced inversion as it is, is *itself a witch*. Shakespeare explores not only the witch potentialities that lie in woman beneath the polite exterior but also the qualities of the unconscious that Ulanov discusses. These are deeply linked, through our infant experience, with the mother, as the source of 'being,' and the breast. What of Mother Earth, the original source of all 'being'? Does she have witch qualities, too? Does this mean that human nature, which sprang from that source, is essentially bad? These are the questions that are asked in *Timon of Athens*.

In a deep metaphorical sense, *Timon of Athens* is about the breast: Bad Breast and Good Breast, but mostly bad. It is about giving and taking. In this very primitive sense, the play is also about money. For as Freud understood, gold is feces or, extending the symbol, blood and milk—the "inner contents" that we give out or receive. Gold is a symbol of inner contents; and to understand the metaphorical complexities of *Timon of Athens*, we need to examine its meanings in terms of very primitive experiences of inner substance and the relationship of this to the whole earth as breast— that is, to the problem of reality, in 'being-in-the-world', of whether we can find and leave the world in 'being', or whether we shall eat it up.

In the first scene, Timon's bounty has a magical quality. It has brought to his house the poet, the painter, the jeweler, and the merchant:

POET:
                    See,
Magic of bounty, all these spirits thy power
Hath conjured to attend!

The "world" is in the beginning both pregnant and beautiful: Yet,

POET:
                    How goes the world?
PAINTER:
It wears, sir, as it grows.

We grow weary of the world the more we know it. We use it up; we empty the breast.

POET:
                    Ay, that's well known.
But what particular rarity? What strange,
Which manifold record not matches?

The appointments made at the house are a record of the multiplicity and strangeness of those products that Timon's richness yields. The poet speaks of his verse as an outpouring of inner contents:

Our poesy is as a gum which oozes
From whence 'tis nourishèd.

Thus, poetry is like the output of a breast. The "giving" that is the subject of *Timon of Athens* is about the kind of giving that Shakespeare as a poet himself was capable of. The resentment against man that the play perhaps expresses has to do with Shakespeare's deep dissatisfaction about the way his genius was received. The poet's language is, of course, something of a caricature of a self-regarding literary man's euphuistic and aphoristic manner; but it also expresses something of a bitter and anguished cynicism about art:

> our gentle flame
> Provokes itself and like the current flies
> Each bound it chafes.

The burning energy of creativity, like a river, wears away the boundaries of the stream and overflows.

The creative output, a product of female-element bounty, is like Timon's fortune. And Timon's fortune is like a hanging breast, in the subdued image:

> His large fortune,
> Upon his good and gracious nature hanging,
> Subdues and properties to his love and tendance
> All sorts of hearts.

The poet has a conceit, of Timon being favored in his turn by Fortune, who is also a breast, throned on a huge mount:

> The base o' th' mount
> Is ranked with all deserts, all kinds of natures
> That labor on the bosom of this sphere.

The response to the bountiful breast, Timon's or Fortune's, is to "eat." In the company, there is one who sees this—the strange, "churlish" philosopher who penetrates pomp. He speaks only a blunt truth:

APEMANTUS:
I scorn thy meat. 'Twould choke me; for I should ne'er flatter thee. O you Gods, what a number of men eats Timon, and he sees 'em not!

This eating already has been given a sexual connotation:

TIMON:
Wilt dine with me, Apemantus?
APEMANTUS:
No, I eat not lords.

TIMON:
And thou shouldst, thou'dst anger ladies.
APEMANTUS:
O, they eat lords. So they come by great bellies.

Today, psychoanalysts report patients' dreams of the *vagina den-tata*, (the woman's genital as a hungry mouth). Here, sexual love is seen as a hungry eating, the product of which is pregnancy—an infantile view of sex, as we know from Melanie Klein (1957). This explains the connections in *Timon of Athens* between sexuality, rapaciousness, and giving and taking. These are linked in all of us by the primitive or bodily oral fantasies of infancy, from which emerges the witch archetype.

The infant view of sex—that it is a kind of eating—is one that includes the possibility of murder, since what is eaten disappears. The infant has this fantasy at the time when he fantasizes about consuming the breast. Thus, Apemantus can speak of the parasitism on Timon as a kind of murder:

It grieves me to see so many dip their meat in one man's blood. . . .
.   .   .   .
I wonder men dare trust themselves with men.
Methinks they should invite them without knives.

There is nothing in the action thus far to suggest such latent violence. What Apemantus is making vocal are the unconscious motives in parasitism and the breast symbolism of feasts, hospital-ity, and ambition:

The fellow that sits next him now,
parts bread with him, pledges the breath of him in a
divided draft, is the readiest man to kill him. . . .
If I were a huge man, I should fear to drink at meals,
Lest they should spy my windpipe's dangerous notes.
Great men should drink with harness on their throats.

The harness would protect, but it would also curb the "eating" or "taking" impulse. At the primitive level of unconscious fantasy, what Shakespeare is exploring are the primitive body impulses underlying envy and gratitude. The parallels with the witch archetype are obvious.

There is an analogy in Shakespeare's imagination between Timon and Christ (and between Timon's feasts and the Last Supper). But Christ was one who also poured out his blood to the world, like the poet, as Timon pours out his bounty. Each is a form of the beneficent breast, and both suffer the consequences of envy. As in the religious cult of the witch, these parallels are a blasphemous inversion of a Christian myth that has deep symbolic elements. The throwing of the warm water over the assembled diners obviously represents a "urinary attack" of the kind Melanie Klein finds in infantile fantasy, by contrast with Christ's blood at communion.

Alcibiades is a kind of parallel to Apemantus—a man of action who is to purge Athens, as Apemantus is a purgatorial philosopher. (At this feast, Apemantus eats roots and drinks water only.) The eating theme continues with Alcibiades. Again, primitive fantasy underlies the exchange:

TIMON:
You had rather be at a breakfast of enemies than a dinner of friends.
ALCIBIADES:
So they were bleeding new, my lord, there's no meat like 'em.

Later, in a speech to the flattering lords, Timon declares: "We are born to do benefits."

At this moment, there are two masquelike symbolizations of the feminine in association with Timon's bounty. One is a joke about weeping, in an excess of bonhomie:

TIMON:
O joy, e'en made away ere't can be born! Mine eyes cannot hold out water, methinks.
APEMANTUS:
Thou weep'st to make them drink, Timon.
SECOND LORD:
Joy had the like conception in our eyes

And at that instant like a babe sprung up.
APEMANTUS:
Ho, ho! I laugh to think that babe a bastard.

The second is the entry of a masque of ladies, led by Cupid, and dressed as Amazons. Apemantus declares that this is to

spend our flatteries to drink those men
upon whose age we void it up again
With poisonous spite and envy.

Apemantus sees the underlying unconscious impulses—the emotional and body impulses. When a Lord cries "My Lord, you take us even at the best," Apemantus declares, "Faith, for the worst is filthy; and would not hold taking, I doubt me." Man is not pure beneficence, as his body is full of filth (feces). And at the end Apemantus says:

What a coil's here,
Serving of becks and jutting-out of bums!

Timon, as a senator says, "flashes now a phoenix." He behaves as a legendary, indestructible creature. In trying to be wholly Good Breast and all-giving, Timon errs in not recognizing ambivalence, give-and-take, the opposite to love in hate (Bad Breast), and the way gratitude can turn to envy. Timon fails to see the way an all-eating relationship can turn into one that destroys the object, by eating up the source of bounty entirely—the breast is devoured completely. As we shall see, it is a recognition of all that the witch stands for that will restore these other aspects of reality to the picture.

Timon's giving has ceased to have substance behind it. As J. C. Maxwell points out in his essay *"Timon of Athens,"* published in 1948, Timon has mismanaged affairs and has ruined himself by giving beyond his means before the play begins. His land is "engaged," forfeited and gone, and the "greatest of his having lacks a self / To pay your present debts." His guests have virtually "eaten" him:

The Insights Applied: Shakespeare's Anguish Over Woman

STEWARD:
So the gods bless me,
When all our offices have been oppressd
With riotous feeders.

Now the riches have gone, it seems the breath by which he gave them might follow:

the world is but a word;
Were it all yours to give it in a breath,
How quickly were it gone!

And as for the flattering sycophants:

Ah, when the means are gone that buy this praise,
The breath is gone whereof this praise is made.
Feast-won, fast-lost: one cloud of winter show'rs,
These flies are couchd.

The primitive imagery underlying *Timon of Athens* as a play about the breast belongs, of course, to the oral stage. It is in keeping with the metaphorical theme of the play that Flavius (who is the Horatio or Kent in this work, focus for the solid common-sense view) should see both Timon's giving and the followers' flattery as mere "breath." (In the background are the primitive feelings of the infant about breath and 'being,' which primitive peoples reflect in their theories about the soul escaping in a yawn.)

Timon thinks of appealing to the senate, but Flavius warns him that they are cold to such appeals. Their inner substance becomes earthy and thus full of ingratitude:

TIMON:
These old fellows
Have their ingratitude in them hereditary
Their blood is caked, 'tis cold, it seldom flows;
'Tis lack of kindly warmth they are not kind;
And nature, as it grows again toward earth,
Is fashioned for the journey, full and heavy.

Thus, ingratitude is linked with a decline toward death, while gratitude belongs to life as to the Good Breast.

Servants waiting for money from Timon are addressed by Flavius thus:

Why then preferred you not your sums and bills
When your false masters ate of my lord's meat?
Then they could smile, and fawn upon his debts,
And take down th' int'rest into their glutt'nous maws.

Timon comes among them in a rage, and we have a foretaste of his madness. Significantly, he speaks as if the creditors claims are claims on his blood, his bodily substance:

TIMON:
Cut my heart in sums! . . .

. . . .

TIMON:
Tell out my blood! . . .

. . . .

LUCIUS' SERVANT:
Five thousand crowns, my lord.

TIMON:
Five thousand drops pays that.

The pain of forfeiture is real because Timon's affection for his syco-phants is genuine. What he cannot bear is the confused recognition that they falsified emotion and loyalty. The primary question is not just quantities of money but the way "interest" evokes the authen-ticity of relationship. There has been already a hint of the greatest betrayal of relationship—Judas betraying Christ.

FIRST STRANGER:
            Who can call him
His friend that dips in the same dish?

The feast Timon provides is (as a student suggested to me) a parallel to the Last Supper. The dishes contain only warm water, Barmeci-dal food. Timon calls the guests

You knot of mouth-friends! Smoke and lukewarm water
Is your perfection.

He calls them wolves and bears and curses Athens. As I have suggested, they are subject to an attack from a bodily substance (urine).

Now, without the walls, Timon pronounces what amounts to a witch's curse on Athens, seeking by his spell to reverse all beneficial processes:

> Matrons, turn incontinent!
> Obedience fail in children! Slaves and fools,
> Pluck the grave wrinkled senate from the bench
> And minister in their steads!

Associated with Timon's Lear-like assault on all social conventions and values is a witchlike desire that innocence should be corrupted:

> To general filths
> Convert, o' th' instant, green virginity!
> Do't in your parents' eyes! . . . Lust and liberty
> Creep in the minds and marrows of our youth,
>
> That 'gainst the streams of virtue they may strive
> And drown themselves in riot!

In the next scene, Flavius is talking to servants who feel a great loyalty to Timon; and he proclaims that Timon's only weakness has been to be good:

> Poor honest Lord, brought low by his own heart,
> Undone by goodness! Strange, unusual blood,
> When man's worst sin is he does too much good!

It may seem thus to Flavius; but, of course, Timon's giving has been unreal, in that he took no realistic notice of the extent of his estates. But goodness, as with the mother, involves giving out and so makes one vulnerable. The giver, like the mother, is always liable to be "eaten." As we have seen, Timon now suffers the consequences; and so that love, betrayed, becomes the reverse of Christ's forgiveness and atonement. The love is "eaten" up by envy, hate, and malice. Witchlike, it turns its energy against man and urges on man's sexual energies a corruption that will destroy him.

In act 4, scene 3, the earth virtually becomes a witch and the forces of nature witchlike:

TIMON:
O blessed breeding sun, draw from the earth
Rotten humidity; below thy sister's orb
Infect the air!

Like one bewitched, Timon inverts all values and hates man (and himself):

There's nothing level in our cursèd natures
But direct villainy. Therefore be abhorred
All feats, societies, and throngs of men.
His semblable, yea himself, Timon disdains.
Destruction fang mankind!

Timon gives way to oral hate. He is like an infant who, expecting Good Breast and identifying with it, finds that the breast does not fulfill the promise envisaged for it but has become Bad Breast. Thus, the infant flips over into hate and seeks to destroy the breast and the whole world with it.

Timon digs into the earth as into a breast and there seeks roots. He finds gold, which is both inner contents and the *radix omnium malorum:*

Roots, you clear heavens! Thus much of this will make
Black, white, foul, fair . . .

Interestingly Timon echoes in this speech the witches in *Macbeth*. What he recites is virtually a spell, again invoking the reversal of all values. Earth herself is now a whore:

Come, damnèd earth,
Thou common whore of mankind, that puts odds
Among the rout of nations, I will make thee
Do thy right nature.

The earth yields gold, and gold corrupts. Nations are at odds because the earth offers mineral deposits; thus, Mother Earth is the cause of man's dissention—that is her true nature. But what stands out most from this speech is Timon's intense image of disgust with woman.

> This is it
> That makes the wappened widow wed again;
> She whom the spital-house and ulcerous sores
> Would cast the gorge at, this embalms and spices
> To th' April day again.

As with Lear's outburst, the intensity of physical repulsion is excessive—riches make the widow nubile again. But why is she so repellent? It can hardly be because she is old and wizened. Is she syphilitic because she caught the disease from her late husband? Rather, I believe the combination of succulent sounds and repulsive images evoke a subliminal vision of her in sexual intercourse. The implication is that even someone accustomed to a leper-house and ulcerous sores would find her so repulsive that he would throw up."[6] The words "embalms" and "spices" make her into a living corpse—married on an April day like an Easter bride. The w's in "wappened widow wed" emphasize the disgust as one moves one's lips saying the words. ("Wappened" means stale, and the flapping sound suggests loose skin on bones.)

This widow is surely herself a witch—that is, an archetypal image of that filthy and disgusting state that is at the opposite pole to the kind of woman to whom we would like to relate. Timon, who declares himself "*Misanthropos*, and hate[s] mankind," declares that gold can make even such a creature marriageable. Of course, the very expressiveness itself has an element of caricature. But we cannot avoid a certain sense that Shakespeare himself is obsessed with extravagant fantasies of hateful and corrupt woman (or Bad Breast), in which woman's body becomes something like a corpse (as in Hamlet's remarks in the graveyard scene and the references to the sun breeding maggots in a dead dog). In the next few lines, Phyrnia, a whore, cries to Timon:

> Thy lips rot off!

Not only is this a reference to syphilis but the words relate to the consequences of suckling at Bad Breast. Then Timon responds:

> Be a whore still. They love thee not that use thee;
> Give them diseases, leaving with thee their lust.
> Make use of thy salt hours. Season the slaves
> For tubs and baths; bring down rose-cheekèd youth
> To the tub-fast and the diet.

The "tub-fast" was a cure for sexually transmitted diseases. The imagery is full of feelings of repulsion at mechanical, cold, and loveless sex and has the feel behind it of unresponsive or impinging breast-feeding, experienced as hate.

A good deal of Timon's spleen is directed against innocence and youth. There is no reason for this in the action of the play because the senate are old men and the flatterers by no means youthful. Nor in the logic of the drama does there seem to be any good reason for Timon's anger to turn itself against human sexuality as a result of the cold response to his "giving." There is a general tendency in Timon to assault all human values and bonds and to seek to bring down vengeance on all, believing in his misanthropy—as did Lear —that since all offend by their hypocrisy, none does offend. All are equally deserving of contempt and vituperation.

But why should whores be urged to inflict their diseases on men and especially on youth? The lines are full of disgust and a witchlike malignancy. The men who use the whores are to leave their "lust" with them—presumably, their semen. Beneath the lines is an undercurrent of disgust. The professional hours of the whores are "salt hours," which suggests the bodily exhudations of sex and also the smarting feelings of excessive sexual activity. "Season the slaves / For tubs and baths" suggests something like rubbing salt into a ham and peppering and spicing it for pickling—all of which make sexuality seem a cold but desperately stimulated activity, which ends in "the tub-fast and the diet," painful attempts at physical cure. All this may be seen as the expression of Timon's sick rage directed against Athens; but in its intensity, it seems also to reveal a certain vibration in Shakespeare such as we may also note when Hamlet confronts his mother and when Lear speaks of woman. And this vibration, in light of psychoanalytical insights, has to do with a certain kind of dread of the body in sex and has to do with eating and the fear that within the excited body there is a malignant corruption. Behind this, as I have suggested, there seems to lie a physical dread that has its roots in bad experiences of the breast— of the breast experienced as hateful.

Timon of Athens appears partly as a means to enable Shakespeare himself to express this sexual or Bad Breast dread. In other words, the play may be an "excuse" to indulge in a certain obsessional exploration of horror at human sexuality and fleshy contact. Because of this, parts of the play become almost a caricature. Timon's next speech is a case in point. To Alcibiades Timon recommends mercilessness:

> Let not the virgin's cheek
> Make soft thy trenchant sword; for those milk paps
> That through the window-bars bore at men's eyes
> Are not within the leaf of pity writ,
> But set them down horrible traitors.

In this we have a suggestion of compulsive voyeurism, an obsession with bare breasts that seem predatory and threatening ("bore at men's eyes") and are "horrible traitors." Sexuality—the sexual urge itself—seems here a tremendous threat to security. Because of these strange dynamics, the verse becomes so grotesque it seems likely to provoke a giggle rather than a sense of horror:

> Spare not the babe
> Whose dimpled smiles from fools exhaust their mercy:
> Think it a bastard whom the oracle
> Hath doubtfully pronounced thy throat shall cut,
> And mince it sans remorse.

The word "mince" here makes the kind of impulse to denature (so dreadful in Lady Macbeth) seem ridiculous.[7] Timon goes on, into a kind of surrealistic vituperation, which also by its exaggerations (and in a sense its irrelevance) seems merely grotesque)—merely *grand guignol*. The urgings essentially seem irrelevant to the themes of gratitude, bonds, and values:

> Hold up, you sluts,
> Your aprons moutant. You are not oathable. . .

178

> . . .Be whores still;
> And he whose pious breath seeks to convert you—
> Be strong in whore, allure him, burn him up
> Let your close fire predominate his smoke,
> And be no turncoats. Yet may your pains six months
> Be quite contrary! And thatch your poor thin roofs
> With burdens of the dead—some that were hanged,
> No matter; wear them, betray with them. Whore still;
> Paint till a horse may mire upon your face.
> A pox of wrinkles!

The commentaries that I have consulted seem baffled by this verse, which is so full of concentrated hostility. "Aprons mountant" is not difficult. Taking a term from heraldry, it means "often lifted up" (for purposes of being mounted).

In his assault on values, Timon urges the prostitutes to resist all attempts to redeem them. If anyone should try to reform them, they should (like witches) burn him up—alluring him, seducing him, and then consuming him with disease. When he assails them, they should direct the close fire of their allure so that it predominates over the (hellfire?) smoke with which he is threatening them. They must not betray their profession (by leaving the field of battle in disguise).

The Arden edition of Shakespeare suggests that the puzzling lines

> Yet may your pains six months
> Be quite contrary!

are a curse. Timon is wishing on them painful menstruation, for six months. But "contrary" means in the opposite direction, so the lines suggest that their efforts to seduce this zealot will, in six months' time, have quite the opposite effect to his original intentions, condemning him to the consuming hell of venereal disease. And as for the whores, their own hair will fall out and become dead; they will have to wear wigs made from the heads of executed felons—using these to seduce further customers.

We have here horrible images of women who burn men (by the scalding pains of disease that are, again, the "sulphurous pit"), wear the hair of dead convicts, and are marked with pox. Yet, they defy this physical corruption by painting their faces:

Paint till a horse may mire upon your face.

The suggestion is surely one of hideous desperation. The deceptively painted face is so inhumanly depersonalized that it is like the street, and a horse may defecate on it without effect; while the make-up is so grossly applied that it looks as if a horse has excreted on the woman's face. (The "soilèd horse" in *King Lear* is fed with purging food and seems to be excreting in the sexual act.)

There could be no more terrible expression of utter revulsion from the feminine. Earlier, the virgins' breasts are menacing, "boring" at men's eyes, and betraying them. Now, we have the perverted image of a desire to see a horse excrete on a woman's face, while she is wearing a wig from a dead—hanged—head and is gloating on having given a man syphilis! Timon is, of course, mad. But is he also the mouthpiece for a psychopathological hatred of femininity in Shakespeare himself? If Shakespeare had not experienced some deeply disturbed state of dread of woman, the verse could not have such power; and surely no other writer has ever written with such appalling force about such a subject.

The following lines delineate all the horrors of syphilis and its effects, which brought to the Renaissance such a dread of corruption—even as men became aware of their angel-like capacities:

TIMON:
Consumption sow
In hollow bones of man; strike their sharp shins,
And mar men's spurring. Crack the lawyer's voice,
That he may never more false title plead
Nor sound his quillets shrilly. Hoar the flamen,
That scolds against the quality of flesh
And not believes himself. Down with the nose—
Down with it flat; take the bridge quite away—
Of him that, his particular to foresee,
Smells from the general weal. Make curled-pate ruffians bald . . .

That your activity may defeat and quell
The source of all erection.

Syphilis consumes; it eats away inside the hollow bones. It causes painful nodes on the shinbone (and so inhibits men spurring on, in sexual riding) and ulceration of the larynx. It whitens the hair (of priests who proclaim against lust and yet indulge), causes decay of the bridge of the nose, and causes hair loss. The individual who seeks his own self-interest—seeks to "foresee" his "particular"—seeks out on a scent that is contrary to the general welfare. But he only sees better because his nose is gone; and he "smells" well enough because he is rotten with sexual disease (a very complex, punning piece of verse). "Erection," surely, has a double meaning. It means both the upright pattern of social organization and the male physical sexual erection, which the whores will undermine by making the organ rotten.

It is hardly surprising that, having plunged so into the deepest loathing of man's creative powers, Timon should now turn to address the earth and urge her to become a great witch, beginning with an attribution of oral intensity to nature in response to man's unkindness:

That nature, being sick of man's unkindness,
Should yet be hungry!

At any level of ordinary realism, the connections in *Timon of Athens* among giving, gold, inner substance, sexuality, the creativity of nature and the earth, hunger, procreation, murder and evil make little or no sense. All are unified, however, by unconscious themes. It even seems absurd and perverse for a tragic hero, ruined by his own reckless generosity and spurned by his erstwhile enemies, to run mad around the countryside, abusing whores, wishing sexual corruption and mayhem on Athens, and vilifying nature and the earth.

The word "perverse," however, gives us the clue. The symbolism of Timon's verse and the expanded metaphor of the play can only be understood properly in terms of the origins of the various expressions here of the experiences of "inner contents"—giving and hunger, in the fantasies of very primitive life. They draw on the first experiences of the infant at the breast, when he is like Timon, "eating a root"—sucking at the earth-source. Primitive feelings and fantasies of this kind, about inner and outer, often are found in the symbolism of sexual perversion.

The parasites come to Timon.

> To gratulate thy plenteous bosom. Th' ear,
> Taste, touch, smell, all, pleased from thy table rise;
> They only now come but to feast thine eyes.

Interestingly, a connection is made here (by Cupid in the masque) between feeding at Timon as at a breast and voyeurism, the delight in watching women. (We may recall the lines previously quoted about the virgin's breasts "boring" at men's eyes and proving treacherous.) Timon now addresses the "plenteous bosom" of the earth, which is treacherous because it generates abhorred births as well as benign ones. Here, there is a dreadful fear, to which Shakespeare yields himself by imagining through Timon's madness that the same creature power in nature that has made life can become witchlike and generate evil.

The Kleinian concepts of envy and gratitude are deeply relevant here. As I have tried to show in my analysis of Mahler's Ninth Symphony, the achievement of a sense of meaningful 'at-oneness' with the world requires the achievement of gratitude, in a triumph over hate and envy. Hate remains a problem because it is "out there" in the world as a menace that, like the wolf in *Little Red Riding Hood*, threatens all security of existence. Once we find that hate is merely an aspect of our own ambivalence and is "embraced," or loved, as a component of human nature—and of nature itself—there can be reconciliation and peace, as at the end of the first movement of the Ninth Symphony.

Timon's trouble is that "the world"—that is, the world of man —has shown no gratitude, despite his extravagant giving. It is as if giving out bountiful love generates no response. In the poet Shakespeare, this concept aroused the dread that generous love could not redeem the world, bringing that benign sense of love and meaning that can be brought (as in *The Rime of the Ancient Mariner*) by the outflowing of love and the redeeming influence of the moon-mother's power (the antiwitch). Instead, since human nature is dominated by hate and envy and Bad Breast, the earth itself will be spoiled. The earth will be hungry and hating—thus, witchlike in the reversal of its proper functions:

> That nature, being sick of man's unkindness,
> Should yet be hungry! Common mother, thou
> Whose womb unmeasurable and infinite breast
> Teems and feeds all. . . .

Suppose this infinite mother of all took on the envious—or hateful—qualities of man, such as Timon has experienced? Suppose man's nature, revealed by the (murderous) rejection he has experienced, was a dynamic of nature—of the earth mother herself?

> whose selfsame mettle
> Whereof thy proud child, arrogant man, is puffed
> Engenders the black toad and adder blue,
> The gilded newt and eyeless venom'd worm.

Significantly, the riot of abhorred and malignant creatures begins to sound like a category of items for a witch's spell. Timon begs;

> Yield him who all the human sons doth hate,
> From forth thy plenteous bosom, one poor root!

For the rest, earth is to

> Ensear thy fertile and conceptious womb;
> Let it no more bring out ingrateful man!
> Go great with tigers, dragons, wolves and bears;
> Teem with new monsters whom thy upward face
> Hath to the marbled mansion all above
> Never presented!—O, a root! Dear thanks!—
> Dry up thy marrows, vines, and plough-torn leas,
> Whereof ingrateful man, with liquorish drafts
> And morsels unctuous greases his pure mind,
> That from it all consideration slips.

183

The Insights Applied: Shakespeare's Anguish Over Woman

Man is not, of course, brought out of the earth, except in a general sense that the products of the earth that he eats become him. But the image is of an earth mother teeming. It would be better to create voracious animals, whose voracity is natural to them, than to generate man, who demonstrates such ingratitude. Man, with the products of the earth—wine and meat—becomes completed by the very oiliness of food, so that his mind can no longer concentrate on the proper issues.

There follows a strange and stagey "flyting" between Timon and Apemantus, the philosopher—to see which can outdo the other in abuse and cynicism:

TIMON:
Were I like thee I'd throw away myself.

Apemantus tells Timon that while he asks nature to dry up her womb and deny man, the truth is that Timon is now in the position of being a sycophant to a nature that is, in fact, extremely cruel and will reject him:

hinge thy knee
And let his very breath whom thou'lt observe
Blow off thy cap.

In his madness, Timon has sought to humanize nature, to make her a mother figure. He will find nature indifferent to him:

APEMANTUS:
What, think'st
That the bleak air, thy boisterous chamberlain,
Will put thy shirt on warm? Will these mossed trees,
That here outlived the eagle, page thy heels
And skip when thou point'st out? will the cold brook,
Candied with ice, caudle thy morning taste
To cure thy o'er-night's surfeit?

Apemantus is trying to demolish the pathetic fallacy that nature "cares." Man tries to make the cold air his valet, but it is cold and indifferent. Man supposes that, like a child in a fantasy, he can make the old trees skip at his command—but they will not. We cannot make nature ours by fantasy and play; it is simply itself. The frozen brook may look like a drink—sugared with ice, to be a cure for a hangover, to clean a furred tongue—but it will merely chill mercilessly. (The contrast is between a child being dressed, who gaily makes the trees skip and drinks a soothing beverage, and a bitter, cold, rejected man who has abandoned himself to the wildness of nature.) The contrast between images of the domestic nursery and the stark wildness to which Timon has abandoned himself is striking and beautiful. Underlying the contrast is the infant's problem of finding reality by vision benign (apperception), and then (as a result of the mother's "disillusioning") finding reality as it really is (perception).

The purpose of this strangely theatrical scene is not clear. Perhaps Shakespeare wanted to distinguish between the assumed and intellectual skepticism of a philosopher and Timon's bitterness generated by his experience of human wickedness. In his next speech Timon tells Apemantus that he has no real reason to hate men and that he has been born in hardship—"sufferance"—and that has made him hard. Suppose Apemantus had been born in good circumstances; like Timon, he would have become corrupt. Timon has other, more devastating, reasons for his hatred:

> Hadst thou, like us from our first swath, proceeded
> The sweet degrees that this brief world affords
> To such as may the passive drug of it
> Freely command, thou wouldst have plunged thyself
> In general riot.

"Swath" is presumably the first cut in a field of hay; the "passive drugs" are those things that make life bearable.[8] If he had been able to command these forms of high life, Apemantus would have

>   melted down thy youth
> In different beds of lust, and never learned
> The icy precepts of respect, but followed
> The sug'red game before thee.

These lines strangely echo Apemantus's about the "candied stream." Shakespeare seems to be pondering the nature of those forms of

discipline and chastening experience that may save man from corruption and despair. Yet, in *Timon of Athens*, he seems to be able
to find very little on which to base any hope of the triumph of
goodness. Here Shakespeare suggests through the mouth of Timon
that nothing can be worse than the experience of loyalty and devotion that is suddenly devastated:

> But myself,
> Who had the world as my confectionary,
> The mouths, the tongues, the eyes, and hearts of men
> At duty, more than I could frame employment;
> That numberless upon me stuck, as leaves
> Do on the oak, have, with one winter's brush,
> Fell from their boughs and left me open, bare
> For every storm that blows—I to bear this,
> That never knew but better, is some burden.

The undercurrent is one of eating happily ("confectionary"), with
the "mouths" of men "at duty," and then experiencing sudden and
terrible rejection, leaving him with a dreadful sense of vulnerability
and open to every storm. Here, again, we have the theme of Good
Breast turning to Bad Breast. In retaliation, Timon turns his oral
hate on all mankind:

> That the whole life of Athens were in this!
> Thus would I eat it.
> *[Gnaws a root.]*

—and at this point Apemantus offers Timon better food, which he
rejects.

The rest of the scene is like an abusive quarrel, full of oral hate,
between two children who are engaged in attempts to outdo one
another in insults. The scene ends with Timon throwing a stone at
Apemantus like at a dog:

TIMON:
Where feed'st thou a-days, Apemantus?
APEMANTUS:
Where my stomach finds meat; or rather, where I eat it.

TIMON:

Would poison were obedient and knew my mind!

APEMANTUS:

Where woulds't thou send it?

TIMON:

To sauce thy dishes.

. . . .

TIMON:

. . . If thou wert the lion, the fox would beguile thee; if thou
wert the lamb, the fox would eat thee. . . . If thou wert the
wolf thy greediness would afflict thee. . . . What beast couldst
thou be that were not subject to a beast?

The theme is of the whole world being full of creatures beguiling
and eating one another. It is the world of the witch who possesses
the archetypal, voracious hunger and of the infant who has felt
such dread of Bad Breast that he can never find confidence in the
benignity of good.

Timon is unable to find the means by which to find gratitude and
redeem the world. Devastated by oral hate, he seeks the ultimate
regression of death. He seeks to be laid where only the sea will
perform a massive reparation—or, at least, ablution:

I am sick of this false world, and will love naught
But even the mere necessities upon't.
Then, Timon, presently prepare thy grave
Lie where the light foam of the sea may beat
Thy gravestone daily.

In the scene with the bandits, Shakespeare returns to the theme
of men "eating" men.

BANDIT:

We are not thieves, but men that much do want.

TIMON:

Your greatest want is, you want much of meat.
What should you want? Behold, the earth hath roots.

They declare that they cannot, as Timon advises them, live on berries. Timon answers, "You must eat men."

Timon gives the bandits gold, to "enable" them:

Here's gold. Go, suck the subtle blood o' th' grape
Till the high fever seethe your blood to froth,
And so scape hanging.

But such a person, drinking himself into a fever, only escapes hanging by drinking himself to death, when he can, because money gives him the power. Timon urges the bandits to thieve more, just as he has urged the whores to whore more. The principle is that this is the nature of nature; they are great witches, all:

The sun's a thief, and with his great attraction
Robs the vast sea; the moon's an arrant thief,
And her pale fire she snatches from the sun;
The sea's a thief, whose liquid surge resolves
The moon into salt tears; the earth's a thief,
That feeds and breeds by a composture stol'n
From gen'ral excrement. Each thing's a thief.

The picture of all things as takers, as thieves, is so horrible it almost persuades one bandit to give up his profession. Timon gives them the gold he has found while seeking roots and gives gold to his loyal steward, too, even as he urges him to leave him and to hate mankind.

The false poet and painter now appear, having scented that Timon has found gold and is to return to his proper place in Athens once again. Timon sets them at one another, promising them gold, and then drives them out. When the senators come to offer Timon back his place in the city, Timon declares:

You witch me in it.

Timon weeps, but he will not return. It is too late. In response to their demand that he should help Athens by his authority to resist Alcibiades, Timon declares that he does not care. He does not rejoice in the common wrack:

> My long sickness
> Of health and living now begins to mend,
> And nothing brings me all things.

He has gone over into nihilism and the death-circuit of suicide; it is this that will cure his sickness. He has a remedy for any of the Athenians who suffer

> griefs,
> Their fears of hostile strokes, their aches, losses,
> Their pangs of love, with other incident throes
> That nature's fragile vessel doth sustain
> In life's uncertain voyage.

His "kindness" is to offer a tree in his garden, on which they can hang themselves. He asks the senators to tell Athens:

> Timon hath made his everlasting mansion
> Upon the beachèd verge of the salt flood,
> Who once a day with his embossèd froth
> The turbulent surge shall cover.

Despite Timon's hate and torment, this is an image of immense tranquillity and atonement. The sea, reflecting in its surge the turbulent soul of Timon, will lave the grave daily with a froth that is "embossed"—studded, as it were, with jewels full of value, the value of reparation. The sea, the great Thalassal mother, will purify Timon in death—even as in his life she, too, was a thief and taker. The massive "rejection" Timon has suffered is at an end.

In the final scenes, the universal massacre threatened by Alcibiades is averted. Only the enemies of Timon and Alcibiades, who shall be indicated by the senators, shall perish. Thus, the heart of man *is* redeemable. Timon's suicide and his grave are an act of imagination:

> yet rich conceit
> Taught thee to make vast Neptune weep for aye
> On thy low grave, on faults forgiven.

The indication of the reparative effect of the final act of imagination is evident. In the end, despite himself, Timon commits himself to an eternity of love, which shall redeem his hate. Yet only in this final act of imaginative conceit does Timon allow the possibility of redemption—redemption of self and world from the destructiveness of those elements in the unconscious and in the world at large to which we attach the name of *witch*.

CHAPTER 9

Marina in *Pericles*:
Hope and Continuity

Shakespeare was capable of confronting the worst that human beings
are capable of. He was able to explore the great cruelty and evil
that woman, the traditional embodiment of love and goodness in
her ideal aspect, was capable of. In his exploration, he unleashed
material that at times seems uncontrollable and out of proportion
to the matter at hand.

Why should not a woman who looks pure give way to riotous
sexual enjoyment? What threat is there in that? Why should a
woman, who knows nothing of her husband's bad deeds, not enjoy
sexual love in his bed? At times we glimpse in Shakespeare's writings an excited dynamic directed in fear and hatred against the
libidinal object and, we may suspect from psychoanalytical theory,
in projection against his own female element and its libidinal proclivities. At the unconscious level, Shakespeare was afraid of the
hungry woman in himself—of the witch in himself and her ability
to corrupt the individual's relationship with the world. I have suggested that this was a common unconscious theme of the time, in
the atmosphere of disillusionment at the end of Elizabeth's reign
and at the beginning of James's corrupt reign.

The Insights Applied: Shakespeare's Anguish Over Woman

But Shakespeare's plays are distinguished from Jacobean tragedy and the usual revenge play by one important characteristic: despite lapses, he did not lose hope in human nature; he did not lose hope in the future. There can be no doubt of the existential struggles Shakespeare went through to achieve this positive view of human life. We may examine this in terms of the symbolism of the late plays and the female element in them. There is an astonishing purity in the significant women of these plays, but this is no aging man's sentimentality. These women survive despite the direct threats and menacing forces of evil. There is sometimes irony in the presentation of their response ("Oh brave new world") but no bitterness; instead, there is a tender admiration for the courage of new generations (as expressed in the name Miranda).

⭑ These women symbolize the female element. In the plays in which there are agonizing dealings with time, they suffer dreadful circumstances: they are saved from rape; captured by pirates; lost at sea; thrown into the sea in barrels; become fugitives in war; are wrongfully condemned; and are continually faced with treachery, evil, and death. They are often lost and then refound. But when they are tested in the ultimate tests of love, devotion, and integrity, they triumph and are blessed. We may say that they represent the ultimate triumph of Shakespeare's faith in female-element 'being', which is integral to a belief in the future. Like Prospero, Shakespeare witnesses with gratitude their creative flowering in love (in Melanie Klein's sense, of taking joy in the achievements of others who come after you). This creative generosity, of being able to let others go into their new future while blessing them, is the harvest Shakespeare won through the immense travail of his poetic labor throughout his life.

One of the most moving scenes in Shakespeare is the one between the king and his long-lost daughter Marina, in *Pericles Prince of Tyre*. The play itself has the air of having been worked on by hands other than Shakespeare's, but it has at times the masquelike quality of his later plays. As with *The Tempest*, *The Winter's Tale*, and *Cymbeline*, a certain stylized distance is created; and we are obliged to suspend our disbelief more willingly than we are, for instance, with the great tragedies.

Marina in *Pericles*: Hope and Continuity

But Shakespeare tries our disbelief in other ways. Is it possible that a girl like Marina could resist exploration, as she does in the brothel in Mytilene? We can easily believe that the governor of the country, Lysimachus, would set foot in a brothel, asking for virgins ("have you that a man may deal withal and defy the surgeon?"). But can we believe he would be resisted successfully by a young virgin, in the name of human values? Of course, we have to be very careful how we answer that question, for it is testing our capacity to trust in human goodness. How does anyone respond to this princess's forthright tone?

MARINA:
If you were born to honor, show it now;
If put upon you, make the judgment good
That thought you worthy of it.

Lysimachus, in response to Marina's tone, rapidly adopts one of true humanity:

Had I brought hither a corrupted mind,
Thy speech had altered it.

And Marina speaks with the authority of Shakespeare's secure sense of what corruption is. Lysimachus goes away "cold as a snowball; saying his prayers too." But Marina also defeats the brothel keeper who threatens her virginity, and the language here has all the force of Shakespeare's moral antipathy to the human being who corrupts another:

Thou holds't a place for which the painèd'st fiend
Of hell would not in reputation change
Thou art the damnèd doorkeeper to every
Cloistrel that comes enquiring for his Tib
To the choleric fisting of every rogue
Thy ear is liable. Thy food is such
As hath been belched on by infected lungs.

With a touch of Falstaff, Boult answers, like every brothel keeper, that it is only a way of making a living. Would she have him go to

193

the wars where a man may serve seven years, lose a leg, and have
not enough money in the end to buy himself a wooden spoon?

MARINA:
Do anything but this thou doest. Empty
Old receptacles, or common shores, of filth;
Serve by indenture to the common hangman.

What is enacted in these scenes is the power of a consciousness
that has exceptional integrity to penetrate, through the power of
language, to any soul. In Marina, Shakespeare embodies his own
poetic quest for truth and values. Ironically, when Pericles's ship
sails in, the governor Lysimachus, whom we have just seen resisted
by Marina in the brothel, suggests that this same girl might be the
one who could relieve the king in his speechless misery of bereavement.

We may, I believe, interpret this balletic plot thus: Shakespeare
is saying that his own soul, like that of Pericles, has lost its hold on
life because of the death of the female element. Both the mother
female element and the daughter female element are involved—
that is, belief in the woman of now, of maturity, and the woman of
the future. The daughter female element is threatened with the
deepest degradation and so is tested to the ultimate. The test of the
daughter female element is also a test of Shakespeare's own belief
in the creative future of human beings and his faith in humanity. If
only that daughter female element could speak to his dumb soul. If
only they could *find* one another, he could regain joy in life and
hope. A new dimension to his art is needed, and in the later plays it
is music. Music is important in *Pericles* (as it is in *The Tempest* and
at the revival of Hermione in *The Winter's Tale*) because music
speaks—again, in a feminine way—directly to the soul, to 'being.'

One of the great achievements of Shakespeare's late finding of
hope for humanity is in his recognition of the suffering endured by
the young and his sense of a common perplexity. In the anguish
Shakespeare feels about the human condition, he recognizes the
common predicament in life—such as even the innocent girl en-

dures because she is human. It is this that provides an antidote to sentimentality.[1]

Marina begins by saying to Pericles:

> She speaks,
> My Lord, that, may be, hath endured a grief
> Might equal yours, if both were justly weighed.

She speaks of her own feminine intuition that is prompting her:

> But there is something glows upon my cheek,
> And whispers in mine ear, 'Go not till he speak.'

Marina's care for her estranged and dumb father is a woman's care, as for a child. As we watch, this is deeply moving. Marina and Pericles discuss parentage and similarities of face and figure. What is aroused in us in this exchange is a reminiscence of creative reflection—that is, gazing into the mother's face with the hope of being seen. Certainly, the scene explores the mystery by which we know a face and know a person in his or her uniqueness.

I have suggested that in these later plays Shakespeare is embracing his female element. After some tentative discussion of the truth of Marina's predicament, Pericles says:

> Tell thy story.
> If thine considered prove the thousand part
> Of my endurance, thou art a man, and I
> Have suffered like a girl. Yet thou dost look
> Like Patience gazing on kings' graves and smiling
> Extremity out of act.

The language is clearly Shakespeare's and reflects his late intensity. There is a clear reference to male and female elements, and Pericles is identifying deeply with his daughter. What is achieved by the identification, or sympathy, is that sense I have spoken of earlier, of a generous appreciation of what the young, the representatives of the next generation, can suffer. This recognition helps overcome Shakespeare's dreadful sense of time ("calumnious time") and enables him to achieve that generosity and gladness that provides the escape from time into hope for the future. Thus, we have the beautiful image of the bereaved king seeing his daughter as Patience. She is a creature capable of studying the graves of kings who have fallen to time in the long historical perspective; and yet, she does not become bitter nor obsessed with extreme severity and duress. She is able to put extremity out of countenance and to substitute for bitterness the smile of pity and acceptance.

Dramatically, the progress of the revelation is accomplished beautifully, and I can never read it without tears coming into my eyes. Yet why the scene should be so moving is ineffable. Perhaps it is because the scene is so "impossible": the daughter believed to be dead, entombed, and mourned for but really exposed to degradation and yet triumphing over it, now revealing herself and proving herself the daughter restored, to such joy that Pericles asks to be given a physical pain to relieve the unbearable torrent of joy that flows through him, in case they kill him:

> O Helicanus, strike me, honoured sir,
> Give me a gash, put me to present pain
> Lest this great sea of joys rushing upon me
> O'erbear the shores of my mortality
> And drown me with their sweetness.

I suppose our response is due to a sense that only very rarely, if ever, in life are impossible hopes realized, particularly hopes for those who are lost or dead. Pericles is so mad with joy that he hears the music of the spheres and then falls into a shocked slumber, in which he witnesses a vision of Diana, "Goddess Argentine," who in a masquelike way celebrates chastity. After all this, the reconciliation between the mother (who is recovered after being thrown overboard in a barrel) with the king is something of an anticlimax.

The plot is not believable; yet, the play is so moving because we interpret it symbolically as the enactment of a rediscovery of something that has been lost. The sea, of course, is important; thus, it is significant that Pericles's daughter is called Marina. The sea symbolizes that mysterious creative power that is woman. It is significant that both women rise again out of the sea; they are both the *Stella Maris*.

Marina in *Pericles*: Hope and Continuity

What is reborn from the sea is hope for the future of life. The pain and joy we experience as we respond to this play—without knowing why—is the pain and joy Shakespeare experienced as he fought and struggled to hold onto his hope for mankind and to "give" mankind its future—by developing a positive attitude to the daughter figure, the future-creating potentiality in himself, his daughter female element.

Identification with this struggle and the symbolism by which it was achieved generated one of T. S. Eliot's greatest poems, "Marina."[2]
The clue to the meaning of Eliot's poem is in the lines

> This form, this face, this life
> Living to live in a world of time beyond me; let me
> Resign my life for this life, my speech for that unspoken,
> The awakened, lips parted, the hope, the new ships.

Here we must talk about the achievements of gratitude, which is a kind of contented giving out and allowing there to be continuity of life—accepting our own death. The continuity will be achieved by others; thus, the achievement of a belief in the future and hope for the future requires the acceptance of our own death. Only if we can feel sufficient confidence in human nature at large can we achieve gratitude in this sense; and this, in turn, requires a triumph over envy (as Melanie Klein [1957] made clear)—for envy is the feeling of wanting to destroy or take away from others satisfactions and achievements that one feels one has not had oneself. Accepting one's mortality is bound up with achieving a feeling that one has had one's share of the satisfactions of life, including the satisfaction of the sense of meaning. Envy (as in Mahler's Ninth Symphony) brings the threat of the collapse of all meaning, and envy leads to hate. Love and gratitude are intertwined in that they are an escape from envy and a means toward meaning. Thus,

> Living to live in a world of time beyond me

means that the face of Marina speaks of continuity, of life going on in the time beyond the protagonist's death. The desire is to move beyond Pericles's dumb, grief-stricken, sterile, and petrified condition to resign that life, in outgoing gratitude, for the life embodied in her. Marina's female-element capacity for 'being' is mysterious and so "unspoken." It is expressed in those parted lips, a lovely image of youthful potential. Perhaps here we feel the voice of Eliot, struggling with "speech" and cherishing the land of hope symbolized by Marina, which is all hope for developments as yet unspoken (antepredicative):

The awakened, lips parted, the hope, the new ships.

—the line is all hope.

Marina feels some warmth on her cheek and a voice instructing her. In Eliot's "Marina," we feel he is responding to a call from some mysterious female prompting. (There is no suggestion that this is a hint from a spiritual world like the hints in the "Four Quartets," though the voice of the bird is important in both.)

And woodthrush calling through the fog

Although the voice speaking is presumably that of a protagonist —Pericles—there seems little doubt that the voice speaking is lost (like Eliot in "The Waste Land" among rocks, on strange shores, in a fog *("Quis hic locus, quae regio, quae mundi plaga?")*.[3] The "images" that "return" seem to come from those memories of childhood that are so important as a sign of renewal in the "Four Quartets":

Whispers and small laughter between leaves and hurrying
feet
Under sleep, where all the waters meet.

This later realm is surely the unconscious or, perhaps, the springs of 'being'. There are memories of those ecstatic childhood moments (also recorded in "Cape Ann" and the other New England poems). Whereas in the "Four Quartets" the search is for another world "behind" this world, to which spiritual authority defer, in "Marina" the "face" that speaks of love and hope is within:

I made this, I have forgotten
And remember.

. . . .
Made this unknowing, half conscious, unknown, my own.

In one sense, "this" is the boat in which the protagonist, Pericles, has set out to look for his lost daughter; but he cannot have made this "unknowing" or "unknown." In another sense, it is "this form, this face, this life" that he has "made" and that is "my own." "Marina" is a narcissistic poem. Yet, the quest is not locked in narcissism, for something is discovered. There is a recognition of a dynamic and a vision that is integral to the life world.

What is this face, less clear and clearer
The pulse in the arm, less strong and stronger—
Given or lent? more distant than stars and nearer than the eye

These lines surely point to the enigmatic perplexity of the female-element being within oneself. They point to the great mystery, which escapes one's grasp. It is both clear and not clear, as familiar as one's pulse, both stronger and less strong, and unfindable either as a gift or as something for which one is a temporary custodian. This sense of a love object both being known and part of one, and yet a distant mystery of 'being' in its own right, is conveyed powerfully in *Pericles*.

By contrast, the sought reality of love, the assurances of the senses and of bodily animal existence belong to death:

Those who sharpen the tooth of the dog, meaning
Death
Those who glitter with the glory of the hummingbird, meaning
Death

Hate is death. The attachment to the outer glories of the world is death.

Those who sit in the stye of contentment . . .

Mere comfort and satisfaction are death.

Those who suffer the ecstasy of the animals . . .

199

Mere bodily ecstasy is death. (Perhaps here we hear the echo of the brothel scenes.) All these once seemingly substantial worldly engagements only exacerbate mortality and

> Are become unsubstantial, reduced by a wind,
> A breath of pine, and the woodsong fog
> By this grace dissolved in place

They are dissolved by the urgent need to find love and meaning, which are found through the discovery of the lost female element; and in embracing the female element, one embraces continuity and hope. It is the symbolization of this primary quest that makes Eliot's "Marina" such a beautiful poem.

CHAPTER 10

Cymbeline

As a play *Cymbeline* creaks. Clearly, it was a botched-up job be-tween several playwrights. However, there are moments in the play that are clearly Shakespeare's, and there are moments related to his deeper themes—not least about woman.

We can make some sense of the play by suggesting that it has to do with something like this: reparation and continuity depend upon establishing a confidence that the dissociations caused by jealousy can be overcome (thus yielding a confidence that the undermining of an adequate grasp of appearance and reality can be overcome).

The crucial theme of the play where we are concerned is the theme relating to Posthumus's departure abroad, Imogen's reaction, and Iachimo's treachery. In the strange language Imogen uses to tell of her husband moving away from her sight, we have, perhaps, early on in the play an echo of the theme of "calumnious time" from *Troilus and Cressida*:

I would have broke mine eyestrings, cracked them but
To look upon him till the diminution
Of space had pointed him sharp as my needle;

Nay, followed him till he had melted from
The smallness of a gnat to air, and then
Have turned mine eye and wept.

The intensity of physical attention here evokes the need to attend
to an appearance—to hold the loved one in one's eye—and the
painfulness of such an attempt.

The problem is to hold one's trust to a unique being. Posthumus's
fatal error is to put a material price on such trust. Iachimo wisely
says, "If you buy ladies' flesh at a million a dram, you cannot
preserve it from tainting." To wager on one's love (as Lear found)
is corrupt and evil.

Act I, scene 6, contains some lines that have Shakespeare's characteristic ring and which express his kind of intense moral feelings
on matters of trust and sexuality. Iachimo has come to Imogen
bearing expressions of trust and affection and her husband's com-
mendation of himself. But he is also there to win his wager, that he
can seduce Imogen. When he sees her, however, he is deeply disturbed and expresses his own dread of the effects of lust. First he
expresses incredulity—that men cannot distinguish between good
and evil even though the distinction should be plain enough:

What, are men mad? Hath nature given them eyes
To see this vaulted arch and the rich crop
Of sea and land, which can distinguish 'twixt
The fiery orbs above and the twinned stones
Upon the unnumbered beach? and can we not
Partition make with spectacles so precious
'Twixt fair and foul?

Although Iachimo is a participant and virtually causes the action
of the play, he surely speaks here chorically. We may even say that
Iachimo is a mouthpiece for Shakespeare: "What, are men mad?"
The lines have dramatic immediacy because they convey the
impression that Iachimo is overcome by the beauty and modest
bearing of Imogen. But they go far beyond this, raising questions of
men's perception of the world. If men are capable of perceiving the
rich beauty of the world, of distinguishing between the sun and

moon, and are even capable of picking out two similar stones among the "unnumbered" millions on a beach, surely they can see the difference between this wife and the general run of women?

Again, there is a contrast drawn between man who is capable of reason and godlike apprehensions and the animal nature to which he belongs. The incapacity to distinguish beauty and goodness in his world that man sometimes reveals cannot be a fault in the (animal) eye, for apes and monkeys would be able to distinguish. "Idiots" would be "wisely definite" in this case, Iachimo says. Nor can the problem be a matter of the appetite. Here, Shakespeare expresses his disturbance about the subject of the (animal) oral voraciousness that always seemed to him to threaten values and meaning:

nor i' th' appetite—
Sluttery, to such neat excellence opposed,
Should make desire vomit emptiness,
Not so allured to feed.

In contemporary terms, we would say that Shakespeare is exploring the problem of our relationship to the ideal object and the libidinal object. When we see the ideal alongside the libidinal, we ought to find that desire itself recoils and generates a physical revulsion—throwing up, as it were, a vacancy, a deprivation of all bodily impulse rather than an attraction to feed on the object. But the violence beneath the surface of this language indicates again the association in Shakespeare's mind between woman and nothingness. In his anguished perplexity over appearance and reality, Shakespeare explores the area of experience every human being has had—of having the breast presented at a certain moment when there was, in the baby, an intense vision that needed to be "filled in," so that the baby's creation of the world and the reality of the world met. Problems of the ideal and the libidinal derive from that primitive experience of the mother, as do many sexual problems.

What Shakespeare is rendering here is the torment of a man who, for a monetary wager, has committed himself to an act of lust. Thus, Iachimo meets Imogen with a hungry eye. But what he meets is admirable beauty, modesty, loyalty and goodness—an ideal vision rather than a libidinal object. The contrast threatens him with nothingness, with losing the human capacity to value. He feels there should be in him a physical revulsion, which will make his hunger as nothing. But the conflict, where there should be harmonious meeting, also threatens to destroy Iachimo's world, as, indeed, it nearly does destroy Imogen's. In the next few lines, we have one of those extravagant, surrealistic outbursts that arise from some deep anguish in Shakespeare:

IACHIMO:
                    The cloyèd will—
That satiate yet unsatisfied desire, that tub
Both filled and running—ravening first the lamb,
Longs after for the garbage.

The psychology here is profound. The thought of defiling (to "sluttery") the magnificent Imogen ought (Iachimo has said) to make his desire throw up emptiness, to have paralyzed his lust. Instead, the evil impulse allures. Thus, Iachimo with gloom begins to contemplate the outcome; in his words he echoes Shakespeare's sonnet on lust. When the will that impels him is "cloyèd" (that is, satisfied in its craving), it will impel him, having butchered the lamb, to seek for fouler satisfactions. Again, we have an association between woman and death; the underlying metaphor is the abattoir. A man's will that has satisfied itself in lust feels even more hungry, like a tub in the butcher's shed that is filled with blood and is running over. Having eaten the lamb, he longs to be filled with the ordures of the shambles.

Contemplating in imagination the assault on Imogen, then, Shakespeare evidently had powerful unconscious fantasies. They may be associated with infant fantasies of "emptying" the breast. The voracious will of dissociated lust (dissociated by the wager, which reduces Imogen to an object) is, in light of these fantasies, bloodthirsty and finds its satisfaction (as does the consumer of pornography) in fantasies of slaughtering, penetrating bodies, spilling their blood, and taking the filth out of them. There is a preoccupation with "inner contents," and, as we have seen, Shakespeare often reveals that he is disquieted by the feeling that woman's insides are filthy.

Yet, Iachimo presumes that he will long for filthier violations if he is successful in violating Imogen. (In real life, of course, such fantasies are sometimes acted out in violent sexual crimes.) If we recall Ann Belford Ulanov's previously discussed analysis, Iachimo is dwelling on the attributes of the witch, who is bloodthirsty, who hungers for garbage, and so on.

Alas, *Cymbeline* offers little by way of solution to the intense emotions aroused. The lovely song "Fear no more the heat o' th' sun" is a gem, which seems to convey a sense of relief in the thought that in death one may be beyond the torments of lust and cruelty and beyond harm. The cumbersome plot allows little insight, though there is a moment, in act 2 scene 4, in which Shakespeare touches upon male projection. Posthumous, whose fault it is that any question of his wife's disloyalty should arise and who is deceived by Iachimo, berates all women and even declares that all the bad qualities in man derive from woman:

> Could I find out
> The woman's part in me! For there's no motion
> That tends to vice in man but I affirm
> It is the woman's part. Be it lying, note it,
> The woman's; flattering, hers; deceiving, hers;
> Lust and rank thoughts, hers, hers; revenges, hers;
> Ambitions, covetings, change of prides, disdain,
> Nice longings, slanders, mutability,
> All faults that man may name, nay, that hell knows,
> Why, hers, in part or all, but rather all.
> For even to vice
> They are not constant, but are changing still
> One vice but of a minute old for one
> Not half so old as that. I'll write against them,
> Detest them, curse them.

The Insights Applied: Shakespeare's Anguish Over Woman

Shakespeare, who had such problems with his own female element, here shows a man who is recognized by the audience as one who has wronged woman and abused his wife. Posthumus projects his own weaknesses over woman, rejects his own female element, and becomes misogynist, when he should look, instead, into his own soul for the faults.

CHAPTER 11

Measure for Measure
and Female Experience

Measure for Measure is a perplexing play. In one sense, we may take the title to mean "let the punishment fit the crime." The Duke says:

'An Angelo for Claudio, death for death!'
Haste still pays haste, and leisure answers leisure,
Like doth quit like, and Measure still for Measure.

Yet, the tenor of the play is quite different. It commends mercy to us, and in the end no one suffers a severe penalty for his offence. There is only one death in the play—that of Ragozine, a condemned pirate. And there is only one act of sexual communion, between Angelo and his betrothed, Mariana, whom he supposes to be Isabella. This is a histrionic trick and so, too, are many things in the play—stays of execution, disguises, and substitutions. In this, there is an extraordinary discrepancy between the grave seriousness of the dramatic poem and the "play" that the drama is.

The play element of the play centers on the Duke. Even at the end, knowing that Claudio is not dead, he plays with Isabella:

207

> O most kind maid,
> It was the swift celerity of his death,
> Which I did think with slower foot came on,
> That brained my purpose.

On her part, Isabella simply falls in with the Duke's advice to be comforted:

> That life is better life past fearing death,
> Than that which lives to fear. Make it your comfort,
> So happy is your brother.
>
> ISABELLA:
> I do, my lord.

The playfulness of the Duke is a "given" in the play, which we must take. It is like the playfulness of Prospero, and both are personas with whom the poet himself identifies closely. The Duke is a testing figure, commanding and controlling events; and he has a divine quality. In trying to understand the play, we must simply accept Shakespeare's belief in, and endorsement of, this quality of divine right in a ruler. When this is revealed, there is no gainsaying it.

> ANGELO:
> O my dread lord,
> I should be guiltier than my guiltiness
> To think I can be undiscernible,
> When I perceive your grace, like power divine,
> Hath looked upon my passes.

Throughout the play there is a "Thou-God-seest-me" quality about the Duke's omnipresence and all-awareness, and the analogy with the Divine witness should be clear.

This is one quality of the play that belongs to Shakespeare's time —the part religion played in medieval and Renaissance life and to Shakespeare's own beliefs. The other question to be borne in mind is that of fornication as a sin.

We tend to judge questions of sexual conduct in humanistic terms; for example, as to whether a person feels his or her integrity to be infringed upon by seduction or rape. *Measure for Measure* cannot be understood unless we bear in mind the religious—that is, medieval Catholic—belief in an actual purgatory, an actual hell, and the condemnation of fornication as a sin that could affect one's consignation to purgatory and hell. This is manifest in Claudio's reflection on being executed for the sin of fornication:

> and the delighted spirit
> To bathe in fiery floods. . . .

And those here:

> or to be worse than worst
> Of those that lawless and incertain thought
> Imagine howling!

—those are the damned. It could be that when one was dead, because of one's disobedience of the Ten Commandments, one could be in a worse state than the worst of the damned. This is the dreadful context in which Shakespeare looks at human sexuality, frailty, treachery, and lust, as well as in the realistic, humanistic perspective of, for instance, the world of Falstaff.

At the other extreme, there is the secular, humanistic view:

MISTRESS OVERDONE:
Well, what has he done?
POMPEY:
A woman.
MISTRESS OVERDONE:
But what's his offence?

The reply is indicative: "Groping for trouts in a peculiar river." That is, the man's offence is only like a kind of poaching, and this is why there is such a public fuss about it. Lust and sex come up against the organization of society, heirdom, rights, property, and inheritance.

Thus, there must be laws in society governing sexual conduct. The questions then arise: On what are these laws to be based? How are they to be applied? Who shall implement them? And here we find the great difference between Christian civilization and the civilizations of the Old Testament or of today's Islam. In the Duke's Vienna, more than anywhere, notice must be tempered with mercy: "Let him who is without sin cast the first stone." Or

> man, proud man,
> Dressed in a little brief authority,
> Most ignorant of what he's most assured—
> His glassy essence—like an angry ape
> Plays such fantastic tricks before high heaven
> As makes the angels weep.

Over these issues there are two strands of the play: the main figures enact the question of the values—rooted in religious belief —*by which man can live* despite his own frailty; while the so-called low-life characters enact how man actually behaves, admitting that frailty in a Chaucerian humanistic way.

There is a tension between these attitudes to morality as Shakespeare explores human sexual experience. We would be wrong to take either as conclusive or as capable of being summed up in a maxim or precept. The humanistic strand does not imply that it is impossible for man to be governed by values or by laws. The "higher" moral strand does not conjoin us to live a pure life by religious precept or simply by "pure" mercy and forgiveness. The play seems to urge that a man must try to be loyal to high values, despite the fact that at times his "blood" will "muster" to his heart and defy his intelligence, his reason, religious injunction, and even the threat of hell fire; and to ponder these matters, compassion and realism are both necessary.

Looking at Shakespeare's play from the point of view of present-day philosophical anthropology, we can see, at the one pole, meaning; at the other, what may be called the "rebellion of the codpiece" —and this means death. Although *Measure for Measure* is a comedy, it is, in fact, a gruesome play in which death is continually invoked and is as tangible as Ragozine's head.

The symbolic forum or context where meaning and death meet is the body. The arena for the poetic drama is the human body, with all its sexual proclivities. And what the body threatens in rebellion

is the failure of meaning, of that gravity that distinguishes man. At
his most tempted moment, Angelo says:

> yea, my gravity,
> Wherein, let no man hear me, I take pride,
> Could I, with boot, change for an idle plume
> Which the air beats for vain.

Here we are close to Shakespeare's own deepest dread, which we
find in his sonnets, in *King Lear*, and elsewhere, of the possibility
that the reality sense, and the sense of meaning is bound up with it,
may collapse because relationship itself has broken down—not least
because of a collapse of trust. This trust is bound up with the
reflection in the 'other's' face, and its failure is marked by the song

> Take, O take those lips away,
>   That so sweetly were forsworn;
> And those eyes, the break of day,
>   Lights that do mislead the morn;
> But my kisses bring again, bring again,
> Seals of love, but sealed in vain, sealed in vain.

These lines echo the line "Set me as a seal upon thy heart" from
The Song of Songs, and they are echoed throughout the works of
Shakespeare, which seem to suggest some terrible experience of
being betrayed by a face. See, for example, these lines from *Macbeth*: ("There is no art / To find the mind's construction in the
face.") It is significant here that the only sexual act takes place in
the dark; and the woman is supposed to be the novitiate Isabella, a
virgin, but she is actually the man's intended wife, though he does
not know it. Analyzing the situation in terms of object-relations
psychology, we can perhaps suggest that Angelo is himself the split-
off "pure" self but one whose other libidinal self bursts out. This
other self seeks to exert his will as lust on the ideal split-off woman,
Isabella the novitiate. In the event, he has sexual congress with his
wife: "He is your husband on a pre-contract." That this is a "play"
by which Shakespeare is working out, in creative fantasy form, the
problem of sexual relationship between man and woman may be
suggested by the Duke's lines:

> O place and greatness, millions of false eyes
> Are struck upon thee; volumes of report
> Run with these false, and most contrarious quest
> Upon thy doings; thousand escapes of wit
> Make thee the father of their idle dream,
> And rack thee in their fancies.

Human beings at large require myths, this seems to say, and "great ones" must necessarily enact these myths, for the people to relate to one another and discuss. But why "false eyes"? Is it that the observation of the people threatens to falsify the choices and acts of the great ones? Or do they falsify these afterward, in "report"?

Measure for Measure is perhaps Shakespeare's most serious comment on sexual morality in relation to the make-up of men and women and between religious belief and humanistic values. How does the play—its "upshot"—appear in light of phenomenological insights into the nature of woman and human sexuality?

A great deal of the play is about justice; and with much of it we can easily, if uncomfortably, concur. Justice, applied too coldly and ruthlessly, can be cruel; sexual lapses are excusable if we remember our own perplexities ("Judge not that ye be not judged"). Anyone who sets himself up as a pure superjudge may be projecting over others something he fears in himself: "most ignorant of what he's most assured." And we recognize our own weaknesses in Angelo's wicked assault on Isabella's virtue; our cowardice in Claudio's misery that Isabella will not trade her body for his life; and our disillusionment in Isabella when Claudio upbraids her for it. We admire the Duke's speech on the emphemeral qualities of death, but we do not give assent to it. (We would like Falstaff's comment on it.)

> Be absolute for death: either death or life
> Shall thereby be the sweeter. Reason this with life:
> If I do lose thee, I do lose a thing
> That none but fools would keep.
>
> · · · · · · · · · · · · · · ·
>
>   Thou hast nor youth nor age,
> But as it were an after-dinner's sleep,
> Dreaming on both.

As we listen to these lines, we are aware that the Duke is offering consolation. He is doing the best he can to produce arguments in favor of detaching oneself from life, letting life go. This is how we ought to feel about attachment to life. Throughout the play, the Duke stands for this kind of philosophical detachment. He may even seem to us to be like Prospero, in the role of the artist trying to plumb the realities of existence to the depths—trying this approach, trying that. There are today some producers and critics who believe that the Duke is a sinister figure who manipulates events to such an extent that he actually creates the problems that arise. They say he must have known that Angelo was emotionally corrupt and so irresponsibly risks the lives of his subjects. But this, surely, is to reject the "given" of the play: without the Duke's play with the situation, we would have no play. He has, it is true, neglected the government of the state in the sphere of morality, but then it can be surely assumed that he wishes to withdraw and observe, in order to take up this problem with realism, having learned more about it from observation. Thus, in one sense, the Duke is an agent in a "felt" philosophical dialogue. The underlying questions are whether moral lapses deserve death, what kind of punishment death is, and what happens after death in eternal punishment for sins of the flesh. There is a conflict between the approach of the Old Testament and the New, of "judge not that ye be not judged." What emerges is a humanistic view of life, of its value, and of its sanctity through the developing sensitivity of the open, enquiring mind. There is a new sense of vulnerability behind such lines as

> Thou 'rt by no means valiant,
> For thou dost fear the soft and tender fork
> Of a poor worm.

and

> The sense of death is most in apprehension,
> And the poor beetle that we tread upon
> In corporal sufferance finds a pang as great
> As when a giant dies.

The Duke's omnipresent participation in the play resembles the role of Pierre Bezuhov in Tolstoy's *War and Peace* (as when Tolstoy renders the sympathetic observation Pierre makes of the ghastly events under the French occupation of Moscow, when civilians are shot under suspicion of being incendiaries). There is in *Measure for Measure* a new awareness of the intense suffering of men, in the face of death and in dying itself—with the dread of the afterlife that is involved. Since sexual fornication is a deadly sin, the question is (as in Isabella's dialogue with her brother) how does firm morality about sexual crime appear in the context of physical dread and the pain of death. Is the sexual lapse, even violation, really a fate worse than death?

What is opened is a new perspective of a humanistic kind, and one can feel Shakespeare's involvement in the problems he approaches in the texture of Claudio's lines:

> Ay, but to die, and go we know not where,
> To lie in cold obstruction and to rot,
> This sensible warm motion to become
> A kneaded clod; and the delighted spirit
> To bathe in fiery floods, or to reside
> In thrilling region of thick-ribbèd ice,
> To be imprisoned in the viewless winds
> And blown with restless violence round about
> The pendent world; or to be worse than worst
> Of those that lawless and incertain thought
> Imagine howling, 'tis too horrible.

It is the vigor of the words evoking physical vitality that make the lines so terrible. The word "obstruction" against "sensible" and "warm motion" conveys a sense of paralysis, even of being buried alive. The same is true of "kneaded clod," since "kneaded" suggests the active work of baker or cook, while the "clod" turns the bread mixture into clay, just as the "warm motion" is turned into "cold" obstruction and into "rot." We feel the glow of being alive, striving against the inert and warmthless quality of dead flesh. The very consonantal quality of the language makes us feel the contrast in our lips: "sensible warm motion" becomes "kneaded clod." The word "delighted" has perhaps changed in its meaning; it meant endowed with delight or affording delight. Is the spirit delighted because it is freed from the body? Or is one of the ambiguities here that the spirit is delivered from the body and so lightened by its liberation? Certainly, it sounds as if the spirit leaps in joy from the cold rotten body but then finds itself plunging into the fiery floods of purgatory, or imprisoned in ice. There are both religious beliefs behind the contemplation—of purgatory and hell—but also humanistic doubts, which are "worse than worst of those that lawless and incertain thoughts / Imagine." Perhaps the freed spirit will find itself merely blown into the winds? The horror is that even as the dying individual feels the body's warm motion being obstructed and while he fears to become a mere trodden lump of clay, the spirit— which he hopes may live on—may find itself in even worse physical torment, trying to find a niche in ice that gathers in thick, ribbed glacial forms, imprisoned or blown in mysterious regions where the spirit's existence seems more fortuitous and abandoned than was the situation of the living man. Here, there is no certainty of being in the hands of God or of being able to deserve the grace of Christ. Claudio's thoughts *are* lawless and uncertain; and so they seem to us closer to the kind of thoughts we have, in a humanistic era, about extinction. Thus, the desire to continue living seems to us, as to Hamlet, much more to be preferred to the acceptance of a fatal punishment. What then of absolute honor?

The problem becomes even more complex now that we find it hard to settle on any solution. Of course, we can see that in the face of Angelo's deeply corrupt treachery to chastity, justice, and human values, there could be no answer in Isabella's giving herself to him. Such a man, caught in the toils of his own evil, would, from a pragmatic point of view, almost certainly put Claudio, if not the woman, to death in the attempt to conceal his sin. But as Claudio begs Isabella to give in to her seducer, her sacrifice does seem lesser, set against the fatal horror that Claudio faces. Her protestations about her honor and her cold masochistic emphases on her chastity seem complementary to Angelo's posture of being a man of "snow broth," and now she seems cold-blooded and even cruel.

We feel confused and certainly cannot easily find a proper solution, while in the meantime concepts, such as honor, have come under question. And beneath the whole drama is that perplexing, eternal question—given man's capacity for lustfulness, perversity, and moral inversion and because of his sexual animal qualities, how can we possibly find anything upon which to rely in human affairs? We are not altogether sympathetic to Isabella when she defies her brother:

> Wilt thou be made a man out of my vice?

And when she cries

> Die, perish. Might but my bending down
> Reprieve thee from thy fate, it should proceed.

she is as inhumanly unbending as Angelo is in his cold legality. Like him, perhaps, there is some human element in herself that she is afraid of—perhaps her own lust?

Our response is mollified, of course, by the knowledge that it is all play. The Duke is present at all times and we know from his exchange with Friar Thomas that he has long-term motives:

> Moe reasons for this action
> At our more leisure shall I render you;
> Only this one: Lord Angelo is precise,
> Stands at a guard with envy; scarce confesses
> That his blood flows, or that his appetite
> Is more to bread than stone.

We know that the Duke is manipulating the action to prove that Angelo is only human and that justice must not be above humanity. Only if we do not forget ourselves can we rule ourselves well.

Our problems, I believe, begin when the Duke hears about Angelo's assault on Isabella, and develops his elaborate plot to put Mariana in Isabella's place and to urge Isabella to go to Angelo at the moated grange and to promise to give herself to him. The lame nature of this plot is indicated surely by Isabella's immediate concurrence ("The image of it gives me content already. . . . I thank you for this comfort").

Questions immediately spring into our minds. If the Duke knew

216

that Angelo had treated Mariana so badly, was it not culpable of him to trust him to reign in his absence? Although she is speaking to a friar, surely Isabella would raise some difficulties: She wouldn't lift a finger to save her brother now; Angelo might assault her on the spot; might it not be another wrong to Mariana? Are the affairs of a woman slighted like that put right by a clandestine deceit? And wouldn't Mariana and Angelo hate one another for the rest of their lives? (I think the members of the *Scrutiny* movement failed seriously to ask these questions because they failed to find woman as she really is and tended to accept male solutions.)

In the play, we suffer agonies over Claudio and the intolerant justice meeted out to him. We do not feel so sympathetic toward Isabella and are inclined to say she is too absolute in refusing to save Claudio's life. Thus, we are relieved when the cunning solution comes up. However, examined in the light of any real concern for human value, the solution is false. It is no solution because it demands such complex inauthenticity all round. The sexual act will be an act of lust, whether the participants are married or not. There will be no authenticity because neither is giving themselves to the other in joy and love—in the meeting of unique beings. Mariana will be in dread of being found out and assaulted. In being taken for another woman, she is taken as second best bed; while Angelo, supposing he is having Isabella, holds her in contempt because he is determined Claudio shall die anyway. It is impossible to imagine a more horrible sexual meeting, in which are annihilated all the values and meanings that Shakespeare strove to uphold in the sphere of sex. The Duke's chirpy chorus

O, what man may in him hide
Though angel on the outward side!

does not hide the lameness of this pantomine nor does the scene of Mariana's sad loneliness. Even after the act, Mariana is to say, " 'Remember now my brother.' " Thus, she maintains a disguise in which she trades her lust for Claudio's life, as Isabella has so virtuously refused to do.

Of course, as the Duke might have anticipated, Angelo sends instructions for Claudio to be executed forthwith. There follows much business with heads, in an ironic passage in which Barnardine proves too drunk to be beheaded. The denouement is complicated by the constant interjections of Lucio, who is each time suppressed by the Duke. All seems devised to distract attention from the impossibility of what occurs.

Isabella is disbelieved and taken off to prison. Mariana confronts Angelo:

> But Tuesday night last gone in 's garden-house
> He knew me as a wife. As this is true,
> Let me in safety raise me from my knees
> Or else forever be confixèd here
> A marble monument.

Just previous to this she says:

> this is the body
> That took away the match from Isabel,
> And did supply thee at thy garden-house
> In her imagined person.

We may compare this moment of revelation with the scene between Pericles and his daughter or between Lear and Cordelia in prison. There is a strange detachment and coldness—a failure of imagination. There is something cold about the word "supply" (satisfy the desires of).[1] It is a mechanical word, with echoes of its origins in the Latin *supplere* (fill). It is a word rather like those breeders use, such as *cover* or *service*.

If we compare Mariana with any male character who is deeply sensitive to his own predicament (such as Hamlet), we will note that she says nothing about the inauthenticity of her situation in taking away the "match" from Isabella by counterfeit means. ("Match" being another cold word: the verb being to procure as a match.) Suppose Hamlet had gone to a woman in disguise in such a way—what a tormented soliloquy we would have had!

Mariana asks only to be turned to stone, if her challenge is not met. In the stern morality of *Measure for Measure*, the woman must display a gemlike standard of chastity and integrity; except where under cover of the marriage codes (as with Angelo's promise), she may practice deceit to gain her ends.

The play's other imaginative failure is Isabella's stern and fatal ✕ impulse in allowing her brother to be put to death—nay, to urge his death so she might preserve her virginity. Despite the subtle attention given in the play to nuances of justice, the dramatist does not confront the problem of what Angelo and Isabella would say to one another about this terrible moment in their lives. This is not a minor shortcoming, since pity and the nature of frail and tender humanity are at the center of the play.

Shakespeare's attention, however, is given to the sufferings of the man. In *Measure for Measure*, Shakespeare shows a significant inability to enter into feminine experience; and this has a good deal to do with his horror of sexuality itself—his fear of appetite as a fatal and destructive impulse:

> Our natures do pursue,
> Like rats that ravin down their proper bane.
> A thirsty evil, and when we drink we die.

His struggle is to resist the impulse to endorse stern and punitive laws, to correct the destructive effects of vice and lust, and to seek for human fairness in justice—even though man is given to animal filthiness. The Duke says to Pompey:

> Do thou but think
> What 'tis to cram a maw or clothe a back
> From such a filthy vice; say to thyself,
> From their abominable and beastly touches
> I drink, I eat.

Beneath this is an association at the unconscious level of the fear of sex as eating. (Why, for instance, should the phrase "cram a maw" have such pejorative energy?) But because the energy directed against lust is bound up with Shakespeare's dread of the lust within himself, it totally detracts attention from one of the most human problems in the play: what about Juliet? She is forgotten, ✕ even as she gives birth. Even when the father of her child is in prison facing execution, she is forgotten. She is even forgotten by

219

Isabella, with her Christian virtues. Nothing is said of her after the Provost is instructed to give her minimal attention. In this, surely, Shakespeare displays some inhibition of his capacities to imagine the experience of woman. And in the end, merely to tidy up the plot, Isabella is married to the Duke without a word and without any consideration of her earlier intense desire to become a chaste nun in renunciation of the flesh. Here are serious failures to hold in mind the inwardness of woman's experience.

CHAPTER 12

Antony and Cleopatra

Every time I read or see *Antony and Cleopatra* I find it in conclusion to be one of those enigmatic works, like *King Lear*, which leave one in tormented suspense. Of course, these creatures, the protagonists, are irresponsible, childish, cruel, impatient, slaves to passion, and self-defeating. Anyone concerned for the good government of men must condemn their indifference to social affairs and their irresponsibilities. On the other hand, it is impossible not to feel at one with Cleopatra when she cries contemptuously, " 'Tis paltry to be-Caesar." At peak moments, she and Antony achieve a nobleness, a vitality, a stature, a dimension of living that is transcendent and superhuman. And this seems a gesture that defies death and mortality.

Of course, there is idealization in this. There is the idealization of the self, of one another, and of love. After one exaggerated speech after Antony's death, Cleopatra asks:

Think you there was or might be such a man
As this I dreamt of?

DOLABELLA:
Gentle madam, no.

Yet, who would be without—who would deny—the magnificent spectacles of Antony's or Cleopatra's deaths, which are not so much a spectacle as an affirmation that certain human attainments, such as a great love, make death insignificant? And yet, it is also undeniable that there is a sense in which these deaths—that death itself —is the natural and inevitable culmination of this kind of burning, hungry love.

If we are aware of the close association in cultural symbolism of woman and death, then Cleopatra is the supreme embodiment of that connection. Yet, she is also a manifestation of the rich fertility of "Nilus' slime."

Throughout the play runs a subdued image, which emerges from the kind of knowledge Shakespeare had of Egypt and the country of the Nile. At certain seasons, the valley was flooded; and in that soil and climate, life swarmed. Besides the vast fertility, corruption also bred. Twice Cleopatra refers to being exposed on the slime of Nile:

Till by degrees the memory of my womb,
Together with my brave Egyptians all,
By the discandying of this pelleted storm,
Lie graveless, till the flies and gnats of Nile
Have buried them for prey!

Rather a ditch in Egypt
Be gentle grave unto me! Rather on Nilus' mud
Lay me stark-nak'd and let the waterflies
Blow me into abhorring!

Toward the beginning of the play Antony speaks of "the fire that quickens Nilus' slime," while in act 2, scene 7, he tells Lepidus of the agricultural system in Egypt:

ANTONY:
Thus do they, Sir: they take the flow o' th' Nile
By certain scales i' th' Pyramid. They know
By th' height, the lowness, or the mean, if death

Or foison follow. The higher Nilus swells,
The more it promises; as it ebbs, the seedsman
Upon the slime and ooze scatters his grain,
And shortly comes to harvest.

LEPIDUS:
Y'have strange serpents there.

ANTONY:
Ay, Lepidus.

LEPIDUS:
Your serpent of Egypt, is bred now of your mind by the operation of your sun: so is your crocodile.

ANTONY:
They are so.

Thus, when Antony calls "where's my serpent of old Nile," he is
calling a Cleopatra who has been bred between the sun and the
mud of the Nile.

In discussing *Timon of Athens*, we have looked at the unconscious concept in Shakespeare's mind of the whole earth—Mother
Earth—being a witch. The images of Cleopatra stretched out and
fly-blown on the mud of the Nile suggest a close affinity between
fertility and corruption. These images suggest that Mother Earth is
a source either of fertility (when seed is sprinkled upon her, "he
ploughed her and she cropped") or of corruption and rottenness.
The latter is, of course, the witch side of woman. She can bring into
being and create, or she can destroy with equal power.

Antony often refers to Cleopatra as a witch:

> The witch shall die.

This is just after he has said that she has

> Beguiled me to the very heart of loss.

Pompey says:

> Salt Cleopatra, soften thy waned lip!
> Let witchcraft join with beauty, lust with both!
> Tie up the libertine in a field of feasts,
> Keep his brain fuming.

A "lethe'd dulness" is the consequence of this witch's spell. Here, two other groups, or kinds of image, are central to the play.

One image is of a lazy, bewitched motion, as in the Nile:

CAESAR:
                    This common body,
Like to a vagabond flag upon the stream,
Goes to and back, lackeying the varying tide,
To rot itself with motion.

ANTONY:
                    the swan's down-feather
That stands upon the swell at full of tide,
And neither way inclines.

Actually, the latter image is in a speech about Octavia, after she has married Antony; and it refers to the division within herself. This situation has a distant touch of Cleopatra in it, and we hear in the metaphor a distant echo of the strange state of suspension of volition that the Nile-witch can induce. Not only in Antony, who is bewitched and paralyzed by Cleopatra's lust, but throughout society and in all man's affairs creeps a rich, lazy state of suspension of volition, emanating from the Old Serpent of the Nile.

This theme of involition may be associated with the other group of images, which clusters around the idea of melting. This melting is both sweet and destructive and fertile and menacing.

    Melt Egypt into Nile! and kindly creatures
    Turn all to serpents!

The word "discandy" occurs twice in association with this sweet melting:

CLEOPATRA:
By the discandying of this pelleted storm . . .

ANTONY:
                    The hearts
That spanieled me at heels, to whom I gave

Their wishes, to discandy, melt their sweets
On blossoming Caesar.

Early in the play Antony declares:

Let Rome in Tiber melt.

And later he cries:

Come, let's all take hands
Till that the conquering wine hath steeped our sense
In soft and delicate Lethe.

At the end, Cleopatra declares that Antony's death

The crown o' th' earth doth melt.

—while she, at her own death, seeks dissolution:

I am fire, and air; my other elements
I give to baser life.

Beneath all these figures there is the underlying fantasy of the dangerous fertility of woman (the mud of the Nile Valley or Mother Earth), a fertility so dangerous that it may rapidly turn into corruption. It is not too fanciful to see in this fantasy a deep dread of menstruation, which is the same as saying that it represents a deep dread of woman's creativity. Since we are discussing these concepts phenomenologically, this means a dread of primary maternal preoccupation—that is, woman's capacity to create our identity and mind. Woman could easily have not created our consciousness; thus, the witch aspect of woman could always display the capacity to reduce us to nothing. It is this dread that underlies Hamlet's obsession with dissolving and nothingness and Lear's terror of the "sulphurous pit" that lurks behind the Centaur image—with its threat of mortality and darkness.

Even in the most beautiful and enchanting picture of Cleopatra, there is a hint of the witch's dreadful power to "empty." Associated with this is an evocation of the desperate quality of lust and sensual indulgence:

> The barge she sat in, like a burnished throne,
> Burned on the water: the poop was beaten gold;
> Purple the sails, and so perfumèd that
> The winds were lovesick.

The word *burn* is repeated in "burnished" and "burned," so the consuming nature of her beauty is suggested. "Burnished" and "beaten" convey the effort that has gone into the display, while the images of the gold poop, the burning image reflected in the water, and the "purple" of the sails suggest something overpowering. The fact that the "winds" become "lovesick" conveys an impression of surfeit, as though even the mere appearance of Cleopatra is exhausting. Using sound, the next lines enact the movement of the rowers:

> the oars were silver,
> Which to the tune of flutes kept stroke, and made
> The water which they beat to follow faster,
> As amorous of their strokes.

The word "beaten" already has occurred in the description of the barge and has evoked a distant echo of sexual assertiveness, now picked up in the quoted passage. It is as though the oars were arousing sexual passion by touching the water. But the movement of the rowing is so clearly given by the rhythm that the subsequent, aroused movement of the water seems to clog the process; the water become amorous seems to swirl after the oars, to inhibit their clean movement.

Similarly, her person "beggars" description, while the fancy outworks nature. The Cupids' fanning seems to make the cheeks glow that it is intended to cool.

> And what they undid did.

This not only enacts the fans moving backwards and forwards; it conveys the enigmatic nature of sexual caresses. They suggest placidity, but they arouse burning lust that is violent until quenched. Then, once quenched, the lust only awaits the next arousal. As Edgell Rickword so marvelously put it in a poem:

Yet it is terrible to feel her stir,
and the continual sense of her that clings
about the mouth entangled in her hair;
and that swift Bird returning to our bed
with sombre throbbing of remorseless wings.
(Rickword, "Obsession")

Passion is continually a progress of "what they undid did" and of doing and undoing, and this ironic touch is latent beneath Enobarbus's depiction. Beneath his description of the women working the barge ("and made their bends adornings" ["bends" meaning here their tendings and their postures]), there is a sexual element, as in

the silken tackle
Swell with the touches of those flower-soft hands.

—which makes the manipulation of the ropes the touching of a penis. And these forms of voluptuousness pervade the air and the city, causing a strange disturbance in the spaces around:

From the barge
A strange invisible perfume hits the sense
Of the adjacent wharfs. The city cast
Her people out upon her; and Antony,
Enthroned i' th' market place, did sit alone,
Whistling to th' air; which, but for vacancy,
Had gone to gaze on Cleopatra too,
And made a gap in nature.

The "perfume hits the sense," the "city cast" the people out, Antony whistles to the air that would have been drawn to Cleopatra, too, had it not been that nature abhors a vacuum. "Vacancy" and "gap" are curious words with which to end such a magnificent description, but Shakespeare is expressing his underlying feeling that in lust there is a "waste of spirit" and that intense sensual voluptuousness merely creates a sense of vacancy and that kind of disturbance in nature.

As we have seen, Shakespeare's central political theme is that of appearance and reality. This is related to trust. How can good government be achieved when the inward and hidden creature lurks behind the exterior—especially in woman ("Yon simpering dame")? In Antony this theme is found throughout. Enobarbus says:

> I see men's judgments are
> A parcel of their fortunes, and things outward
> Do draw the inward quality after them.

—indicating the relationship between the subjective life and objective perceptions. There are some explicit comments on this by Antony, as he approaches the moment of his mistaken death.

ANTONY:
Sometime we see a cloud that's dragonish;
A vapor sometime like a bear or lion,
A towered citadel, a pendant rock, . . .
And mock our eyes with air. Thou has seen these signs;
They are black Vesper's pageants.
EROS:
        Ay, my lord.
ANTONY:
That which is now a horse, even with a thought
The rack dislimns, and makes it indistinct
As water is in water.

Antony goes on to say he is now like that:

> here I am Antony,
> Yet cannot hold this visible shape.

—And he goes on to talk of the effect Cleopatra has had upon him. But not only has she ruined Antony's grasp on reality, she also has robbed him of his sexual identity. In this scene, he cries:

> Oh, thy vile lady!
> She has robbed me of my sword.

But in another scene, Cleopatra actually changes roles with Antony:

Then put my tires and mantles on him, whilst
I wore his sword Philippan.

This castration symbol echoes throughout the play. As psychoanalysts point out, what we mean by castration is really annihilation.
The witch-woman can remove from us all the capacity to deal
effectively, which she gave us in the first place. Antony speaks of

My sword, made weak by my affection.

and throughout the play are references to men being transformed
into women.

CANIDIUS:
And we are women's men.

ENOBARBUS:
       Look, they weep,
And I, an ass, am onion-eyed; for shame!
Transform us not to women.

Thus, manhood is violated:

SCARUS:
Experience, manhood, honor, ne'er before
Did violate so itself.

In pondering the theme of sexual reversal, we need to approach
in a phenomenological way the symbolism of the serpent. The sphere
of the play becomes at one point "a cistern for scaled snakes." In
Freudian terms, this serpent must be a phallus; yet, it is Cleopatra
who is "the serpent of Old Nile." As the witch, Cleopatra is clearly
the phallic woman who steals Antony's sword to wear. But then
this worm becomes death, as she puts the asp like a babe to her
breast. It is as if the fertile but corrupting penis-serpent of the Nile
becomes a baby that "sucks its nurse asleep." The voracious love it
represents appropriately and inevitably leads to death. This is appetite, the universal wolf, at last eating up itself. In another sense,
the threat is female sensuality, dreaded by Shakespeare at an un-

The Insights Applied: Shakespeare's Anguish Over Woman

conscious level, bringing mortality, destruction, and death—as in *King Lear* and *Hamlet*.

These themes in the background make the scene with the Clown in act 5, scene 2, ambiguous and ironic. As we have seen, a rich combination of medieval and Renaissance attitudes generated in Shakespeare a sharp awareness that the most intense energies of living merely exacerbate a sense of mortality. In medieval symbolism, the lapse into sin is juxtaposed with the skull that warns of the eternal consequences after death. In Renaissance symbolism, the skull seems to mock the new heights of individual fulfillment devised by humanistic endeavor. Both bring an awareness of the *Dasein* problem of "being-into-death."

The Clown repeats, "I wish you all joy of the worm," thus implying that the worm is a penis. To "die" was to have a sexual climax. To Cleopatra, her "joy" is to suckle a babe—the death worm is the outcome of her passion for Antony. Thus, the hungry penis of lust finally eats Cleopatra—appetite consumes itself. This strange symbolism vibrates beneath the surface of Cleopatra's exchange with the Clown. As Ann Belford Ulanov and Barry Ulanov (1980) point out, the word *clown* originally meant a peasant, as it does still in Shakespeare. Yet, it also means a buffoon or a fool. According to the Ulanovs, the clown "embodies the reverse of what convention holds up as the desirable durable ego, capable of achievement"; "he exposes the terrible vulnerability of the person who will not acknowledge the human condition" (Ulanov and Ulanov 1980, 5). The Clown *in Antony and Cleopatra* is a clown in this sense, along with Falstaff, Leperello, and Quixote.

The Clown fills us with a kind of terror by his combination of stupidity and penetrating irony:

those that do die of it do seldom or never recover.

At first his words seem to be a joke, until we take from them the chill wind of the truism that when we are dead we are dead forever. (Falstaff is closer to this truth than is Hotspur.)

The Clown says he has heard a good report of the worm from a woman who died of it:

what pain she felt. Truly she makes a very good report o' th' worm; but he that will believe all that they say shall never be saved by half that they do; but this is most falliable, the worm's an odd worm.

The Clown's report is as insane as Sylvia Plath's declaration that she can commit suicide every ten years (in her poem "Lady Lazarus"). But, again, it makes one shiver with the recognition that there is no recollection of pain after death and so no report. And the dreadful comedy is that the Clown speaks of woman's experience of the worms as if it were sexual experience ("shall never be saved by half what they do . . . the worm's an odd worm").

You must think this, look you, that the worm will do his kind.[1]

This remark, too, makes the worm a kind of penis, as does this exchange:

CLOWN:
Give it nothing, I pray you, for it is not worth the feeding.
CLEOPATRA:
Will it eat me?

The devil will not eat a woman, says the Clown, thus hinting darkly at witchcraft:

CLOWN:
. . . a woman is a dish for the gods, if the devil dress her not. But truly, these same whoreson devils do the gods great harm in their women; for in every ten that they make, the devils mar five.

On the one hand, woman is a "dish for the gods"—the kind of human angel for whom Zeus would descend. On the other, woman is spoiled by the devils through appetite, since the Clown's thinking is obsessed with appetite; and this appetite is death.

We ascend to the godlike with Cleopatra's death scene, yet appetite remains an aspect of her character:

CLEOPATRA:
                              Now no more
The juice of Egypt's grape shall moist this lip.

The Insights Applied: Shakespeare's Anguish Over Woman

And even the death that is the culmination of this love affair seems no more than a moment in the sensual game:

> The stroke of death is as a lover's pinch,
> Which hurts, and is desired.

Cleopatra dies on a note of peace because life without Antony and breathing love has no significance for her. She takes her fate magnificently on herself—her choice to die:

> 'Tis paltry to be Caesar:
> Not being Fortune, he's but Fortune's knave, . . .
> A minister of her will. And it is great
> To do that thing that ends all other deeds,
> Which shackles accidents and bolts up change;
> Which sleeps, and never palates more the dug,
> The beggar's nurse and Caesar's. . . .

Here, to lie at the breast of Mother Earth and to merely exist in compromise with circumstance is contemptible. Cleopatra embraces a different baby, as the Clown tells, whose "biting is immortal." Thus,

> Dost thou not see my baby at my breast,
> That sucks the nurse asleep?

> As sweet as balm, as soft as air, as gentle—
> O Antony! Nay, I will take thee too:
> What should I stay.

The other side of Cleopatra's sensuous, passionate life is the feeling that this world is too contemptible to be endured. In Antony's absence, "this dull world" is "no better than a sty." Life is "this knot intrinsicate." Yet, she dies with other illusions, too:

> Methinks I hear
> Antony call: I see him rouse himself
> To praise my noble act.

And when Iras falls, she is jealous:

> If she first meet the curlèd Antony,
> He'll make demand of her, and spend that kiss
> Which is my heaven to have.

Perhaps she still believes that in heaven their love will make other lovers jealous, as Antony urged Eros:

> Where souls do couch on flowers, we'll hand in hand,
> And with our sprightly port make the ghosts gaze.

There is, however, very little strong sense of an afterlife (as there is in Chaucer's *Troilus and Criseyde*). Rather, one feels that Antony is being prophetic, when he says

> I will be
> A bridegroom in my death, and run into't
> As to a lover's bed.

In that relationship death is the inevitable consummation, despite the aspirations of the spirit to transcend life into air and fire.

I realize that I have not given a fully adequate account of this great tragedy. (There are, for instance, the two important scenes in which messengers are attacked; and these are scenes that reveal much of the psychopathology of the protagonists.) I have tried only to relate the play's themes to Shakespeare's unconscious perplexities about woman. Again, the fundamental question is the reconciliation of the libidinal and the ideal:

> For vilest things
> Become themselves in her, that the holy priests
> Bless her when she is riggish.

Considering the deep perplexity one is left with at the end of the play, it may seem surprising that I believe that in *Antony and Cleopatra* Shakespeare achieved his most remarkable coming to terms with the problem of woman. The poet admits, as it were, his dread of the "vile" in woman's animal lustfulness; and he confronts the witch, darkness, hate, and evil. Yet, by the end of the play we do not feel we want to reject woman or control her; we do not condemn either Antony or Cleopatra. We feel neither the loathing nor the bitterness that *Timon of Athens* arouses in us. Instead, we feel these twain are magnificent and full of a transcendant vitality. It is true of Antony that

> his delights
> Were dolphin-like, they show'd his back above
> The element they lived in.

The perspective of our awareness of male and female is extended, albeit into darkness and destructiveness and, at times, into meanness, cruelty, and stupidity. Yet, even the deaths of Antony and Cleopatra are a human glory; and love has an endurable, if tormented, meaning. We end the play glad of love and sexuality, if in some dread of the havoc they may cause. But we are given no encouragement to be revolted by humanness, passion, or woman. On the contrary, we learn a great deal about ourselves that is painful. We also learn, however, that as beings—and woman is a focus of "being"—we can achieve meanings that are stronger than death.

CHAPTER 13

Othello and Notes on Woman in Other Plays

The best book I have read on Shakespeare's *Othello* is Jane Adamson's *Othello as Tragedy: Some Problems of Judgment and Feeling* (1980). In it Adamson follows the approach of Sam Goldberg, whose book *An Essay on King Lear* (1974) urges us to allow the play to work upon us so as to allow ourselves to suffer and to be bewildered. Adamson finds *Othello* to be a painful play because it reveals too starkly that if we commit ourselves to love, we become vulnerable. We are vulnerable not only in our dependence upon the loved one but in discovering, in our need to be loved, weaknesses and evils within ourselves. The play is a complex web in which individuals are painfully concerned with who they are (particularly in the light of others' eyes), of the way in which they are confirmed by the regard of others, and, in the extreme, by love ("and if I love thee not, chaos is come again").

The anguish is about how, given the need to love and be loved, a distortion of consciousness in the realm of love (which is such an intangible experience, subject to all manner of fantasy and delusion) can lead to dynamics of destruction, that can turn against others and against oneself. In *Othello* the central image is the primal scene—the sexual act (with the marriage sheets on the bed) that is the act of death. Surely, the most primitive unconscious fears are aroused by this act, not least when the male protagonist is associated with blackness, cruelty, and evil. (The blackamoor was associated with such qualities in the Elizabethan mind, whatever one thinks of such dangerous color prejudices.)

Adamson believes, rightly I think, that many critical approaches, however useful they have been in illuminating aspects of the play, have tended to take up positions which are, in the Freudian sense, defences. The Victorian critic A. C. Bradley idealized the noble Othello in his *Shakespearean Tragedy* (1904) , while F. R. Leavis saw Othello as a self-deluding egotist. Both are thereby defending themselves against empathy, against recognizing in Othello their own human proclivities—to be sensitively vulnerable on the one hand and to be so out of touch with reality as to be brutal, cruel, and unjust, and murderous on the other. Leavis declared that this tragedy was lesser than the other tragedies, and I believe Adamson is right in challenging this assertion. If one opens oneself to *Othello* as Adamson urges us, I believe we may find it to be very modern and, in the tradition of English literature, seminal. One can detect the influence of *Othello* in George Eliot's *Middlemarch*, Henry James's *The Portrait of a Lady*, and Edith Wharton's *The Reef* because of the play's subtle and dreadful illumination of the darkness and cunning in the human psyche and the weaknesses in our emotional make-up (which we need to confront in order to understand ourselves, not least in the sexual life).

My purpose in this book is to indicate some of the deep anxieties about woman and sexuality in Shakespeare's later plays. As one ponders passages in which these anxieties become apparent, a number of themes emerge that link the problems of woman and sexuality with the other great themes of Shakespeare's mature work. One such theme is the difference between appearance and the inner reality; for example, Shakespeare writes of a woman whose "face presages snow," yet "goes to it with a riotous appetite." The woman dressed in silk and fur can have a wolfish heart. A Desdemona can seem to be

> A maiden never bold;
> Of spirit so still and quiet that her motion
> Blushed at herself.

—that is, a woman whose graceful movements were so inviting that she blushed even to move and yet seems to have an imperfect judgment. Brabantio says that it is strange that she should "fall in love with what she feared to look on." He goes on:

> It is a judgment maimed and most imperfect
> That will confess perfection so could err
> Against all rules of nature, and must be driven
> To find out practices of cunning hell
> Why this should be.

What he is saying is that it must be magic that Othello has used to attract Desdemona, for no one whose judgment has not been maimed or is imperfect could believe it could have happened naturally. But Iago says:

> Foh! one may smell in such a will most rank,
> Foul disproportions, thoughts unnatural—
> . . . .
>   I may fear
> Her will, recoiling to her better judgment,
> May fall to match you with her country forms,
> And happily repent.

—which suggests that it would be "normal" for Desdemona to marry a white Venetian, and she may (if she reverts to "better judgment," an insult to Othello) decide that it was wrong to marry a black man. Not to marry someone of her own "clime, complexion and degree" is a mark of "a will most rank" and "foul disproportions." Of course, Iago is thrusting subtle and evil persuasions into Othello's mind about the possibility of Desdemona being inwardly foul and so likely to be unfaithful. But in both passages, there is a preoccupation with the chaste and beautiful exterior and the woman's urge to be "tupped" or "bolstered" by a black man, making "the beast with two backs" with him. Copulation is seen as the kind of thing toads do:

> O curse of marriage,
> That we can call these delicate creatures ours,
> And not their appetites! I had rather to be a toad
> And live upon the vapor in a dungeon
> Than keep a corner in the thing I love
> For others' uses.

Later, Othello says:

> But there where I have garnered up my heart,
> Where either I must live or bear no life,
> The fountain from which my current runs
> Or else dries up—to be discarded thence,
> Or keep it as a cistern for foul toads
> To knot and gender in.

This is one of the themes in Shakespeare's dramatic poetry concerning the relationship between man and woman—the woman's outward fairness, the ideal image of woman, and the toadlike capacity of woman, following her appetite and copulating like an animal, a reptile, a soiled horse, a fitchew, or a toad.

But Othello's speech also makes it clear that the threat to a man is considerable if he gathers up all his heart and invests it in love, that emotional relationship that then becomes the source of his being. If this source becomes occupied by repulsive animality (to Othello the repugnant animality of unfaithfulness, of course), that the man becomes something less than a toad living on vapor in a dungeon. He becomes nothing, nothing human or capable of prowess: "Farewell the tranquil heart! Farewell content! Othello's occupation's gone!"

Antony has such a moment when he speaks of the way the clouds dissolve, as "water does in water." If a love is lost, then chaos comes again and the wrack in which one sees oneself figure "dislimns." The great threat of woman, then, is that one may take her as a pure, ideal, goddess figure who offers a fundamental source of nourishment for one's being; but if something foul corrupts her, then the idealized dependence upon her may become so betrayed that the individual is threatened with going out of existence. Instead of an angel she becomes a witch, capable of removing life rather than creating it. Therefore, she must be "chopped into messes," or suffocated.

Perhaps one may suggest here a phenomenological link with the primal scene. It is the mother who is one's world in infancy; the suckling idealizes her at the breast, our alma mater. But then this ideal mother goes over to a grunting and raucous physical sexuality with the father. From the combined parents comes the sound (and for some infants the sight) of frenzied activity, savage breathing, moans, and seemingly tormented periodicity. The child does not know what it means. If it means anything, it seems to mean violence. It could mean death or murder. The only way the child can imagine sexual hunger is as a form of eating, and so the child may fear that the parents are eating one another. The child is strangely jealous, yet knows that if he tries to interfere, the parents will turn on him. The child then fears (if Melanie Klein [1932] is right) that the combined parents will eat him—that is, destroy him.

Thus, behind the idealized woman is another danger: the more one becomes fascinated by her, the more terrible will be one's dread of going out of existence through her secret, duplicitous proclivity for entering into animal copulation with another—the father. Thus, one is left utterly at the mercy of a rejection or hostility that threatens one's existence. This is what is acted out in the murder scene in *Othello*. The father kills the mother in sex; but in the process, of course, Othello kills himself, as Adamson (1980) points out. Othello is not only the father, he is "us"—each of us in the audience. We identify with his attempt to control the female appetite and to destroy the suspected toadlike engendering danger in woman. But because he loves Desdemona and cannot live without her, he puts an end to his own life as well. There is nothing for him to do but commit suicide.

This is the enigma of love: One needs it more than anything else in the world, to confirm one's identity and to be a rich source of meaning and "being." Yet, the dangers within love are such that love always has the potential to destroy one.

The Insights Applied: Shakespeare's Anguish Over Woman

I have suggested throughout this book that there must have been intense personal preoccupations in Shakespeare that impelled his imaginative explorations of these deep themes of love, appearance and reality, and 'being' and 'nonbeing.' The problem is, of course, that we know so little of his life. Even more importantly, we know so little of his personality.

However, what we do have are the sonnets, and I was fascinated recently when teaching *Othello* to find some illuminating comments in R. J. C. Wait's *The Background to Shakespeare's Sonnets* (1972). Wait draws our attention to a particular continuous sequence of sonnets, 109–25, which seem to have the object of explaining and excusing Shakespeare's apparent disloyalty to the Earl of Southampton, in favor of persons who seemed likely to prove to be more valuable patrons (probably Sir Philip Herbert and Lord Cecil of Essendon). They seem to relate to events that took place in the latter half of June 1604. (*Othello* is dated 1604.)

In these sonnets, Wait finds elements that are found in the plays of Shakespeare's dark, or tragic, period: "Not only love, sex and friendship but all idealism, truth and integrity were cynically and painfully called into account" (Wait 1972, 194). Wait believes that the real tragedy of the sonnets is "what the friend makes him discover about himself":

> that it was Shakespeare who could have been the one who was "false of heart," "have looked on truth askance and strangely," and have "sold cheap what is most dear." (194)

It was after the publication of the sonnets in 1609 that the mood in Shakespeare's writing changed. Instead of sinking into Jacobean pessimism and a sense of being overwhelmed by corruption, Shakespeare wrote his later plays in which he expressed a new hope in the potentialities of human nature.

Wait traces the story from 1592, when Shakespeare found both a patron and a friend in the shape of an idealistic and virginal youth who was at the same time a wealthy aristocrat and a scholarly critic. Friendship developed into an intense love that could not be reciprocated by the young Southampton. Just as Shakespeare was publishing a poem on the theme of Adonis's disdain for sexual dalliance, the model for the poem turned the tables on him by accepting the embraces of Shakespeare's own mistress. Unable to admit that the beautiful youth was growing up into a virile and rakish young man, Shakespeare adopted an attitude of exaggerated humility and fondness, while also reproving the youth and showing anger at his showing favor to a rival poet.

In 1594 Shakespeare rejoined his actors under the patronage of the Earl of Derby, but the latter soon died. Shakespeare swallowed his pride and returned to the patronage of Southampton. The latter, now in control of his inheritance, gave Shakespeare a sum sufficient to enable him to purchase a partnership in his company, thus setting him on the road to success.

While Shakespeare flourished after 1594, Southampton fell increasingly into trouble, until in 1601 he was sentenced to death with the Earl of Essex. The poem "The Phoenix and the Turtle" mourns the death of the two earls.

But Southampton was reprieved, on the grounds that he was a foolish dupe of Essex. In Sonnet 117, Shakespeare reveals that he was one of those who shrank from Southampton when he lay condemned:

> Accuse me thus, that I have scanted all
> Wherein I should your great deserts repay;
>
> . . . .
>
> That I have hoisted sail to all the winds
> Which should transport me farthest from your sight.

Sonnet 119 is full of bitter remorse and speaks of his tears being distilled from "limbecks foul as hell within"—within his own impure motives:

> What portions have I drunk of siren tears
> Distilled from limbeckes foul as hell within,
> Applying fears to hopes and hopes to fears,
> Still losing when I saw myself to win!

It is time that he speaks of "ruined love, when it is built anew, / Grows fairer than at first," but he seems surely to be "cheering himself up," for in Sonnet 120 he says:

> For if you were by my unkindness shaken,
> As I by yours, you've passed a hell of time,
> And I, a tyrant, have no leasure taken
> To weigh how once I suffered in your crime.

Shakespeare had come to seek the favor of the opposing party, Cecil and the Pembrokes, and even Lords Grey and Cobham. And Shakespeare was aware of his disloyalty to one who had been convicted for that very act. But while Shakespeare was the most successful playwright of his time, Southampton was still striving to make a mark at court and was short of means. But Southampton could not expect to be patronized by Shakespeare, and Shakespeare's response to him was guilty and confused. Wait summarizes what the sonnets say about their relationship:

(a) My love for you is undying, and not dependent on your one-time good looks;

(b) To sharpen my appetite for you I have tried out other associations;

(c) Because of economic circumstances I have had to appear to follow others;

(d) When I saw others and followed them, it was because they all seemed to be facets of you;

(e) When I followed others, it was to test your regard for me;

(f) Because I had a surfeit of your goodness, I followed others by way of taking a nasty medicine to cure me of the surfeit;

(g) You were once very unkind to me, by stealing my mistress, so you should not mind my unkindness to you;

(h) I am not as bad as all that, and I do not see why I should be criticized by someone worse;

(i) I gave away your notebook with the fair copy of the Sonnets because I could remember all my love for you without their aid;

(j) My love for you has remained constant and never faltered, unlike that of people who are constantly thinking about the vicissitudes of the court.

(196)

Not all these positions can be reconciled with one another, and Shakespeare's defence is inconsistent. But this, says Wait, is how human beings are when they try to explain away past behavior. But the confusion and dismay, Wait suggests, lie behind the horror and disillusion of *King Lear* and the unmitigated gloom of *Macbeth*. The contradictions in the sonnets, he suggests, underlie *Measure for Measure* and *Othello*.

Wait suggests that the somberness of the plays written at that time reveal that Shakespeare's expression of affection was not productive. *King Lear, Macbeth, Measure for Measure,* and *Othello* are about the deep contradictions in human nature; and behind them ✗ Wait finds the contradiction between the idealized picture of Southampton in Shakespeare's mind and the painful experiences he had experienced since their golden days, as recorded in the sonnets. Not least, in this inner conflict is the problem of Shakespeare's guilt at the way he had treated Southampton. Because of these experiences Shakespeare became appalled by human nature, particularly by the weaknesses and proclivities for evil *in himself*. It was these anguished torments, of trying to reconcile the good and angelic in man with his capacity for baseness, sensuality, grossness, and destructiveness—as in sexuality—that impelled Shakespeare's great art in its exploration of human reality.

The greatness of *Othello* lies in its terrifying portrayal of how justice is impossible, unless men are able to sustain a certain reality sense. The same problem, of course, is explored through the character Leontes in *The Winter's Tale*. In *Othello* the theme focuses on the word *cause*. As Adamson points out, when Othello murders Desdemona he speaks of her death as not something he has resolved upon but as an act in which he is the instrument of an impersonal power—justice—which is "out there," fixed and distant like the "chaste stars." Murder seems but a bloodless sacrifice ("pluck thy rose"; "put out the light"), and there is no shrinking or anguish in him nor an awareness of the consequences of his cruel and unjust execution of his woman. He seems totally unable to find her reality. In his "story," Othello is portrayed as brave; but nothing could be more cowardly than killing without pity a defenceless woman without giving her a chance to clear herself. Afterward, the reality of what Othello has done seems to strike him with astonishing force, as if the truth had penetrated a film of illusion: "Oh Desdemon! dead Desdemon! dead! Oh! Oh!" Both his bravado and his self-justification are preposterous, as Adamson claims.

But Othello's murder of Desdemona must seem to us like some of those psychopathological manifestations we read about in our own newspapers, as when murderers believe they are "called" to destroy prostitutes or when suicides wipe out their own families, including the children. In such horrifying acts, the perpetrators, like Othello, must have lost all sense of the other reality of the human beings they have attacked. They have projected onto their victims their own fantasies and are attacking in them elements within themselves. This proclivity in Othello goes with his need to live in his "story"—that is, his macho image of himself as a warrior.

Shakespeare's realization of this kind of consciousness is superb and extremely complex. Othello uses images that belong to a topography larger than himself and which seems, like his tales about the Anthropophagi by which he wooed Desdemona, to require a certain kind of performance, like a great stage set:

Never, Iago. Like to the Pontic sea,
Whose icy current and compulsive course
Ne'er feels retiring ebb, but keeps due on
To the Propontic and the Hellespont,
Even so my bloody thoughts, with violent pace,
Shall ne'er look back, ne'er ebb to humble love,
Till that a capable and wide revenge
Swallow them up.

                    Now, by yond marble heaven,
In the due reverence of a sacred vow
I here engage my words.

Such an individual, as Shakespeare sees, is extremely dangerous; and in the ridiculousness of the elaborate, pompous comparisons—Pontic and Propontic—he caricatures the way in which such an individual exports his emotional problems into a mythological landscape and justifies his failures of the reality sense, by invoking a "marble heaven." It is a horrifying portrait of aggrandized self-deception. (It was that, of course, that T. S. Eliot found so dreadful about Othello.)

The truth about himself was that Othello perceives here:

Othello and Notes on Woman in Other Plays

> Haply, for I am black
> And have not those soft parts of conversation
> That chamberers have or for I am declined
> Into the vale of years—yet that's not much—
> She's gone.

"Conversation" means here more than talk. It refers to the whole of civilized behavior. Othello glimpses that his color sets him apart from Venetian civilization and that he, being a warrior, is not good at civilian life and the emotional existence. There also are subtle hints at his lack of sexual prowess, or at least his fear of impotence, a subtle contrast with what men tend to believe at large about "old black rams" and the mythical lustfulness of the black man.

Behind the theme of justice and how it fails is a recognition of great psychological importance. We can only be just insofar as we perceive and embrace the reality of the other person. This problem is of the greatest importance with woman, and it is about woman that man is liable to fall into totally unrealistic self-deceptions. There has been, of course, neither place nor time for Desdemona to perpetrate one sexual act of disloyalty, let alone the many of which Othello suspects her. The reality of woman, of which Emilia speaks, is something that Othello fails to grasp in his impulse toward idealizing his wife and his love:

> Let husbands know
> Their wives have sense like them: they see, and smell,
> And have their palates both for sweet and sour,
> As husbands have. What is it that they do
> When they change us for others? Is it sport?
> I think it is: and doth affection breed it?
> I think it doth. Is't frailty that thus errs?
> It is so too. And have we not affections,
> Desires for sport? and frailty, as men have?
> Then let them use us well: else let them know,
> The ills we do, their ills instruct us so.

This is a strong claim for equality, in the spirit of the Wife of Bath. Women have both a libidinal urge and component, and they are as frail as men. It is a speech to set against Othello's claim to be the servant of justice in his murder of Desdemona. But to accept that women are no more than human requires emotional security in a man—to allow woman to be herself. Othello's urge is to exercise control over woman because she is so dangerous. And woman is dangerous because in placing himself in her hands, through such intense and idealizing love, he exposes his vulnerability. Thus, when Othello first suspects that Iago can "prove her haggard," he thinks in terms of control, like a falconer over a wayward bird:

> If I do prove her haggard,
> Though that her jesses were my dear heartstrings,
> I'd whistle her off and let her down the wind
> To prey at fortune. . . .
>   O curse of marriage,
> That we can call these delicate creatures ours,
> And not their appetites! I had rather be a toad
> And live upon the vapor of a dungeon
> Than keep a corner in the thing I love
> For others' uses.

The word "thing" almost escapes our notice. Yet, if we ponder the speech, it is strange, for Othello talks about Desdemona as if she were some alien creature utterly apart from him, deprived of human qualities, rather than a human being with whom he has shared intimate and sympathetic communion. She is characterized as a dangerous predator or a mere "thing" with a "corner" that can be used by others. This speech leads to the immense depersonalization that dominates Othello's mood when he slaughters Desdemona. In that moment, she is an alabaster form, a rose, which impersonal justice impels him to destroy. Othello's hint at possession after Desdemona's death virtually associates this tendency with a kind of perversion, in which the woman has become a fetishistic object to be destroyed:

> Be thus when thou art dead, and I will kill thee,
> And love thee after.

Othello and Notes on Woman in Other Plays

Othello is a terrifying play (Dr. Johnson wrote that it is not to be endured) because it shows the capacity for consciousness to be corrupted, particularly in those who are capable of idealizing (or being "noble"). From the experience recorded in the sonnets, Shakespeare explores the theme of our vulnerability when we commit ourselves to a relationship and reveal our deepest needs to ourselves. The self-dramatization in this play, with which F. R. Leavis (1952) was so preoccupied, is not so much a manifestation of the inability for true tragic experience but a compensation for insecurity, as Adamson (1980) argues. On her part, Desdemona shows almost as little understanding of the 'other', her husband, as Othello shows of her. This is perhaps most apparent in her persistence in Cassio's cause and her "artless perseverance," as Samuel Johnson called it. Yet she says, with feminine perception, "I saw Othello's visage in his mind"; and both she and Emilia show awareness of the problem of delusive fantasies in men ("I nothing know, but for his fantasy"). One awful feature is Desdemona's passivity, to which Adamson points, in the face of Othello's injustice and violence. In her uncensoring love, Desdemona tries to prevent Othello from becoming known to himself. Emilia says:

Thou hast not half that power to do me harm
As I have to be hurt.

These lines indicate that painful aspect of the play that explores how, when people's view or grasp of themselves and of each other becomes corrupt, what pain and destruction follow. Can there be any hope for justice when human consciousness is thus vulnerable?

The worst aspect of the play is that it is in the very heart of love that the corruption is thrust. Iago says, "So will I turn her virtue into pitch," and he makes this "the net that shall enmesh 'em all." It is with this possibility that Shakespeare strives. Iago's realism here is a challenge:

When she is sated with his body, she will find the error of her choice. [She must change, she must.]

Is Iago's realism, his references to salmon's tails and cod's heads, his coarse mention of clyster-pipes and kissing fingers, the true human reality? Obviously not. Although Iago is hideously convincing, like Edmund, we gradually come to see that he manifests schizoid moral inversion: "evil be thou my good." The reality with which we are concerned primarily is not the gross physically sexuality that is our essential truth as it may seem from much modern literature. The central problem is the need for love. It is the contortion of this need that causes the pain, agony, and death. Iago hates love and tries to cause the maximum possible chaos and destruction there, in that center: "When I love thee not, chaos is come again." Iago's is a consistent assault here, which emanates from schizoid moral inversion and hate. It is his consistency that makes him seem too "honest," and he has the devil's luck. While declaring to his victim

> I would not have your free and noble nature,
> Out of self-bounty, be abused. Look to 't.

—it is just that abuse he perpetrates. Iago's instrument is the vulnerability of the image of woman in the consciousness of man, for that powerfully important image in our minds can be so easily corrupted—dangerous conceits are in their nature poison.

So great is our need to see our image in the face of woman, and to see an image in woman that draws out the highest qualities of our being, that here we find ourselves in the greatest danger. Phrases throughout the play indicate this problem: "Let me see your eyes"; "Look in my face"; "Your mystery, your mystery." Here, in the need for reflection, we may experience the deepest betrayal. It is here that "lilies that fester smell far worse than weeds," and

> O thou weed,
> Who art so lovely fair, and smell'st so sweet,
> That the sense aches at thee, would thou hadst ne'er been born!

The effect of betrayal there can make life impossible because our own image to the world becomes humiliated. We may feel that this may serve

> to make me
> A fixed figure for the time of scorn
> To point his slow unmoving finger at!

The threat of emotional failure can lead to the destruction of our world, so that

Methinks it should be now a huge eclipse
Of sun and moon, and that th' affrighted globe
Should yawn at alteration.

Othello is such a painful play because we do not like being shown our vulnerability, in our need to love and be loved, nor to be brought to recognize that this vulnerability centers on the image of woman.

Any critic tackling Shakespeare's art is bound to feel a desperate sense of inadequacy, since the playwright created a world that seems unfathomable. Indeed, the fact that Shakespeare's poetic dramas are unfathomable is the reason why they continue to delight us all our lives. I have concentrated on what seem to me to be the important phenomenological themes—the unconscious problems with woman's image and the relationship of the images of woman to the question of the meaning of life. Toward the end of his creative career Shakespeare achieved a great triumph, which was to find a belief in continuity—that is, a belief that new generations would appear on earth to carry on re-creating values and meanings. It is this achieved faith in humanity that is manifest in the rhythms of Ferdinand's speeches to Miranda in *The Tempest* and Florizel's to Perdita in *The Winter's Tale*.

There is much more to say, of course, about Shakespeare's women themselves. What shall we say of that blague, *The Taming of the Shrew*, which seems almost a vehicle for the final propaganda speech by Katharina, expressing the wisdom of keeping woman under control:

A woman moved is like a fountain troubled,
Muddy, ill-seeming, thick, bereft of beauty.

The need for woman to be submissive to her husband is given a political analogy:

And when she is froward, peevish, sullen, sour,
And not obedient to his honest will,

249

> What is she but a foul contending rebel
> And graceless traitor to her loving lord?

To be subservient is made to seem natural:

> Why are our bodies soft and weak and smooth,
> Unapt to toil and trouble in the world.
> But that our soft conditions and our hearts
> Should well agree with our external parts?

The pat rhyme, however, gives it away a little. The audience is aware that this is the dramatic offering a piece of male propaganda to which not all the company gives assent without irony, so that it is like the opening lines of Chaucer's *The Merchant's Tale*: "all ready, sir, quoth she." The lines are spoken by a boy actor, and the irony is obvious by the next line: "Come, come you froward and unable worms."

We feel much more sympathetic toward the possibilities of relationships as portrayed in Benedick and Beatrice, in *Much Ado about Nothing*, where we hear exchanges that have the passion and rhythm of real engagement between man and woman:

BEATRICE:
Is 'a not approved in the height a villain, that hath slandered, scorned, dishonoured my kinswoman? O that I were a man! What? bear her in hand until they come to take hands and then with public accusation, unconvered slander, unmitigated rancor—O God, that I were a man! I would eat his heart in the market place.

BENEDICK:
Hear me, Beatrice—

BEATRICE:
Talk with a man out at a window!—a proper saying!

BENEDICK:
Beat—

BEATRICE:
Princes and Counties! Surely a princely testimony, a goodly count, Count Comfect, a sweet gallant surely! O that I were a man for his sake! or that I had any friend would be a man for

my sake! But manhood is melted into cursies, valor into com-
pliment, and men are only turned into tongue, and trim ones
too. He is now as valiant as Hercules that only tells a lie, and
swears it. I cannot be a man with wishing; therefore I will die
a woman with grieving.

BENEDICK:
Tarry, good Beatrice. By this hand I love thee.

BEATRICE:
Use it for my love some other way than swearing by it.

The dispute is about justice. Claudio has been as unjust to Hero
as Othello was to Desdemona, too hasty to condemn and reject her.
Beatrice's response is extreme: she demands cold-bloodedly that
Benedict should "kill Claudio"—that he should challenge him to a
duel. She asks for the conventional response of the man, in honor,
to avenge the wronged woman's reputation. But the excesses of her
passion are womanly, too, while Benedick's response in his bewilderment is, she declares, less than realistic—he is all words. It is
great comedy because the two characters originally pretended to be
above passion, intimacy, and such complex tangles of response and
action. Here they are in a deep mess, the grounds of which are in
hopeless love, into which they have been tricked by ironic play on
the susceptibilities of their humanity.

But the row itself is superbly done; and the deeper they fall into
the contentious mess, the more we love them and see in them the
realities of the relational life. In D. H. Lawrence's *Women in Love*,
we have some marvelous exchanges like this, between Birkin and
Ursula Brangwen, as in the lane, when she throws the rings down
in the mud. It could even be that Lawrence learned how to handle
such a scene from his reading of *Much Ado about Nothing*. Certainly, such a heroine as Beatrice, with her "felt-life" realism,
stands strongly behind the English novel (a point made by Q. D.
Leavis in her remarkable essay "The Englishness of the English
novel" [1983]).

We are deeply moved by these heroines, as we also are, perhaps
without knowing why, by Viola in *Twelfth Night*, during her famous exchange with the Duke in act 2, scene 4. There is music and

the enigmatic song about death sung by "the spinsters and the knitters in the sun, / And the free maids that weave their thread with bones":

> Come away, come away, death,
>   And in sad cypress let me be laid.

Viola is disguised as a man (played, of course, by a boy actor), while she is serving the Duke as a messenger in his suit to Olivia, who in turn has fallen in love with Viola, supposing her to be a man. We are in a complicated tangle of switches of gender, and what we experience is a sense of how both men and women inevitably suffer because of the fatal development of the power of love. The Duke discusses the difference between man's passion and woman's:

> There is no woman's sides
> Can bide the beating of so strong a passion
> As love doth give my heart.

The histrionic opportunity is great, of course, for the woman acting the part of Viola to make it clear that nothing could be further from the truth. In addition, the simple movement of the verse shows Shakespeare's a marvelous capacity to identify with his woman:

> My father had a daughter loved a man
> As it might be perhaps, were I a woman,
> I should your lordship.

And what's her history, asks the Duke?

VIOLA:
> A blank, my lord. She never told her love,
> But let concealment, like a worm i' th' bud,
> Feed on her damask cheek. She pined in thought;
> And, with a green and yellow melancholy,
> She sat like Patience on a monument,
> Smiling at grief.

Viola then nearly gives herself away:

252

> I am all the daughters of my father's house,
> And all the brothers too, and yet I know not.

We find tears coming into our eyes, and we hold our breath. The mode of thought is so womanly; and yet, because she is dressed as a man, we have that deep sense of the common experience in both sexes of being in love and hoping for circumstances in which there can be a movement toward recognition of the condition. Yet, in these circumstances, it seems hopeless. The scene has the same gripping quality as the scene in Tolstoy's *Anna Karenina* when Koznyshev fails to propose to Varenka (part 6, sections 4 and 5) or, indeed, when Levin proposes to Kitty and is rejected. And in the Duke's question lies the grave undercurrent:

> But died thy sister of her love, my boy?

Such polarities between us belong to the sphere of *sub specie æternitatis;* and the warm, sympathetic involvement we experience with this courageous woman fills us with a sense of the value and substance of human emotion and the meaningfulness of love.

The significance of love and the way in which it can be transmuted into marriage is, as Leo Salingar (1974) has argued, the essence of the comedies. In the end, this theme enabled in Shakespeare to express the hopefulness we experience in the relationship in *The Winter's Tale* between Florizel and Perdita in a context that relates it to the ever-renewing cycles of the seasons:[1]

> I wish you
> A wave o' th' sea, that you might ever do
> Nothing but that, move still, still so,
> And owe no other function.

The way time is dealt with in his later plays suggests that Shakespeare was seeking to achieve a new sense of time, in which a perception of continuity and renewal could be achieved and a reconciliation to his own mortality. The later plays also reflect a hopefulness about future generations—a gladness for them and a sense that they could re-create the meanings for which he strove. (The use of music in the plays relates to this attempt to transcend time.) The need for the heroines to be treated with awe and respect and within a courteous and sanctified acceptance of marriage as a stabilizing state of grace is highly important. So, too, is the profound respect for woman. For example, Hermione's restoration to life at the end of *The Winter's Tale* marks a highly significant celebration of the rediscovery of the female element and of the poet's faith in woman's essential goodness and creativity. It is extraordinary how, even in a bad production, this seemingly impossible scene still has a deeply moving effect upon us, even though we cannot understand why.

We may say, I believe, that an underlying problem for all of us is the embracing of both our male and female elements. Shakespeare himself seems to have had serious difficulties with the integration of his female element, and he had deep insights into the problem of men who could not find in themselves a rich "female" side. He often links this kind of man with the Romans, who seemed to him, from contemporary accounts of Roman civilization, devoted to male "doing"—that is, the Romans were tough, cold, and efficient yet inadequate in dealing with human beings in their social setting. The Romans in *Antony and Cleopatra*, for instance, are practical and effective; but we respond warmly to Cleopatra's contempt: " 'Tis paltry to be Caesar." One theme of the play is "let Rome in Tiber melt." This irresponsible relinquishing of practical affairs seems attractive as a gesture toward a higher level of living that transcends the "sty" of ordinary, mundane existence. To be manly, to the extent of enduring privation as Antony has, drinking "the stale of horses" in arduous campaigns, seems of doubtful value. And yet there is the threat of being "unmanned," so that Antony's dealings with Enobarbus, justice, and loyalty—on which good government depend—become undermined. The threat to stability is perhaps underlined by Cleopatra's playful enquiries into the emotional state of Mardian, the eunuch. The problem is to modify the so-called macho stance of the warrior, without being castrated or becoming impotent.

Coriolanus is a great play that addresses this theme, which is related at the unconscious level in a most perceptive way to the influence of woman, particularly in the upbringing of children. In this play, the Roman state is a great machine:

> you may as well
> Strike at the heaven with your staves as lift them
> Against the Roman state, whose course will on
> The way it takes, cracking ten thousand curbs
> Of more strong link asunder than can ever
> Appear in your impediment.

The language of the play, which examines this mechanistic capacity in human beings, is blunt, ugly, and consonantal, like the muscular flesh of the protagonist who is himself a war machine:

> his sword, Death's stamp,
> Where it did mark, it took. From face to foot
> He was a thing of blood, whose every motion
> Was timed with dying cries.

In his poetic contemplation of the problem of "being," Shakespeare is thinking of the way in which brute force seems to establish a man's image. Like Othello, Coriolanus "lives in" his "story" and in reports of his prowess. In the famous description of the crowds pushing and shoving to "eye" him, it is clear that he sets off the same kind of physical energy by his mythological appearance:

BRUTUS:
> All tongues speak of him, and he bleared sights
> Are spectacled to see him. Your prattling nurse
> Into a rapture lets her baby cry,
> While she chats him; the kitchen malkin pins
> Her richest lockram 'bout her reechy neck,
> Clamb'ring the walls to eye him. Stalls, bulks, windows
> Are smothered up, leads filled, and ridges horsed
> With variable complexions.

Yet this image is all false male "doing": When Coriolanus is invited to show his wounds to the people in the market place, he cannot do it. It seems to him a humiliation, which he cannot tolerate. In our terms, he cannot bear to come down from his posture as a war machine to accept his common humanity with the rest of mankind. Fundamentally, this reveals a childish weakness. It is characteristic that among Cariolanus's last words are the childish boast "Alone I did it. Boy?" The phrase becomes, at the level of the preparatory school, a catch phrase.

In his mind Shakespeare has the image of a child brutally wrecking a butterfly, destroying frail life in the way a child might who has not yet learned, through the imagination, to feel concern and reverence for life. The butterfly image occurs three times in the play. First, in Valeria's account of the behavior of Virgilia's son, so like his father, Coriolanus:

> I saw him run after a gilded butterfly, and when he caught it, he let it go again, and after it again, and over and over he comes, and up again; catched it again; or whether his fall enraged him, or how 'twas, he did so set his teeth and tear it! O, I warrant, how he mamocked it!
> VOLUMNIA:
> One on's father's moods. . . .
> VALERIA:
> Indeed, la, 'tis a noble child.

The second reference to butterflies is

> they follow him
> Against us brats with no less confidence
> Than boys purusing summer butterflies
> Or butchers killing flies.

Although the women—wife and mother—admire the child's brutality, as if this "mood" represented strong male capacities to grit one's teeth and do valiant acts, the references to boyish, confident preoccupation with petty destructiveness and the indifference to life put a large question mark behind this kind of ardour. And then, finally, Menenius says:

> There is differency between a grub and a butterfly; yet your butterfly was a grub. This Marcius is grown from man to dragon. He has wings; he's more than a creeping thing.

—which raises the question of what is natural and what is unnatural in a man. He goes on, "When he walks, he moves like an engine. . . . There is no more mercy in him than there is milk in a male tiger."

Shakespeare is contemplating whether or not it is natural for man to be so singularly male. He sees that Coriolanus's posture toward the world lacks something profoundly important: mercy, for one, and then the imaginative capacity to identify with others (a very female capacity) that makes us human.

But how did this incapacity to have "milk"—the milk of human kindness—develop in Coriolanus, so that he seems to have grown into a dragon rather than a man? The clue is in the discussions between the mother and the wife about how they regard the prowess of their sons and husbands. Volumnia declares that for a wife it should be better to see her man fighting than making love to her:

> If my son were my husband, I should freelier rejoice in that absence wherein he won honor than in the embracements of his bed where he would show most love.

She believes that it is in battle that a man proves himself a man. She would rather have eleven sons die nobly for their country, "than one voluptuously surfeit out of action." In this we—and Shakespeare—perceive a strange impulse in the mother to substitute physical prowess in male "doing" for love. This is underlined by Volumnia's lines

> The breasts of Hecuba,
> When she did suckle Hector, looked not lovelier
> Than Hector's forehead when it spit forth blood
> At Grecian sword, contemning.

We may see in Volumnia the impinging mother who offers her child a form of male "doing" instead of normal feminine responsiveness, thus failing to equip her son with that sympathetic human responsiveness on which the moral life and the capacity to live with others depend. Thus, while Coriolanus accomplishes his feats in battle "to please his mother," that is about all he can do. In all other spheres, he is intractable and incapable. Although his mother persuades him

257

to go to the market place, he cannot cope with that kind of open situation. He cannot drop his defences, fearing that "when steel grows soft, as that parasite's silk" he may become too vulnerable. Yet, inevitably, when he does give way to compassion (ironically, at the pleas of his wife and mother), he is doomed. The great warrior, lacking feminine sensitivity as a complement to his capacity for courageous action and prowess, is fatally impotent when dealing with the larger human questions of politics, government, justice, and community.

There is a great deal more to say about *Coriolanus*, but I have said enough to indicate how profoundly Shakespeare here plumbs the problem of the taboo on tenderness. The play reminds me of a display I saw on the Fourth of July, in which a truck, bearing a group of sad old ladies, was decorated with a banner along the side that proclaimed "proudly they gave their sons." Perhaps we find it no longer possible to tolerate such a message. If so, then this is a great advance because it indicates that we no longer feel we can endorse this kind of false celebration of male prowess that hides its weaknesses behind jingoism or patriotism, in the service of a state that seems like an impersonal machine. To be willing to accept our gentleness, our vulnerability, and our female-element capacities is a mark of strength not weakness. Shakespeare shows well where the weaknesses lie, in a human make-up that cannot find its female qualities.

Epilogue

I should like to end by saying that I do not wish to push Shakespeare into the realm of philosophical anthropology. We do not read Shakespeare for his philosophy or his anthropology, though we do appreciate his insights—for his art explores the nature of 'being.' Shakespeare's sonnets provide a useful corrective. To read any one of them is to reveal an engagement with human experience that is extremely complex. I shall conclude by looking at one or two of the sonnets and by asking what it is they illuminate about problems of gender and sexuality.

There is no doubt that if we read Shakespeare's Sonnet 94 we must think about human psychology, morality, and experience.

> They that have pow'r to hurt and will do none,
> That do not do the thing they most do show,
> Who, moving others, are themselves as stone,
> Unmovèd, cold, and to temptation slow;
> They rightly do inherit heaven's graces
> And husband nature's riches from expense.

Epilogue

Only, at this point, we begin to feel perhaps that within this sonnet is an ambivalence. Does it mean what it says, straightforwardly— that people who control themselves so tightly and keep their powers and inner intentions so secret should be commended? Are they the ones who rightly inherit "heaven's graces?" In light of contemporary psychoanalysis, we may feel that a severe superego perhaps hides suppressed desire or rage. And if we have read *Measure for Measure*, we shall have the deepest doubts about admiring—as the opening lines of this sonnet seem to urge us to admire—the Angelos of this world.

"They are the lords and owners of their faces"—yes, but "there is no art / to find the mind's construction in the face"; and man may be "most ignorant of what he's most assured—his glassy image." Are they the owners merely of their faces and not of themselves?

Others but stewards of their excellence.

To be lord and owner of one's face may mean only that one may seem fair and good while being inwardly corrupt. Will one then be, compared with others, the owner of one's own self, compared with those who are only temporary managers of their own excellence? Our response to this sonnet requires that we pick up resonances from other sonnets and, indeed, from the whole Shakespearean obsession with appearance and reality, the fair exterior and the darkness within, and the troubled or corrupt inwardness.

There is now an abrupt change of imagery and tone for the sextet. The octet, as I have said, seems to be ambivalent, as if the poet was not convinced of the truth of what he was saying or was being sardonic. A great deal depends on what we suppose he is saying to W. H., the "only begetter" to whom the sonnets are dedicated. After reflection, I believe Shakespeare is desperately urging W. H. not to cause some kind of havoc by entering into a sexual relationship that will almost certainly have a disastrous outcome.

He (W. H.) has the power to cause that havoc but will not—so Shakespeare hopes. If he doesn't cause such harm, even though he looks as if he might, then he will be his true self. Even though others are stirred by his beauty, he may well remain cold and above

260

temptation. If he does so, he will inherit "heaven's grace" and make the best use of his own riches, storing them up for the future. He will be in command of his own face, which will display his real self, by comparison with others who will only be temporary tenants and managers of their rich potentialities. Yet, even if one reads the lines as straight injunction to the young man, as a beseeching, there is a strong current moving the other way—as we realize if we remember Angelo—in the recognition that even if the young man developed the power to be "very snow-broth" there would be something deceptive and false about it. There would be in it a denial of human truth.

Thus, the sonnet is Blakean in its suspension of opposites. And in going on to advise the young man not to enter into a dangerous sexual alliance, there is more than a hint of sexual disease on the one hand and of hate in the emotional life on the other—the hate that, as Blake realized, could corrupt from within.

> The summer's flow'r is to the summer sweet,
> Though to itself it only live and die.

To fulfill oneself, it is not necessary to be seen or responded to by others. Even the flower that blooms unseen and wastes its substance on the desert art is sweet to the summer season in its *Selbstdarstellung* (manifestation of inner character on the surface):

> But if that flow'r with base infection meet,
> The basest weed outbraves his dignity.

A flower may be a fine and sweet thing; but if it becomes sick, then the most humble weed will become superior to it and will seem to be more worthy than the now-degraded flower.

> For sweetest things turn sourest by their deeds;
> Lilies that fester smell far worse than weeds.

The last line brings one up with a horrified shock because the word "fester" suggests pus and suppuration, and for such a fleshly condition to smell so bad suggests serious sickness of the body. Yet, the body behind the image of the lilies is, by that symbolism, a pure flesh—white and holy. For it to stink worse than stink wort seems

a rapid and appalling change; yet, it happens because a pure thing
rots more rapidly and catastrophically *because* of its purity. That
"purity," then, seems to be put in quotation marks because it was a
false purity that denied implicitly its weedlike proclivities (as Angelo did). The purity hid a suppressed corruption that now bursts
forth. This refers back to the earlier lines of the poem: sweet things
turn sourest because of the things they do, which are, in sweetness,
putting themselves in the way of infection—that is, by engaging in
sexual love. A horror of sexuality lies beneath the surface of the
poem, which takes its energy from a dismay that this beautiful boy
seems about to put himself in danger of sexual corruption. Oddly
enough, having read *Timon of Athens*, one cannot escape wholly
from a feeling that, like Timon, Shakespeare is fascinated by the
possibility of purity deliberately seeking corruption. And if we know
our Blake and are familiar with psychoanalytical literature, we
know that in this strange sonnet Shakespeare is embodying through
language deep and perplexing human truths, not least the impulse
we all have to deliberately corrupt ourselves. We may note the
same complex contradictions in Sonnet 99.

> The forward violet thus did I chide:
> Sweet thief, whence didst thou steal thy sweet that smells,
> If not from my love's breath? The purple pride
> Which on thy soft cheek for complexion dwells
> In my love's veins thou hast too grossly dyed.
> The lily I condemnèd for thy hand;
> And buds of marjoram had stol'n thy hair;
> The roses fearfully on thorns did stand,
> One blushing shame, another white despair;
> A third, nor red nor white, had stol'n of both,
> And to his robb'ry had annexed thy breath;
> But, for his theft, in pride of all his growth
> A vengeful canker eat him up to death.
>> More flowers I noted, yet I none could see
>> But sweet or color it had stol'n from thee.

Shakespeare's Sonnet 99 is about love, and so mangled has love
become in our thinking that even the topic needs a gloss. In rela-

tionships between man and woman, we may have today easier sex. However, psychotherapists tell us that many of their patients still find something missing—satisfaction for the need for love. As Rollo May writes in *Love and Will*, (1969) the existentialist therapist believes (because that is what he finds) that the primary need is for love as a source of meaning. Easier sexuality in our time, often an act of will, has even become in some spheres the sign of a new taboo on tenderness. Such a taboo has developed in the context of a new puritanism that suppresses the love need in a new way—that is, by insisting on sexual activity as a sign of health even when love is no nearer.

This is one good reason for attending to love poetry of the past: to examine what insights into this area of experience may be found in it. In Shakespeare's sonnets there is much torment about love, but it is about *love*. (The torment of "mere" sex is expressed in Sonnet 129.) But many of the sonnets are about the reality of the love need—even when the symbolism of the poem is in a conventional mode, as in Sonnet 99 where Shakespeare uses the symbolism of flowers. In discussing a poem such as this, one implicitly acknowledges the importance of human emotional needs, which are universal and continuing. One also recognizes that the aspirations and beauties of love are accompanied by much pain and difficulty.

The final two lines sum up at the conventional level the theme of the sonnet.

> More flowers I noted, yet I none could see
> But sweet or color it had stol'n from thee.

The usual use of flower imagery in love poetry is to assert that the woman has drawn into her features all the beauties of nature and yet transcends them. But in this sonnet, Shakespeare makes the fanciful assertion that the flowers have stolen their colors and sweetness from his love. Underlying this conceit is a good deal of painful and tormented feeling.

He chides the violet and takes a condemnatory attitude to the other flowers, some of which are, he says, "condemned" and have in consequence suffered. The sonnet was written at a time when people were hanged for theft; thus, a thief who was caught and

Epilogue

convicted was doomed to die in a horrible way. This aspect of Elizabethan life lurks forcibly behind the poem and raises an important historical-sociological question. Can we, living in a time when people try to forget pain and death, to hide unpleasant aspects of existence, but mercifully have become more humane in law, be as serious about the subjective life as the Elizabethans?

The violet is "forward," and this introduces the element of time. Violets bloom early in spring, but they do not last long. Linking the violet with the love's breath thus introduces an undercurrent of mutability and the brevity of life. This, too, contributes to the seriousness that underlies the sincerity here, despite the playful conceits. The violet can only have stolen its sweet perfume from the love's breath. In doing so, the violet has taken on some of the loved one's mortality.

> The purple pride
> Which on thy soft cheek for complexion dwells
> In my love's veins thou has too grossly dyed.

"Pride," of course, has an extra resonance because pride was one of the seven deadly sins. The violet, it seems, is trying to look human and to be proud of it; but the color it has stolen, by dyeing its cheek with the loved one's blood, is too gross. By implication, human sweetnesses and color are too gross for the flowers, and this gives the poem a strangely ominous undercurrent. This has a very subtle effect, of a literary kind. It is as if the poet is saying "we customarily bring flowers into the human aspect and talk (say) of flowers in cheeks. Suppose we turn this humanization about and talk about cheeks in flowers or purple blood in the petals of violets. The effect is to grossen the flowers!"

Thus, the lily, which has stolen the whiteness of the loved one's "hand" is "condemned" for stealing it. The lily appears pale because it is condemned to death. The fluffy, wound-up buds of marjoram may have a pleasant perfume, but they are guilty because of that "stol'n." Perhaps we see in the background the heads of hair of hanged people? It is difficult for us to imagine the horror of public spectacles of judicial death and even more difficult to imagine being familiar from daily experience with executed corpses. Here, the roses are like people on the way to Tyburn.

> The roses fearfully on thorns did stand,
> One blushing shame, another white despair.

Roses have thorns, and this (especially to the child) is perplexing and disturbing. (See Sonnet 35: "Roses have thorns, and silver fountains mud.") That they have thorns is playfully explained in terms of the roses being guilty because they have stolen their scent and color from the loved one. Therefore, they must stand on tenterhooks, condemned to death in the tumbril. The red rose is blushing with guilt; a white rose is pale with the despair and dread of going to the gallows. The third rose, which is pink or some intermediate color, has, in addition, stolen the loved one's perfume. Despite the rose's pride in this (like the violet's pride in dipping its petals in the loved one's blood), the flower is eaten up by a "vengeful canker."

Now the question arises. Why should love be associated with such sinister undercurrents? And here we must surely, if we are to understand why the poem moves us, explore the unconscious. Why should a canker, in revenge, destroy a rose because it has stolen the breath of the loved one? We cannot answer this, I believe, unless we enter into the area of unconscious life and examine the oral aspects of primitive layers of the psyche.

The poem assumes that the poet enjoys the fair aspect of the beloved—the red, white, pink, and purple—and enjoys her breath. Of course, there are the appetitive focus of his desire. But the flowers are accused of grossening themselves, putting themselves in fear, and being eaten by canker. Thus in psychoanalytical terminology, the flowers are *taking* in an oral way, and the underlying dynamic is envy. The "vengeful canker" is the envy that lurks beneath gratitude and that has all the passionate taking qualities of primitive oral desire. Behind the poem is the fear, such as we all feel, that our love hunger, like the flowers, may "eat" the beloved and that, even when we feel pride in the possession of our love, some "vengeful canker" may consume us to death. Blake's "Sick Rose" is perhaps the most powerful expression of this ambiguous aspect of love—of ambivalence, the admixture of love and hate.

Epilogue

Beneath the flower symbolism of Sonnet 99 is an expression of the ambivalence in the human soul, the way gratitude in love (the poem is full of giving away) is commingled with hate (the poem is also full of taking). That which seems to belong to the living moment, which reassures us we are alive, also belongs to decay and death. Indeed, love always exacerbates the drive of time toward death—the problem of 'being-unto-death'.

The poem, as a completed artifact, yields some satisfaction in the face of all these disturbing awarenesses. The form itself, the playful conceit, and the arresting imagery still the dynamic of 'being-unto-death' and so assert the *Dasein*—the feeling of having been meaningfully "there." The more the poem penetrates into the disturbing aspects of existence, the greater the satisfactions it yields. The poem offers a meaning that may be snatched from the flux.

The poem thus attends with a particular gravity to fundamental human needs—for love, for bridging the gulf between one and another, and for meaning. It is a strange mixture of male and female and dread and joy. It relates the quest for love to the attempt to "construct something upon which to rejoice" in the face of death.

Thus, the poem takes us beyond the conventional facades of our manic or blunted life that is sunk in mere routine or forgetfulness. By the excitement of our response, it faces us with problems of love, hate, death and mortality, and the perplexities of gender.

By its success as a poem, it seems to triumph over these by the power of the imagination. In this, we are drawn to participate. We have to work in order to grasp

> The lily I condemnèd for thy hand . . .

in all its fullness of comparison and ambiguity. (The qualities of the hand have been given to the lily, which then takes on a human quality of being condemned. The lily is pale because of it and is white with its acknowledgment—as at funerals—of mortality and death.) The poem forces us to think imaginatively about relaxational experience.

Thus, we are not presented simply with realities—that is, the disturbing truths of human existence—in mere morbidity. We take part in striving for meaning—the meaning that love can yield. And this is another kind of involvement, in the subtleties of rhythm, the "voice" of the poem, its play with conceits, and its turning of the tables on convention. And so we are involved in its imaginative triumph; we share art by which meaning may be established.

This is surely a most valuable lesson at a time when all around us there is a collapse of meaning, in a civilization in which sources of meaning are becoming increasingly scarce and much of our lives tends toward the meaningless.

We cannot, however, extract anything that helps us to form a set of moral precepts. There are many lines that are memorable speech and undoubtedly will stick in our minds all our lives. Although the sonnet is often beautiful (sometimes in a terrible way), we cannot easily claim that this art has done us good. What it has done is to give us some insight into the kind of experience we may find within ourselves or encounter in life. It offers insights. Thus, insofar as it contributes to our ponderings about the nature of love, it helps us with the complex problem of meaning in existence. But, as so often, the memorableness may not be at one wholly with the setting. Thus, in *Othello*, the memorable and beautiful line

When you shall these unlucky deeds relate . . .

actually comes in a speech (Othello's last) by which we are made to feel that the character is presenting himself in a completely false light—that is, in terms of his own "story." Even then Othello still deludes himself about the nature of his disastrous act and evades the reality of it—so that (as Leavis said in a lecture once) we want to kick him.

The very beauty to which we respond in Shakespeare's poetry comes from some of his deepest perplexities about woman and love. Our recognition of the negative dynamics in our unconscious feelings about woman should not, therefore, daunt us.

As Ann Belford Ulanov puts it in "The Witch Archetype" (1977), we should regard the witch as an indication of potentialities rather than as a threat:

Epilogue

The witch arouses our imaginations to new visions of the nature of the psyche. She personifies energies that connect us with unsuspected unconscious potentialities. (5)

In other words, from the perspective I have been following throughout this book, the phantom woman is a part of our own inner makeup, however much she is derived from our experience of the mother. Thus, exploring her nature is part of the discovery of ourselves, and as we explore that nature we find mysterious and dark aspects of our own inner lives. If our fear of the phantom woman is projected out into the world, in false modes, then we shall contribute to the destructiveness in the world; and woman herself in society may suffer, as D. W. Winnicott points out. But if we can come to terms with the phantom woman within ourselves and acknowledge these elements within ourselves as belonging to us, then we may find positive resources we have never before known. Indeed, could Shakespeare have achieved his great sense of continuity and gratitude—such as he expresses through Ferdinand and Miranda, or Florizel and Perdita, or in Marina—had he not confronted the witch woman in *Timon of Athens* and elsewhere? Perhaps that is the difference between Shakespeare's view of humanity and that of the Jacobean dramatist who saw woman in such a dark light (for example, Beatrice in Middleton and Rowley's *The Changeling*).

What we can see is that certain writers—such as Shakespeare, Blake, and Lawrence—when confronting woman are engaging with the deepest problems of existence, because woman symbolizes the whole living reality of the cosmos.

Finding woman and respecting, or "allowing" her mystery is bound up with our capacity to find and "allow" Mother Earth; thus, this is bound up with our very relationship to reality. It is the mother who, by reflecting us, brings us to find ourselves in a meaningful cosmos. As Karl Stern argues in *The Flight from Woman* (1965), there is a complex and closely woven connection between our attitudes to woman and to the universe. The earth itself is like a great breast or mother; and if we have an adequate attitude to woman, we shall feel the earth to be benign and shall live *with* the earth and not exploit her.[1] Those who have not had an adequate experience with the mother and cannot relate to woman tend to

Epilogue

feel alienated. Stern traces this alienation through Descartes and Schopenhauer to Sartre and shows how each feels progressively alienated because of a deepening psychopathological inability to relate to woman or find her. In consequence, since the seventeenth century knowledge itself has become masculinized and, therefore, dominated by the mathematical and the abstract. Those female, intuitive, 'being' modes of knowing and perceiving have been distrusted and lie in abeyance. This is one of the deepest problems of our world and of Western civilization. Our task is, like Lear's, to refind the feminine and "take upon us the mystery of things."[2]

Notes

INTRODUCTION

1. For the author's views on this paper, see Holbrook, "Truth, Campaigns, and Freedom," 54.
2. And there are ideologues within ideologies. A student complains that in one section of the examination paper where she had expected to answer questions on Freud and Virginia Woolf, there were only questions on a certain segment of French feminist writers—about whom the main proponent of the course, who conducted the seminars for this paper, had refused to discuss because she did not believe in them.

CHAPTER I

1. Ann Belford Ulanov, in "Witch Archetype," 3, reports on an organization called W.I.T.C.H. (Witches International Terrorist Conspiracy from Hell), which lauds aggressive women and asserts the value of the witch qualities in woman that society has outlawed.
2. See Ann Belford Ulanov, Feminine in Jungian Psychology, 18; and Ann Belford Ulanov and Barry Ulanov, Religion and the Unconscious. The animus in the poetry of Sylvia Plath also is worth considering; it is often dead or malignant but by no means a spring of soul.

271

Notes

3. See Winnicott, "The Split-off Male and Female Elements to Be Found in Men and Women—Theoretical Influences," in *Playing and Reality*. Guntrip discusses Winnicott's paper in *Schizoid Phenomena*, 249ff. Presumably, Guntrip used the paper I have in typescript, which also was published in *Forum* (February 1966). The version in *Playing and Reality* is somewhat abbreviated.
4. See Ann Belford Ulanov, *Receiving Woman*, chap. 4.
5. For a parallel case, see Khan, "To Hear with Eyes." Chap. 16 in *Privacy of the Self*. It is interesting that Winnicott considered his case study here to be relevant to Hamlet's predicament.
6. I have examined these fears by looking at the work of schizoid individuals in literature and music, notably Dylan Thomas, Sylvia Plath, and Gustav Mahler. See especially my analysis of Plath's poem "Poem for a Birthday," in David Holbrook, *Sylvia Plath: Poetry and Existence* (London: Athlone, 1976), 23–64.

CHAPTER 2

1. Some of these experiences are beautifully described by Len Chaloner. See Chaloner, "Me and Not-Me." Chap. 2 in *Feeling and Perception*.
2. To be able to accept "acceptable madness" is an important necessity in other realms. It is important in grief to allow oneself to go somewhat mad. There is a kind of reckless madness in sexual life, while all kinds of creativity may involve something approaching it. It is a fear of this extension of experience into what usually is suppressed for the individual's own comfort that causes psychoanalysis itself to be rejected, attacked, and suppressed.
3. Winnicott refers to the following papers that address this problem: L. Kanner, "Autistic Disturbances of Affective Contact"; L. Bender, "Childhood Schizophrenia"; and M. J. Mahler, "Problems of Infant Neurosis."
4. I have used these insights in my studies of Sylvia Plath, Dylan Thomas, and Gustav Mahler. These insights are crucial to our understanding of the problem of the fear of woman, which originates in the experience of what seems to be hate from woman. The important phrase is that "impingement is experienced as hate." It seems that impingement was what D. H. Lawrence experienced with his mother.
5. The word "psyche" would be better here than the word "psychology," which surely means a study of *the* mind, whereas Winnicott clearly means *a* mind.
6. See Holbrook, "How Do We Know a Child?" Chap. 5 in *Education and Philosophical Anthropology*. See also David Holbrook, *Further Studies*

Notes

in Philosophical Anthropology (Aldershot, England: Gower, 1988), chap. 5.

7. See Khan, "Reparation to the Self," 93.
8. See Winnicott, *Therapeutic Consultations in Child Psychiatry*, 391. These phenomenological concepts are unfamiliar to the academic mind, and I sometimes despair of every getting them across in literary discourse. People in ordinary walks of life—especially the so-called ordinary, good mother—have no such difficulty. One morning in a baker's shop, a mother was holding a baby who gazed at me with his blue eyes and chuckled. "What penetrating stares they have," I exclaimed. "Yes," said the young married woman who serves me in the shop, "it's as if they were looking into your inner mind, isn't it?" As Winnicott says, "the mother knows."
9. I have discussed the symbolism of mirrors in this respect in the work of Sylvia Plath. See Holbrook, *Sylvia Plath* (see chap. 1, n. 6), 142. There are other related symbols. In the writings of D. H. Lawrence I do not find the mirror to be a predominant symbol. What I do find is an omnipresent manifestation of the mother's face—especially in the *Moon*—and many various manifestations of the maternal principle—in flowers, in beasts, and in the many faces of woman. Mirrors are important symbols of the mother's face and eyes in Lewis Carroll's *Alice's Adventures in Wonderland* and *Alice through the Looking Glass*, as well as in works by C. S. Lewis and George MacDonald.
10. See Stern, *Flight from Woman*, 18. There, Stern's emphasis is close to that of Winnicott and others, to whom I have referred in earlier works.
11. My eldest daughter's second baby was born exactly on the next anniversary of the date that a previous baby that miscarried might have been born.
12. See Edmund Husserl, *Erfahrung und Urteil. Untersuchungen zur Genealogie der Logik* (Prague: Akademia Verlagsbuchhandlung, 1939); and Karl Jaspers, "Kausale und verständliche Zusammenhänge zwischen Schicksal und Psychose bei der Dementia Praecox (Schizophrenie)." *Z.f.d. ges. Neurol. und Psychiat.* 14 (1913): 158–263. For a discussion of the main work of Husserl and Jaspers in their historical setting, see Holbrook, "A Hundred Years of Philosophical Anthropology." Chap. 4 in *Education and Philosophical Anthropology*.
13. Perhaps one of the cruelest and most symbolic of all such customs is "female circumcision," which is a mutilation of the clitoris that destroys the capacity for sexual pleasure. Symbolically the operation is an attack, out of fear, both on the male element in the woman and on her libidinal fulfillment.
14. The phrase Holy Mary syndrome was used by Freud to describe to Gustav Mahler his idealization of his wife, Alma. Mahler said to his wife that if only she were ugly he could love her. Dickens also displayed

Notes

an inability to accept love from a woman unless she was maimed in some way, as with Lizzie Hexham. See the entry for the Holy Mary syndrome in the appendix to David Holbrook, *Gustav Mahler and the Courage to Be* (London: Vision Press, 1975), 255.

15. Much of this is dramatized in the brothel chapter in *Ulysses*, not least Bloom's sexual ambiguities.

CHAPTER 3

1. See Holbrook, *Human Hope*, 49–60.
2. Tolstoy is an author who is profoundly aware of the female way of knowing. This is evident, for example, in his portrayal of Kitty with her baby in *Anna Karenina*.
3. The appeal of the "thinking machine" lies in the fact that it never had a mother. If man were a Cartesian machine, he would not possess those problems that stem from his experience of the feminine; thus, he would possess no emotional or existential life.
4. Each child will be different, a problem some women cannot face, which can lead to disastrous consequences such as those explored by Winnicott in the split-off female-element case history discussed on page 14–16.

CHAPTER 4

1. See Guntrip, *Personality Structure and Human Interaction*, 420ff. Fairbairn's internal psychic dynamics include the *libidinal ego*, the *antilibidinal ego*, and the *central* (or *false*) *ego*. The *object* (the mother) is divided into *exciting object* and *rejecting object*, while there is also the *regressive ego*, the *oral needy libidinal ego*, and so on. There is no doubt that human nature is so complex that such a complex system may be necessary. However, with Fairbairn's elaborate system, I find that the effect is to dissolve into confusion rather than to help insight.
2. Some years ago, a young man in Paris was arrested for eating his girlfriend. See the *Times* (London), 17 June 1981.
3. This is not the place to discuss the question, but surely the passionate debate today about women priests belongs to these unconscious issues: Woman is too impure to conduct the sacrament, it is felt, because she menstruates. Her creativity cannot be tolerated.

CHAPTER 5

1. Another example can be found in Gustav Mahler's *Kindertotenlieder*, especially in "Wen der Mutterlein."

Notes

2. The "flimsy thing" has evident analogies with the brother's christening robe. As a child, Barrie lived with the problem that his mother talked to a dead sibling who was not really there.

3. There are, actually, many literary references in *Peter Pan*. Behind the playfulness, we can recognize certain important moments in Shakespeare. At one moment, for example, Wendy is Cordelia, as when she seems to be dead; but she then gives signs of being alive: Peter cries, "She lives!" See also "the way to dusty death" from Macbeth's famous speech about the futility of life and references to *The Tempest* and the sounds and voices on the island.

4. It is a mark of the period that often in plays and novels young lovers show their love by baby talk. See, for example, how the lovers talk in George Bernard Shaw's *Mrs. Warren's Profession*. It is a very English form of emotional ineptitude.

5. The only reference Coveney gives is to Denis MacKeil, *The Story of J. M. B.* (London: Peter Davies, 1941), from which, presumably, he takes the account of Elizabeth Bergner's influence.

6. There is also, of course, the "other world" of *Peter Pan* that is sometimes so threatening.

7. Goitein draws attention also to the phrase used about Mary Rose, "a finger has . . . stopped her growth"; he believes "the Father" has kept her for himself.

8. An analysis of Sylvia Plath's kind of predicament exposes the dangers here of the regression becoming total and final.

9. See also Ted Hughes's "Song for Phallus," in *Crow* (London: Faber and Faber, 1970), 77. In this poem Hughes writes, "What a cruel bastard God is."

10. Goitein writes, "It is not pleasant being a dream-child. Whatever her parents think must perforce be the thoughts of Mary Rose. . . . All the while attention is being focussed on her image; she lives, indeed she shines forth with the hallucinatory vividness; without it she must die" (Goitein 1926, 192–93).

11. See Bachelard, *Poetics of Space*, passim, on the room as a symbol of the mother's body and other such symbolism.

CHAPTER 6

1. See, for example, the murder of Sir Thomas Overbury, an event in which Thomas Campion was involved. (Campion was suspected of laundering some money in the affair.) I was interested to note recently that Nathaniel Hawthorne, in *The Scarlet Letter* (1850), was fascinated by this murder.

Notes

2. See Freud, "On Hamlet and Oedipus," in *Interpretation of Dreams*, vol. 4, 264–66.
3. Compare these lines with the following from Sonnet 99: "The forward violet thus did I chide."
4. As I read this speech again, the title of one of Knights's chapters in *Drama and Society* came into my mind: "Shakespeare and Profit Inflations."
5. Here, "naught" means naughty but retains a flavor of nothing.
6. "Neck" surely is here, by displacement, genital. A *glue-neck* is a prostitute in underworld cant.
7. Cf. the following lines from *The Winter's Tale:*

> LEONTES:
> to do't, or no, is certain
> To me a break-neck.

CHAPTER 7

1. Before the denaturing speech of Albany, Goneril has just said how different Edmund is from her husband:

> O, the difference of man and man
> To thee a woman's services are due.
> My foot usurps my body.

The Quarto "corrected" reads "A fool usurps my bed." The Folio reads "My fool usurps my body." "Foot" seems most correct. In any case, Goneril is expressing contempt for her husband and a sense that the proper decision is for her to give her body to Edmund—a reversal of proper values under the impulse of voracious lust.
2. See also "Paint till a horse shall mire upon your face," in *Timon of Athens*. Here, the disturbances concerning woman's image may be linked with the phenomenology of coprophilia.
3. As W. B. Yeats's Crazy Jane says, "But Love has pitched his mansion in / The place of excrement" ("Crazy Jane Talks with the Bishop," in *The Collected Poems of W. B. Yeats* [New York: Macmillan, 1979], 254).
4. T. S. Eliot, *Four Quartets* (1944).
5. Samuel Johnson (1709–84) offered criticism of Shakespeare characteristic of his time but was intelligent enough to perceive his genius. His remarks on *King Lear* are made in his edition of *The Plays of William Shakespeare* (1765), the preface to which is one of Johnson's most famous pieces of critical writing.

Notes

1. *Henry IV*, part 1, extends immensely the range of contemplation of human nature after *Richard II* to include everything that is represented by Falstaff and company—lust, cowardice, drunkenness, avarice, and egocentric cowardice—just as Freud extended our range of human proclivities to the great gain of our impulse to ask how such an ambivalent and mixed creature as man can be properly governed.
2. Edmund Husserl (1859–1938) was a German mathematician, logician, and philosopher. He is recognized as the founding father of phenomenology—that is, the study of the phenomena of consciousness. Husserl's aim was to "bracket off" preconceptions and let phenomena present themselves in their own terms.
3. *Walpurgisnacht* (Walpurgis Night) was the night preceding May Day when witches were abroad to worship the devil. The name comes from Saint Walpurgis, a German saint who is supposed to provide protection against the magic arts.
4. On Christmas of 1981, I found myself fascinated by the fact that my plump and attractive grandson of five months was exactly twice the weight of the goose we were going to eat.
5. Otto Gross (1877–1930) was a German sexual revolutionary of the Munich Schwabing movement and was an associate of psychoanalysts such as Carl Jung. He was a lover of Else and Frieda von Richthofen (the latter later became Frieda Lawrence, the wife of D. H. Lawrence).
6. Note the references to vomit in Iachimo's response to Imogen in *Cymbeline* and the physical feelings of Lear toward woman's body: "burning, scalding, stench, consumption."
7. The word "mince" also appears in an odd context in Lear's lines about the "simpering dame" who "minces virtue," though there it means to affect in a mincing way.
8. Compare "passive drugs" with W. B. Yeat's "As recollection or the drug decide" ("Among School Children," in *The Collected Poems* [see chap. 7, no. 3], 213). Yeats's lines are also about the bearableness—or otherwise—of life.

1. For example, in their anguish and in seeking their integrity, the heroines of Elizabeth Gaskell, George Eliot, and Jane Austen enlist our awareness that they are really good and true and not mere sentimental embodiments of maidenly virtue.

Notes

2. F. R. Leavis valued highly this poem of Eliot's, without ever being able to say why. Leavis's reading of the poem, captured on tape, is quite magical. Obviously, Leavis had possessed the poem's meaning—ineffably.
3. The line is Hercules's in Seneca's tragedy *Hercules Furens*. He cries, "What is this place, what country, what region of the world?" as he returns to sanity after having slaughtered his wife and children.

CHAPTER 11

1. Compare the use of "supply" with the following from *Othello:*

> as knaves be such abroad,
> Who having, by their own importunate suit,
> Or voluntary dotage of some mistress,
> Convinced them or supplied them.

CHAPTER 12

1. The "worm" will act according to his nature.

CHAPTER 13

1. I have discussed *The Winter's Tale* at length in a previous work in terms of this larger meaning and do not propose to reconsider it here. Although if I did, I would say more about themes of gratitude and continuity. I would try to relate it to Mahler's quest (in *Das Lied von der Erde* [The song of the earth] and in the Ninth Symphony) to find the connection between love and a sense of the continual re-creation of the relationship between man and the earth, and a sense that, despite the dreadfulness of death, nothing can take away from us the meaning inherent in the fact that *we have been.* See David Holbrook, *The Quest for Love* (London: Methuen, 1964), 127–91.

EPILOGUE

1. See Freud, "The Dream Work," in *Interpretation of Dreams*, vol. 6. In it, Freud relates in a footnote how Julius Caesar had a dream of sexual relations with his mother. The oneiroscopists interpreted this as a favorable omen of his taking possession of the earth.

Notes

2. With women, of course, the problem is different from that in men. Here is a different story and perhaps another book. We might explore this problem in the literature of the Brontës. For example, there is something clearly strange about Charlotte Brontë's image of man. In *Villette* (1853), for example, she gives a marvelous picture of Madame Beck, of the heroine Lucy Snowe, of Polly, and of Miss Genevra. However, the men are much less satisfactory, and she often plays a shadowy game with them—as with Graham who becomes Dr. John. Mr. Paul is a figure who shifts and changes and seems never clearly realized. The hero of *The Professor* (1857) and Hunsden in the same book are by no means as clearly grasped by the reader as is Lucy Snowe; and while Jane Eyre is tangibly "there" as a woman into whose sufferings we enter with great sympathy, Mr. Rochester is a figure from romance who never quite seems humanly real to us (though he does gain in humanness as he suffers).

In Emily Brontë's great novel, *Wuthering Heights* (1847), while Heathcliff is a powerful figure, perhaps he is understood better as an archetypal figure of myth—to be understood, I believe, most adequately if we see him as Emily's own animus, her male element that she was striving to come to terms with and embrace in her whole identity. From her poems we learn of a strange mystical figure to whom she deferred, a kind of godlike man, a mentor, who was the source of her being.

In both these writers we have a fascinating glimpse of women striving with problems of gender, striving to become whole, and striving to find themselves in a meaningful existence with the world. They both have a marvelous apprehension of the underlying wildness and savagery of the world—like the moors in *Wuthering Heights*, which is the outward symbol of the savage and wild elements in human nature, especially in its implacable yearning to find a sense of meaning in existence that will satisfy the deepest existential need.

The quest for wholeness in woman, then, is a very different story; and it involves complex modes in the development of gender. The woman perhaps identifies more easily with the mother, but problems may arise where there are difficulties with the father—as was surely the case with the Brontës. Women writers with a strong male component but who also were confident in their femininity, such as George Eliot, were able to give us marvelous depictions of men as well as women. Others, like Radclyffe Hall, reveal the deep anguish sometimes found in women who cannot find an integrated sense of gender and 'being' in themselves. We may ponder this kind of problem in a writer like Edith Wharton, whose men often are weak and nebulous but whose women often also fall short of fulfillment.

Bibliography

BOOKS

Abbs, P. *Reclamations: Essays on Culture, Mass-Culture, and the Curriculum.* London: Heinemann Educational Books, 1979.
Adamson, Jane. *Othello as Tragedy: Some Problems of Judgment and Feeling.* New York: Cambridge University Press, 1980.
Asquith, Cynthia. *Portrait of Barrie.* London: J. Barrie, 1954.
Bachelard, Gaston. *The Poetics of Reverie.* Boston: Beacon Press, 1969a.
———. *The Poetics of Space.* Boston: Beacon Press, 1969b.
Barrie, James. *The Little White Bird.* London: Hoddler and Stoughton, 1902.
———. *Margaret Ogilvie, by Her Son.* London: Hodder and Stoughton, 1896.
———. *Mary Rose: A Play in Three Acts.* New York: Charles Scribner's Sons, 1924.
———. *Peter Pan: Or the Boy Who Would Not Grow Up.* New York: Charles Scribner's Sons, 1928.
———. *The Plays of J. M. Barrie.* London: Hodder and Stoughton, 1947.
Bennett, Arnold. *The Old Wives' Tale.* New York: Hodder and Stoughton, 1911.
Binswanger, Ludwig. *Being-in-the-World.* New York: Basic Books, 1963.
Bowlby, John. *Child Care and the Growth of Love.* Harmondsworth, England: Penguin, 1953.

Bibliography

Bradley, A. C. *Shakespearean Tragedy*. London: Macmillan, 1904.

Brink, Andrew. *Creativity as Repair*. Hamilton: Cromlech Press,m 1977a.

———. *Loss and Symbolic Repair*. Hamilton: Cromlech Press, 1977b.

Buber, Martin. *Between Man and Man*. London: Routledge and Kegan Paul, 1947.

———. "Distance and Relation." In *The Knowledge of Man*, edited by M. Friedman. London: Allen and Unwin, 1964.

———. *I and Thou*. New York: Charles Scribner's Sons, 1957.

Buytendijk, F. J. J. "Essay on the Phenomenological Approach to Problems of Feeling and Emotion." In *Psychoanalysis and Existential Philosophy*, edited by H. Ruytenbak. New York: E. P. Dutton, 1962.

———. *Phénomènologie de la Rencontre*. Paris: P. Desclée de Brouwer, 1952.

———. In *Readings in Existential Phenomenology*, edited by D. O'Connor and N. Lawrence. Englewood Cliffs, N.J.: Prentice-Hall, 1967.

———. *Woman*. Glen Rock, N.J.: Newman Press, 1965.

Cassirer, Ernst. *An Essay on Man*. New Haven, Conn.: Yale University Press, 1963.

Chaloner, Len. *Feeling and Perception in Young Children*. London: Tavistock, 1963.

Collingwood, R. G. *The Idea of Nature*. Oxford: Clarendon Press, 1945.

———. *Principles of Art*. Oxford: Clarendon Press, 1938.

Coveney, Peter. *Poor Monkey*. London: Rockliff, 1957.

Deutsch, Helene. *The Psychology of Women*. New York: Grune and Stratton, 1945.

Eliot, T. S. "Marina." In *Collected Poems: 1909–35*. New York: Harcourt, Brace, 1936.

Ellmann, Richard. *James Joyce*. New York: Oxford University Press, 1959.

Erikson, Erik. *Childhood and Society*. New York: W. W. Norton, 1959.

Esterson, Aaron. *The Leaves of Spring*. London: Tavistock, 1970.

Faber, M. D., ed. *The Design Within: Psychoanalytic Approaches to Shakespeare*. New York: Science House, 1970.

Fairbairn, W. R. D. *Psychoanalytical Studies of the Personality*. London: Tavistock, 1952.

Farber, Leslie H. *The Ways of the Will*. London: Constable, 1966.

Foudraine, Jan. *Not Made of Wood*. London: Quartet, 1974.

Frankl, Victor. *From Death Camp to Existentialism*. Boston: Beacon Press, 1963.

———. *The Doctor and Soul: From Psychotherapy to Logotherapy*. New York: Knopf, 1965.

———. *Psychotherapy and Existentialism*. New York: Washington Square Press, 1967.

Bibliography

Freud, Sigmund. *The Interpretation of Dreams*. London: Hogarth Press, 1953.

———. *On the History of the Psychoanalytical Movement*. 1914. Reprint. Vol. 1 of *Collected Papers*, 287. London: Hogarth Press, 1924.

Friedman, Maurice, ed. *The Knowledge of Man*. London: Allen and Unwin, 1964.

Fromm, Eric. *Escape from Freedom (The Fear of Freedom)*. London: Routledge and Kegan Paul, 1942.

Gaskell, Elizabeth. *North and South*. New York: AMS Press, 1972.

Grene, Marjorie. *The Anatomy of Knowledge*. London: Routledge and Kegan Paul, 1969.

———. *Approaches to a Philosophical Biology*. New York: Basic Books, 1968.

———. *Dreadful Freedom: An Introduction to Existentialism*. Chicago: University of Chicago Press, 1948.

———. *Introduction to Existentialism*. Chicago: University of Chicago Press, 1959.

———. *The Knower and the Known*. London: Faber and Faber, 1966.

———. *Martin Heidegger*. London: Bowes and Bowes, 1957.

———. *Philosophy in and out of Europe*. Berkeley and Los Angeles: University of California Press, 1976.

———. *The Understanding of Nature*. Boston: D. Reidel, 1974.

Guntrip, Harry. *Personality Structure and Human Interaction*. London: Hogarth Press, 1961.

———. *Schizoid Phenomena, Object Relations, and the Self*. London: Hogarth Press, 1968.

Holbrook, David. *Education and Philosophical Anthropology*. Cranbury, N.J.: Associated University Presses, 1987.

———. *English for Meaning*. Reading: National Foundation for Educational Research, 1980.

———. *Human Hope and the Death Instinct*. Oxford: Pergamon, 1971.

Isaacs, Susan. *The Nursery Years*. London: Routledge and Kegan Paul, 1929.

Jardine, Lisa. *Still Harping on His Daughters*. Hassocks, England: Harvester Press, 1983.

Jung, C. G. *Contributions to Analytical Psychology*. London: Routledge and Kegan Paul, 1928.

Khan, Masud. *The Privacy of the Self*. London: Hogarth Press, 1979.

Klein, Melanie. *Contributions to Psychoanalysis*. London: Hogarth Press, 1941.

———. *Developments in Psychoanalysis*. London: Hogarth Press, 1952.

———. *Envy and Gratitude*. London: Tavistock, 1957.

———. *New Directions in Psychoanalysis*. London: Tavistock, 1958.

Bibliography

————. *Our Adult Society and Its Roots in Infancy*. London: Hogarth Press, 1963.

————. *The Psychoanalysis of Children*. London: Hogarth Press, 1932.

Knights, L. C. *Drama and Society in the Age of Johnson*. London: Chatto & Windus, 1937.

Laing, R. D. *The Divided Self*. London: Tavistock, 1960.

————. *Interpersonal Perception: A Theory and Method of Research*. New York: Springer, 1960.

————. *The Self and Others*. London: Tavistock, 1961.

Langer, Susanne. *Mind: An Essay in Human Feeling*. Baltimore: Johns Hopkins University Press, 1967.

————. *Philosophical Sketches*. Baltimore: Johns Hopkins University Press, 1962.

————. *Philosophy in a New Key*. Cambridge: Harvard University Press, 1957.

Lawrence, D. H. *Kangaroo*. New York: T. Seltzer, 1923.

————. *Sons and Lovers*. New York: Modern Library, 1922.

Leavis, F. R. *The Common Pursuit*. London: Chatto & Windus, 1952.

————. *The Living Principle*. London: Chatto & Windus, 1975.

Leavis, Q. D. *Collected Essays: The American Novel and Reflections on the European Novel*, vol. 1. New York: Cambridge University Press, 1983.

Ledermann, E. K. *Existential Neurosis*. London: Butterworth, 1972.

————. *Mental Health and Human Conscience*. Amersham, England: Arebury, 1984.

Lomas, Peter. *The Case for a Personal Psychotherapy*. Oxford: Oxford University Press, 1981.

————. *True and False Experience*. London: Hogarth Press, 1967.

————, ed. *The Predicament of the Family*. London: Hogarth, 1967.

McCann, J., and B. Ulanov, eds. *The Cloud of Unknowing*. London: Burns, Oates and Washbourne, 1936.

Maslow, Abraham. *Towards a Psychology of Being*. New York: Van-Nostrand, 1968.

May, Rollo. *Love and Will*. New York: W. W. Norton, 1969.

Mead, Margaret. *Male and Female*. New York: Mentor, 1955.

Merleau-Ponty, Maurice. *Phenomenology of Perception*. London: Routledge and Kegan Paul, 1962.

Milner, Marion. *Hands of the Living God: An Account of a Psychoanalytic Treatment*. New York: International Universities Press, 1969.

————. *On Not Being Able to Paint*. London: Heinemann Educational Books, 1950.

Moberley, Elizabeth R. *Psychogenesis: The Early Development of Gender Identity*. Boston: Routledge and Kegan Paul, 1983.

Bibliography

Moustakas, Clark E. *Existential Child Therapy*. New York: Basic Books, 1966.

Naevestad, Marie von. *The Colours of Rage and Love*. Oslo, Norway: Universitetsforlaget, 1979.

Plessner, Helmuth. *Laughing and Crying: A Study of the Limits of Human Behavior*. Evanston, Ill.: Northwestern University Press, 1970.

Polanyi, Michael. *Knowing and Being*. London: Routledge and Kegan Paul, 1969.

———. *Personal Knowledge: Toward a Post-Critical Philosophy*. Chicago: University of Chicago Press, 1962.

———. *Science, Faith, and Society*. Chicago: University of Chicago Press, 1946.

———. *The Tacit Dimension*. Garden City, N.Y.: Doubleday, 1966.

Polanyi, Michael, and Harry Prosch. *Meaning*. Chicago: University of Chicago Press, 1975.

Rickword, Edgell, ed. *Scrutinies by Various Writers*. London: Wishart & Company, 1928.

Roubiczek, Paul. *Ethical Values in the Age of Science*. Cambridge: Cambridge University Press, 1969.

Salingar, Leo G. *Shakespeare and the Traditions of Comedy*. Cambridge: Cambridge University Press, 1974.

Schlipp, P. A., and M. Friedman, eds. *The Philosophy of Martin Buber*. Cambridge: Cambridge University Press, 1969.

Sechehaye, M. A. *Symbolic Realization*. New York: International Universities Press, 1951.

Shakespeare, William. *The Complete Works*. Edited by Alfred Harbage. Baltimore: Penguin Books, 1969.

Stern, Karl. *The Flight from Woman*. London: Allen and Unwin, 1965.

Suttie, Ian D. *The Origins of Love and Hate*. London: Routledge and Kegan Paul, 1935.

Ulanov, Ann Belford. *The Feminine in Jungian Psychology and Christian Theology*. Evanston, Ill.: Northwestern University Press, 1971.

———. *Receiving Woman: Studies in the Psychology and Theology of the Feminine*. Philadelphia: Westminster Press, 1981.

Ulanov, Ann Belford, with Barry Ulanov. *Religion and the Unconscious*. Philadelphia: Westminster Press, 1975.

Wait, R. J. C. *The Background to Shakespeare's Sonnets*. London: Chatto & Windus, 1972.

Winnicott, D. W. *The Child and the Family*. London: Tavistock, 1957a.

———. *The Child, the Family, and the Outside World*. London: Penguin, 1964a.

———. *The Child and the Outside World*. London: Tavistock, 1957b.

Bibliography

————. *Collected Papers: Through Pediatrics to Psychoanalysis*. London: Tavistock, 1958.

————. *The Family and Individual Development*. London: Tavistock, 1964b.

————. *The Maturational Processes and the Facilitating Environment*. London: Hogarth Press, 1970.

————. *The Piggle*. London: Hogarth Press, 1970.

————. *Playing and Reality*. London: Tavistock, 1971a.

————. *Therapeutic Consultations in Child Psychiatry*. London: Hogarth Press, 1971b.

ARTICLES

Bender, L. "Childhood Schizophrenia." *American Journal of Orthopsychiatry* 17 (1947).

Deutsch, Helene. "Ein Frauenschicksal: George Sand." In *Almanach für das Jahr 1929* (Vienna: Internationaler Psychoanalytischer Verlag, 1929).

Goitein, P. Lionel. "A New Approach to Analysis of 'Mary Rose.' " *British Journal of Medical Psychology* 6 (1926): 178.

Harlow, H. F. "Love in Infant Monkeys." *Scientific American* 68 (1959): 200.

Holbrook, David. "Truth, Campaigns, and Freedom." *Encounter* 65, no. 5 (December 1985): 54.

Kanner, L. "Autistic Disturbances of Affective Contact." *The Nervous Child* 2 (1943).

Karpe, Marietta. "The Origins of Peter Pan." *Psychoanalytic Review* 43 (1956).

Karpe, Marietta, and Richard Karpe. "The Meaning of Barrie's 'Mary Rose.' " *International Journal of Psycho-Analysis* 38 (1957): 408.

Khan, Masud. "Reparation to the Self as an Idolised Internal Object." *Dynamic Psychiatry* (November 1968).

Lacan, Jacques. "Le Stadt du Miroir." *New Left Review* (October 1968).

Leavis, F. R. "Justifying One's Valuation of Blake." *The Human World* 7 (May 1972).

Mahler, M. J. "Problems of Infant Neurosis: A Discussion" *Psychoanalytical Study Child* (9) (1954).

Maxwell, J. C. "Timon of Athens." *Scrutiny* 15 (1948): 195.

Salingar, Leo G. "Tourneur and the Tragedy of Revenge." In *Pelican Guide to English Literature*, edited by Boris Ford. London: Penguin, 1955.

Tomlin, E. W. F. "The Concept of Life." *The Heythrop Journal* 18, no. 3 (July 1977).

————. "Biology and Metaphysics." *Books and Issues* 1, no. 2 (1979).

Bibliography

Ulanov, Ann Belford. "The Witch Archetype. *Quadrant, Journal of the C. G. Jung Foundation* 10 (Summer 1977): 5.*
Ulanov, Ann Belford, and Barry Ulanov. "The Clown Archetype." *Quadrant, Journal of the C. G. Jung Foundation* 13 (Spring 1980).+

*+The material in the articles by Ann Belford Ulanov and Barry Ulanov has been incorporated in Ann Belford Ulanov and Barry Ulanov, *The Witch and the Clown: Two Archetypes of Human Sexuality* (Wilmette, Ill.: Chiron Publications, 1987).

Index

Index

Castration symbol, 229
Chaloner, Len, 76, 78
Changeling, The, 131, 268
Chaucer, Geoffrey, 233, 250
Child, preoccupation with, 50
Child and the Family, The, 49
Child, the Family, and the Outside World, The, 49
Christianity, 43, 93, 163. *See also* Religious elements
Coleridge, Samuel Taylor, 43, 56, 72, 75, 78
Coriolanus, 254, 258
Coveney, Peter, 85, 87, 89–90
Creative reflection, mother's capacity for, 24, 25, 61, 65, 66, 72, 73, 74, 77, 82, 84, 92–93, 101, 106, 110, 112; confirmation of identity in, 94; eyes and faces as symbols of, 63–64, 76; mirror phase and, 34–36; primary maternal preoccupation and, 29, 82; and quest for meaning, 62, 268–69
Creativity, 10, 11, 42–43, 87, 225; origins of, 22, 35; and primary maternal preoccupation, 9; rejection of, 46; and ways of knowing, 53, 55, 58
Creativity as Repair, 117
Cymbeline, 192, 201, 205

Dante, 42
"Dead These Twenty Years," 83, 85
Death, 152, 172; in *Antony and Cleopatra,* 222, 229, 230, 233; denial of, 77, 83, 87, 89; in *Hamlet,* 123, 137, 142; lost mother sought in world of, 19, 65, 66, 92–93; and love, 265; in *Measure for Measure,* 210; of the mother, 8, 35, 44, 64, 65, 66, 72, 82; in *Othello,* 236–41, 243–48; in *Peter Pan* and *Mary Rose,* 71–114; as regression, 187; and sex, 109, 137, 142, 149, 150–51, 239; and witch archetype, 161, 162; women associated with, 1–2, 66, 72, 147–48, 150–51, 163, 204, 222
De Beauvoir, Simone, 9, 40, 61
Democritus, 128
Dependence, 17, 28, 35–36, 60, 61, 165, 239; fear of women rooted in, 28, 48–

49; idealization or hatred of women rooted in, 61; and *participation mystique,* 39; terror of, 37, 55, 61, 66
Descartes, René, 8, 32, 44–46, 55, 64, 269
Deutsch, Helene, 42
Dialectical materialism, 57
Dickens, Charles, 17, 33, 47, 50, 89
Dominating mother, 61–62
Domination, 49
Don Juan type of individual, 16
Donne, John, 117
Drama and Society in the Age of Johnson, 132

Eating, 159, 167, 168, 169–70, 171, 174, 177, 186–88, 265; infant's view of sex as, 110, 169, 219, 239; and symbolism in *Antony and Cleopatra,* 229, 230, 231
Edward II, 121
Ego strength, 24
Ego weakness, 17–22
Eliot, George, 63, 236
Eliot, T. S., 55, 151, 197–98, 200, 244
Ellman, Richard, 50–52
Empathy, 11, 16, 44
Empirical psychology, 17
"Englishness of the English Novel, The," 251
Envy and gratitude, 170, 172, 182, 183, 197
Erikson, Erik, 47
Essay on King Lear, An, 235
Eternity, origins of concepts of, 39–40
Ethical Values in the Age of Science, 41
Evolution, 48
Existentialism, 9, 17, 38, 40, 43, 46, 55
Existentialist psychotherapy, 29, 263
Eyes, 63–64, 72, 76

Faces, 63–64, 72
Faerie Queene, The, 150
"Failure in Ego-Development," 18
Fairbairn, W. R. D., 17, 25, 62
Fairy tales, 110, 148, 158, 159, 162, 182; dread of mother symbolized in, 66; face and eyes as symbols in, 64

Index

Index

Index

body of, 64, 65–70; castrating, 65–66, 92; and childhood logic, 4; death of, 8, 35, 44, 64, 65, 66, 72, 82; fear of, 4, 65–66, 77; and participation mystique, 9, 23, 39, 43, 86, 106, 154; and symbolism in *Peter Pan* and *Mary Rose*, 71–114. See also Creative reflection, mother's capacity for; Primary maternal preoccupation

Mourning, 64, 65, 73, 92, 113; and association of women with death, 72

Much Ado about Nothing, 250–51

Music, 253–54

Mysterium tremendum, 42, 106

Narcissism, infant, 26

"Narnia Chronicle, The," 64, 66

Nazi Germany, 49

"New Approach to Analysis of 'Mary Rose,' A," 82

Nihilism, 44–45

Ninth Symphony (Mahler), 19, 182, 197

North and South, 11

Novel, 17

Nursery rhymes, 66

Object-relations psychology, 21, 37

"Obsession," 227

Oedipal material, 25; in Barrie's work, 90, 92, 102–3; in *Hamlet*, 122–23, 138

Ogilvie, Margaret, 83, 87, 90

Old Wives' Tale, The, 22

Omnipotence, 31

Oral features, 172, 186–87; and witch archetype, 147, 159, 160, 162, 164, 166, 181

Othello, 235–40, 243–49, 251, 267

Othello as Tragedy: Some Problems of Judgment and Feeling, 235

Participation mystique, 9, 23, 39, 43, 86, 106, 154

Passivity, 37, 247

Penis envy, 15

Pericles Prince of Tyre, 153, 192–200

Personality Structure and Human Interaction, 17

Personal Knowledge: Toward a Post-Critical Philosophy, 56

Peter Pan, 2, 71–81, 85–86, 89, 106, 108–9

Phallic symbols: in *Antony and Cleopatra*, 227, 229, 230, 231; in Barrie's work, 77, 81, 89, 90, 102, 109, 111

Phantastes, 106

Phenomenology, 38, 40, 41, 43

Philosophical anthropology, 17, 29, 43, 53, 54, 57, 63, 210, 259

Philosophy, 43, 45, 55

"Phoenix and the Turtle, The," 241

Pissarro, Camille, 17

Plath, Sylvia, 1, 8, 19, 64, 72, 82, 231

Play, 22–23; and culture, 34; and identity, 28; and life and work of James Barrie, 73, 77–78, 79, 109; between mother and infant, 24, 29, 31, 58; origins of thought in, 31; symbolism of, 64

Playing and Reality, 23

Plessner, Helmuth, 29

Poetic modes, 11, 17, 47, 55–56; rejection of, 46

Poetics of Space, The, 64

Polanyi, Michael, 26, 42, 56–59

Politics, 48

Poole, Roger, 46

Poor Monkey, 85

Pornography, 12, 51; and witch archetype, 162

Portrait of a Lady, 236

Portrait of Barrie, 105

Portrait of the Artist as a Young Man, 51

Primary maternal preoccupation, 9, 21, 27, 30, 43, 82, 101; and creative reflection, 24; dread of, 225; imaginative play and psychic nurture which develop from, 28, 29; perpetual, 86, 92

"Primary Maternal Preoccupation," 27

Privacy, 21

Projection, 12–13, 92, 191, 244; and feminine element in men, 7; Hamlet's, 141–42; and witch archetype, 130, 166

293

Index

Index

modern science, 32; and sexual behavior, 50–51
Stern, Karl, 8, 9, 16, 32, 37–48, 55, 64, 268–69
Sucking, 159, 160–61, 162
Suicide, 19, 94, 128, 189
Suttie, Ian D., 53
Swift, Jonathan, 62
Symbolism, 23, 109; and transitional objects, 31, 33
Syphilis, 120, 141, 164, 176, 179, 180–81

Tacit knowing, 56, 57
Taming of the Shrew, The, 117, 249
Telepathy, 11, 54, 84, 101
Tempest, The, 192, 194, 249
Therapeutic Consultations in Child Psychiatry, 35
Thomas, Dylan, 1, 19, 82
Time, 39–40, 89, 106–7, 119, 253–54, 264
Timon of Athens, 128, 146, 155–56, 161, 164, 166–90, 223, 234, 262, 268
"Timon of Athens," 171
Tolkien, J. R. R., 64
Tolstoy, Leo, 17, 41–43, 50, 86–87, 214, 253
Tomlin, E. W. F., 48
Tourneur, Cyril, 131–32, 143
Transitional object phenomena, 24, 30–32
"Transitional Objects and Transitional Phenomena," 30
Troilus and Cressida (Shakespeare), 121–22, 140, 147, 201
Troilus and Criseyde (Chaucer), 233
True and False Experience, 18
Twelfth Night, 251

Ulanov, Ann Belford, 9–11, 12–13, 156–64, 166, 205, 230, 267

Ulanov, Barry, 230
Ulysses, 51, 163
Unevoked potential, 19

Vagina dentata, 169
Virgins, 92, 103, 104, 108, 193, 219. *See also* Holy Mary syndrome

Wait, R. J. C., 240, 242–43
Walpurgisnacht, 158
War and Peace, 214
"Waste Land, The," 198
Water-Babies, The, 64, 93
Weaning, 34, 64, 106
Wendy House, 78
Wharton, Edith, 236
Wife-beating, 12–13
Winnicott, D. W., 3, 9–10, 13–17, 20–22, 24–36, 37, 43, 48–49, 54–56, 61, 72, 82, 87, 91, 106, 109, 132, 268
Winter's Tale, The, 140, 192, 194, 243, 249, 253–54
Witch archetype, 37, 65, 66, 117, 128, 146, 150, 191, 239, 267–68; and *Antony and Cleopatra*, 162, 224, 225, 229, 231, 233; dynamics of, 155–90; and *Macbeth*, 113, 146, 160, 165–66, 175; and mirroring power of women, 8; as obverse of creative mystery, 54; and projection, 130; and sexuality, 158, 160, 162, 164, 165, 166, 174, 176–82; and *Timon of Athens*, 155–56, 161, 164, 166–90, 223; woman with male potency represented in, 48
"Witch Archetype, The," 156, 267
Wives and Daughters, 139
Women in Love, 251
Wordsworth, William, 50, 56
Wyatt, Thomas, 121